Secrecy

Books by Daniel Patrick Moynihan

Miles to Go: A Personal History of Social Policy

Pandaemonium: Ethnicity in International Politics

On the Law of Nations

Came the Revolution: Argument in the Reagan Era

Family and Nation

Loyalties

Counting Our Blessings: Reflections on the Future of America

A Dangerous Place

Ethnicity: Theory and Experience (editor, with Nathan Glazer)

Coping: Essays on the Practice of Government

The Politics of a Guaranteed Income

On Equality of Educational Opportunity (editor, with
   Frederick Mosteller)

Toward a National Urban Policy (editor)

*On Understanding Poverty: Perspectives from the Social
   Sciences* (editor)

*Maximum Feasible Misunderstanding: Community Action in
   the War on Poverty*

*The Defenses of Freedom: The Public Papers of Arthur J.
   Goldberg* (editor)

*Beyond the Melting Pot: The Negroes, Puerto Ricans, Jews,
   Italians, and Irish of New York City* (with Nathan Glazer)

Books by Richard Gid Powers

The History of the FBI (forthcoming)

Not Without Honor: The History of American Anticommunism

Secrecy and Power: The Life of J. Edgar Hoover

G-Men: Hoover's FBI in American Popular Culture

Handbook of Japanese Popular Culture (editor, with Hidetoshi
   Kato)

DANIEL PATRICK MOYNIHAN

Secrecy

THE AMERICAN EXPERIENCE

Introduction by Richard Gid Powers

YALE UNIVERSITY PRESS   NEW HAVEN & LONDON

Published with assistance from the Kingsley Trust Association
Publication Fund established by the Scroll and Key Society of
Yale College.

Designed by James J. Johnson and set in New Aster Roman by
The Composing Room of Michigan, Inc.
Printed in the United States of America.

Library of Congress Cataloging-in-Publication Data

Moynihan, Daniel P. (Daniel Patrick), 1927–
    Secrecy : the American experience / Daniel Patrick Moynihan ;
introduction by Richard Gid Powers.
        p. cm.
    Includes bibliographical references and index.
    ISBN 0-300-07756-4 (cloth : alk. paper)
    ISBN 0-300-08079-4 (pbk. : alk. paper)

    1. Official secrets—United States—History—20th century.
2. Executive privilege (Government information)—United States—
History—20th century.   3. Security classification (Government
documents)—United States—History—20th century.   I. Title.
JK468.S4M68   1998
352.3'79—dc21   98-8144

A catalogue record for this book is available from the British Library.

The paper in this book meets the guidelines for permanence
and durability of the Committee on Production Guidelines
for Book Longevity of the Council on Library Resources.

10   9   8   7   6   5

For Irving and Bea Kristol

Contents

Preface

Secrecy was well received, which suggests that a new subject is emerging. In the *American Lawyer*, Floyd Abrams, the leading First Amendment advocate of our age, judged it "the single best book of the year—and then some—about law, government, politics, and American history. And human nature, too. . . . [T]he book describes . . . the baleful impact on our national life of the ever-expanding imposition of governmental secrecy since World War I."[1] In a review in *Foreign Affairs*, Eliot A. Cohen wrote, "From a proud and unrepentant Cold Warrior comes a forceful exposition of two theses: that 'secrecy is for losers,' and, more subtly, that the price paid for victory in the Cold War went beyond blood and treasure to a deformation of democratic norms."[2]

Note Abrams's phrase: "the ever expanding imposition of governmental secrecy since World War I." This, I believe, and I expect Richard Gid Powers would agree, is the source of the interest in our work. Here we are at the end of the century, the Cold War over, yet governmental secrecy, one of the defining institutions of that era, is evidently more salient than ever! What had seemed, what had been assumed to be merely an adjunct to the dreadful conflicts of the age turned out to have a life of its own. Some institutional enquiry was in order.

There was a background. In 1994 Congress established the Commission on Protecting and Reducing Government Secrecy largely from the perception (mine, I suppose) that while the defense budget was going down—base closing was perhaps the most troubled issue in Congress in the early 1990s—the "intelligence" budget was going *up*. I was at that time chairman of the Senate Finance Committee, the committee whose task it was to bring off President Clinton's 1993 budget. It was a formidable, if not unprecedented, goal. We would cut spending and raise taxes by half a trillion dollars (arguably the largest tax increase in world history). The object was to demonstrate that we could restore discipline to public finance. Which we did. The more then was the jolt when reading the paper the next day, as it were, to learn that the administration was asking for another billion dollars for the intelligence budget.[3]

Our commission began work in 1995 and two years later issued a unanimous report. It was time, we wrote, for a new way of thinking about secrecy, which was defined as a form of government regulation. This was liberating. If little was known about secrecy, a good deal was understood about regulation, which we proceeded to explicate. Let the reader judge. The job was considerably enlivened by the decision of the National Security Agency, prompted by John M. Deutch, then director of Central Intelligence and a commission member, to make public the Venona decryptions of Soviet cables sent to and from the United States during the long run of espionage associated with Communist organizations and sympathizers during and after World War II. Americans learned that while the fierce and costly public debate took place over Communist influence and espionage, their government possessed all the essential facts. But kept them to itself. Indeed, early on the Soviets had detected our cryptographic successes. And so the time came when we knew they knew, and they knew we knew they knew. Only the American people did not know.

Bureaucratic behavior. Frederick Seitz, former president of Rockefeller University who in 1970 headed a task force on secrecy for the Defense Science Board (see p. 175), relates an encounter with Admiral Hyman G. Rickover at the time. "Well, while I respect you very much, Fred," said the admiral, "let me tell you that if you have any secrets you *keep* them."[4] To which I would add the one bit of confounding information in the book that follows. The Commission on Protecting and Reducing Government Secrecy published its final report in March 1997. I then undertook to write *Secrecy* for the Yale University Press Annals of Communism series. For all our various discoveries, the one thing the commission never learned was what President Harry S. Truman thought of the revelations in the Venona decryptions, as they would become known.* It was, after all, his administration that had borne the brunt of the charges of subversion. I had met the President through his longtime associate W. Averell Harriman, but could scarce claim to know him. On the other hand, I was an aide to Harriman during his term as governor of New York and was in Washington with him during the Kennedy and Johnson administrations and so had at least an acquaintance with many figures of the Truman era. They never mentioned Venona or its like. And now, with the indispensable help of Louis J. Freeh, director of the Federal Bureau of Investigation, who in May 1997, released a collection of FBI documents on Venona, we found out why.[5] Truman was never told. The chairman of the Joint Chiefs of Staff

---

* In their preface to *Venona: Soviet Espionage and the American Response, 1939–1957*, editors Robert Louis Benson and Michael Warner explain, "The control term 'Venona' did not appear on the translated messages until 1961. In the beginning the information was usually called the 'Gardner Material,' and a formal control term—'Bride'—was finally affixed in 1950. From the late 1950s to 1961 the control term was 'Drug' (Benson and Warner, eds., *Venona: Soviet Espionage and the American Response, 1939–1957* [Washington, D.C.: National Security Agency, Central Intelligence Agency, 1996], p. xxii).

had given explicit orders that he, and only he, would inform the president, if and when he thought it necessary. *He* was General Omar Nelson Bradley.**

And so to our subject. Of the many institutions of American government that emerged in the course of the twentieth century, none has received, in relation to its importance, so little attention as that of secrecy.

As will be discussed, the New Deal of the 1930s brought on a great increase in government regulation as generally understood, and an equally great range of concern. In 1946 the Administrative Procedure Act was enacted with provisions for discovery, due process, and the like. As early as 1935 the *Federal Register* had been established to publish all public regulations. President Carter even decreed that his cabinet members actually read all such decrees issued by their departments, although one by one they begged off. The task was too great. Still this regulatory regime answers to most democratic standards.

Not so secrecy. To repeat, the report of the commission began: "Secrecy is a form of government regulation. Americans are familiar with the tendency to overregulate in other areas. What is different with secrecy is that the public cannot know the extent or the content of regulation."[6]

It remains a hidden, humongous, metastasizing mass within government itself. In a recent paper, "On Liberty, the Right to Know, and Public Discourse: The Role of Transparency in Public Life," the economist Joseph Stiglitz argues:

There is, in democratic societies, a basic right to know, to be informed about what the government is doing and why.

** In a review in *Commentary* (December 1998), Richard Perle suggests that this cannot be so, that there is a "metasecret" none of us yet know about. This is surely a possibility. Yet the thesis of organizational behavior does seem to fit what we do know was "Army property." In *Venona*, John Earl Haynes and Harvey Klehr write: "The evidence is not entirely clear, but it appears that Army Chief of Staff Omar Bradley, mindful of the White House's tendency to leak politically sensitive information, decided to deny President Truman direct knowledge of the Venona Project." Think about that (Haynes and Klehr, *Venona: Decoding Soviet Espionage in America* [New Haven: Yale University Press, 1999], p. 15).

To put it baldly, I will argue that there should be a strong presumption in favor of transparency and openness in government. The scourges of secrecy during the past seventy years are well known—in country after country, it is the secret police that has engaged in the most egregious violations of human rights. I want to talk today about the kind of secrecy that is pervasive today in many democratic societies. Let me be clear: this secrecy is a far cry from that pursued by the totalitarian states that have marred the century that is drawing to a close. Yet this secrecy is corrosive: it is antithetical to democratic values, and it undermines democratic processes. It is based on a mistrust between those governing and those governed; and at the same time, it exacerbates that mistrust.[7]

Almost half a century ago, in 1956, Edward Shils, recently described as "the most learned man in the social sciences" of his time, published *The Torment of Secrecy,* an impassioned yet rigorous account of the turmoil of what we recall as the McCarthy era of the 1950s.[8] If the turmoil was just then subsiding, Shils wrote, "A great society should not allow its partial recovery from a humiliating and unjustifiable lapse from decent conduct to diminish the necessity for the conscientious scrutiny of that lapse."[9]

Shils was not given to illusion. In the 1930s he made clear his contempt for fellow travelers: "the rush of the Gadarene intellectuals" to embrace Communism. Wartime service in the Office of Strategic Services only strengthened his disdain, adding an element of concern. In *Torment* he wrote: "The Communist Party of the United States is and has been malevolent in intent. Its impotence as an effective conspiratorial revolutionary body does not mean that it is entirely harmless. Given the interest of the Soviet Union in penetrating such information on American resources and intentions as are kept secret, and given the subservience of the Communist Party to the Soviet Union, there have been ample grounds for care in dealing with Communists or persons under their influence."

Shils was, however, a cofounder of the *Bulletin of the Atomic Scientists*. He continued: "The scientists, who had worked on the bomb and knew its monstrous powers, felt perhaps more than a little guilty over their role in having produced this necessary tool of destruction and they also knew enough about the inner nature of science and scientists to foresee that the American monopoly of the scientific and technological knowledge which went into the making of the bomb could not be indefinitely maintained."

They hoped for some mode of international control. But before anything could be achieved the Soviet Union detonated its own bomb and the Cold War was on. Soon came some evidence and many charges that they had stolen the secrets. Shils called for a "functional secrecy" that would protect the society from "genuine external danger." What he feared was secrecy that was not functional but symbolic: "part of the war of fantasy which the pure and good conduct incessantly with corruption and evil until the Last Judgment. The secrecy demanded by ideological extremism in the United States and in Soviet Russia, in Soviet China and in the Soviet satellites is not connected with national security except by the occasion which crises provide for fanatics to focus their excited fantasies."[10]

Had Shils been aware that President Truman was not told of the contents of the Venona decryptions he would surely have recognized the rise of bureaucracy as propounded by Max Weber in Germany in 1922.

> The pure interest of the bureaucracy in power, however, is efficacious far beyond those areas where purely *functional interests* make for secrecy. The concept of the "official secret" is the specific invention of bureaucracy, and nothing is so fanatically defended by the bureaucracy as this attitude, which cannot be substantially justified beyond these specifically qualified areas. In facing a parliament, the bureaucracy, out of a sure power instinct, fights every attempt of the parliament to gain knowledge by means of its own experts or from interest groups. The so-called right of par-

liamentary investigation is one of the means by which parliament seeks such knowledge. Bureaucracy naturally welcomes a poorly informed and hence a powerless parliament—at least in so far as ignorance somehow agrees with the bureaucracy's interests. [My emphasis; see Shils's term "functional secrecy."][11]

Note that of the 6,610,154 secrets created in 1997 a tiny proportion, some 1.4 percent, was created under statute, which is to say the Atomic Energy Act.[12] The remainder are pure creatures of bureaucracy, via executive orders.

Joseph Stiglitz has now added an economist's perspective. There are gains to be got.

> Secrecy provides some insulation against being accused of making a mistake. If a policy fails to produce desired results, government officials can always claim that matters would have been even worse but for the government policy. While we all recognize human fallibility, government officials seem particularly loath to own up to it, and for good reason: the public judges mistakes harshly. But there is a vicious circle: given that so little information is disclosed, the public must rely on results in judging government officials. The officials receive credit for good results, whether they deserve the credit or not; and they are condemned for bad results. . . . If outsiders have less information, voters may feel less confident that they will be able to take over management effectively. Indeed, the lack of information of outsiders does increase the costs of transition, and make it more expensive (for society) to change management teams. The fact that the alternative management teams have less information means that there is a higher probability of any proposals that they put forward will be ill-suited to the situation. By increasing the mean cost of transition and increasing the subjective variance, secrecy puts incumbents at a distinct advantage over rivals. . . .
>
> While it may be in the interests of the government as a whole to maintain secrecy, it may not be in the interests of particular individuals. Indeed, that is what gives rise to

the whole problem of leaks. As in the case of other forms of collusive behavior, there are incentives for individuals to deviate. If a secret is shared among a number of individuals, any one of the individuals can reap the scarcity rents for himself by disclosing the information to the press.[13]

Such a situation obtained in 1976 when President Ford agreed to a "competitive analysis" of Soviet strategic strength and intentions.[14] As related by Christopher Andrew, a "B Team" of conservative critics of the CIA supposed "arms control bias" was asked to make an independent analysis of the agency's view, which would in turn be critiqued by an in-house "A Team." The B Team concluded that the nation was in grave peril given the Soviet "drive for dominance." The classified B Team report was delivered December 2, 1976. "Within a few weeks the main conclusions of the report had been leaked to the press."[15] Ronald Reagan, for one, was convinced, and upon becoming president four years later, the B Team was well rewarded both in policy terms and in appointments.

I had been a member of President Ford's cabinet, having returned from a posting in India more than ever convinced of the power of ethnicity in world affairs. Colonial empires did not last. After visiting China on my way home I wrote "Letter from Peking" for the *New Yorker,* which concluded that that regime would be around for some time. So also would the Soviet Union, "until ethnicity breaks it up."[16] By 1979, in *Newsweek,* I proposed that the break up would come in the 1980s. But the B Team had access to classified information and hence far greater authority, albeit one could argue that the analysis was incomplete.

This brings up another thesis in what I dare to call the science of secrecy. Social science, that is. A poor thing, but our own. Ethnicity. In *The Torment of Secrecy,* Shils wrote that the "American visage began to cloud over" when we learned of Soviet espionage. "For a country that had never previously thought of itself as an object of systematic espionage by foreign powers, it was upsetting."[17] Shils, a second-generation American, was seemingly little aware of the near panic over German espionage that accompanied World War I. The Espionage Act of 1917; Theodore Roosevelt going on about the "Hun within our own gates"; Eugene V. Debs going to prison. The German language, German culture, trod down. Even to the lowest of dogs. In 1919 at the Westminister Kennel Club Dog Show, dachshunds were entered as badger hounds.

Espionage is almost invariably associated with diaspora politics. It can lead to panic as with Germans in the First World War; or Japanese in the second. And yet the atomic spies were in the main first- or second-generation Central Europeans. Little was made of this. Chinese will now be watched a bit more closely. Indian nationals also, if I am not mistaken. But American society has pretty much lost its nativist dread. Not enough natives, or so I would hypothesize.

The Venona revelations began with a book, *The Secret World of American Communism* by Harvey Klehr, John Earl Haynes, and Fridrikh Igorevich Firsov, which appeared in 1995. Working in newly opened archives in Moscow, the authors established that the American Communist Party was indeed an instrument of Soviet intelligence. In the course of their work they picked references to Venona. In May 1995, they were invited to testify before the Commission on Protecting and Reducing Government Secrecy, just then beginning its work. They pointed to the anomaly that one could learn about American counterintelligence activities in Moscow, but not in the United States. As Haynes and Klehr recount in their newest study *Venona: Decoding Soviet Espionage in America,* I turned to John Deutch, then director of Central Intelligence, to ask why not. He thought it over, and the following July, in a ceremony at CIA headquarters in Langley, Virginia, the first set of decryptions was made public. This was no small event; the heads of the CIA, the FBI, and the NSA were present, as were the surviving cryptanalysts, including Meredith Gardner, whose existence had been perhaps the best kept secret of all!

There now followed a sequence of rigorous and unprecedented studies. First, in 1996, came a superb compilation, *Venona: Soviet Espionage and the American Response, 1939–1957*, edited by Robert Louis Benson and Michael Warner and published jointly by the National Security Agency and the Central Intelligence Agency. In 1999 Haynes and Klehr followed with their exhaustive and brilliant study of the archive. Simultaneously Nigel West, the British authority on espionage, published *Venona: The Greatest Secret of the Cold War*. In the meantime the indefatigable Allen Weinstein had published, with Alexander Vassiliev, *The Haunted Wood: Soviet Espionage in America—The Stalin Era*, a volume of new nuggets from Moscow archives, including the information that Samuel Dickstein, the Democratic representative from the Lower East Side of Manhattan, the sponsor of various measures that eventuated in the House Un-American Activities Committee, was in fact on the payroll of the NKVD.

Just what the Soviet spymasters and the Democratic congressman were up to is not all that clear. Dickstein had wanted to investigate Nazi influence. But under the chairmanship of Martin Dies, Jr., of Texas the committee proceeded to uncover Communists everywhere, or if not outright Communists, Comsymps, as the term was. In *Congress Investigates,* Michael Wreszin records that Dies "used Dickstein's concern with right wing propaganda groups to launch an assault on the entire spectrum of the Left in America and to smear the New Deal with a Red brush."[18] Francis Perkins was to be impeached. One consequence of all this was a wide distrust of, even disdain for, charges of real Soviet espionage by people who knew. Witness Whitaker Chambers. Another consequence, as argued by Haynes and Klehr, was a near pervasive misreading of Soviet intentions. They conclude *Venona* with this:

This offensive reached its zenith during the period when the United States, under President Franklin D. Roosevelt, adopted a policy of friendship and accommodation toward the USSR. The Soviet assault was of the type a nation directs at an enemy state that is temporarily an ally and with which it anticipates future hostility, rather than the much more restrained intelligence-gathering it would direct toward an ally that it expected to remain a friendly power. Stalin's espionage offensive was also a significant factor contributing to the Cold War. By the late 1940s the evidence provided by Venona and the sources of the massiveness and the intense hostility of the Soviet espionage attack caused American counterintelligence professionals and high-level American policy-making officials to conclude that Stalin was carrying out a covert assault on the United States. The Soviet espionage offensive, in their minds, indicated that the Cold War was not a state of affairs that had begun after World War II but a guerrilla action that Stalin had secretly started years earlier. They were right.

But surely they were wrong not to insist that the President know and *understand* what was going on. Secrecy has its costs; in this instance incalculable costs.

Notes

1. Floyd Abrams, "Bedside Reading,"*American Lawyer* 20, no. 10 (December 1998): 79.

2. Elliot A. Cohen, "Recent Books," *Foreign Affairs* 77, no. 5 (September–October 1998): 150.

3. See, for example, R. Jeffrey Smith, "Senators, CIA Fight over $1 Billion," *Washington Post,* July 16, 1993.

4. Frederick Seitz, letter to author, April 15, 1999.

5. These FBI documents, including a memorandum of October 8, 1949, relating the chairman's orders, are available online at *www.fbi.gov–foipa–venona.htm.*

6. Commission on Protecting and Reducing Government Secrecy, *Secrecy: Report of the Commission on Protecting and Reducing Government Secrecy* (Washington, D.C.: Government Printing Office, 1997), p. xxi.

7. Joseph Stiglitz, "On Liberty, the Right to Know, and Public Discourse: The Role of Transparency in Public Life," Oxford University Amnesty International Lecture, Oxford University, January 27, 1999, *www.worldbank.org–html–extdr–extme–jssp012799.htm*, p. 1.

8. Donald Dewey, "Edward Shils: A Last Harvest," *Society* 36, no. 3 (March–April 1999): 75.

9. Daniel Patrick Moynihan, introduction to Edward A. Shils, *The Torment of Secrecy: The Background and Consequences of American Security Policies* (Glencoe, Ill.: Free Press, 1956; reprint, Chicago: Ivan R. Dee, 1996), p. xii.

10. Ibid., p. xviii.

11. Max Weber, "Bureaucracy," in *Essays in Sociology*, translated and edited by H. H. Gerth and C. Wright Mills (New York: Oxford University Press, 1946), pp. 233–34; see also Weber, *Wirtschaft und Gesellschaft* (Economy and society) (New York: Bedminster Press, 1968). Donald Dewey describes Shils's introduction to Weber and the German tradition in sociology as "close to a religious experience" (Dewey, "Harvest," p. 74).

12. The Department of Energy reports that it classified 900,000 pages of material in FY 1997 pursuant to the Atomic Energy Act. The Information Security Oversight Office reports 6,520,154 classification actions in FY 1997 pursuant to Executive Order 12958. In comparing these figures, an average of ten pages per document is assumed, resulting in an estimated 90,000 classification decisions by the DOE: 1.4 percent of the combined DOE–ISOO classification decisions reported in 1997 (Information Security Oversight Office, *1997 Report to the President* [Washington, D.C.: Information Security Oversight Office, 1996], p. 25; A. Bryan Siebert, director, Office of Declassification, Department of Energy, to Steven Garfinkel, director, Information Security Oversight Office, National Archives and Records Administration, Washington, D.C., December 3, 1998).

13. Stiglitz, "Liberty," pp. 10–16.

14. Christopher Andrew, *For the President's Eyes Only: Secret Intelligence and the American Presidency from Washington to Bush* (New York: HarperPerennial, 1996), p. 423.

15. Ibid., p. 424.

16. Daniel Patrick Moynihan, "Letter from Peking," January 26, 1975, accepted for publication in the *New Yorker* but not printed due to Moynihan's appointment to the United Nations.

17. Shils, *Torment*, p. xvi.

18. Michael Wreszin, "The Dies Committee, 1938," in *Congress Investigates: A Documented History, 1792–1974*, edited by Arthur M. Schlesinger, Jr., and Roger Burns (New York: Chelsea House, 1975), p. 2925.

Acknowledgments

This work would not have been possible without the un-precedented assistance provided by members of the intelligence community in all its many branches. I am particularly indebted to William P. Crowell and Robert Louis Benson of the National Security Agency, Michael Warner of the Center for the Study of Intelligence of the Central Intelligence Agency, and Kevin B. Wilkinson of the Federal Bureau of Investigation. Meredith Gardner, who on December 20, 1946, deciphered the Venona cable which first opened the whole world of Soviet espionage in the United States, was an inspiration throughout.

John Earl Haynes of the Library of Congress kept coming up with treasures from the archives. Robert A. Katzmann of the Brookings Institution and the Georgetown University Law Center was a counselor of gentle wisdom combined with relentless rigor.

Eric R. Biel, Michael J. Lostumbo, Richard F. Bland, Joshua A. Brook, and Margaret B. Sloane were endlessly supportive, as was, as ever, Eleanor Ann Suntum.

Introduction

Richard Gid Powers

Secrecy is the first essential in affairs of the State.
—CARDINAL DE RICHELIEU

Every thing secret degenerates, even the administration
of justice; nothing is safe that does not show how it can bear
discussion and publicity.
—LORD ACTON

One more thing, adds Senator Daniel Patrick Moynihan:
"Secrecy is for losers."

Americans, we are told, love and admire winners, hate
and despise losers. That on no less an authority than general
and historian George S. Patton, Hollywood revised spectacular version. Why, then, did the American government, the
hands-down winner in the global battles of the twentieth
century, draw the veil of official secrecy over a large measure
of its Cold War deliberations and decisions? And why has it
clung to that system of Cold War security long after the war
ended, and ended in a victory far more complete than ever
imagined, even by that confident first generation of cold
warriors?

Senator Moynihan, bringing a lifetime of experience as
statesman and social scientist to bear on the problem, has
examined the origins, growth, and significance of secrecy in
American government. In this remarkable book, he proposes that governmental secrecy may be seen as a dark
thread connecting and explaining some of America's most

disastrous Cold War policies. In tracing the history of the American security system, he shines a new light on some of the most familiar, even legendary, events of the Cold War and reveals the critical significance of others that deserve to be better known. Drawing on hitherto unavailable files of the FBI and on discussions with architects of American Cold War policies, he argues that the most baleful consequences of the Cold War—the fissure in American culture that developed during the McCarthy period and the fathomless debts accumulated during the arms buildup of the Reagan years—could have been avoided had it not been for the secrecy that concealed from the American people what the government knew and what it did not know.

How, then, did the United States of America stumble into the shadows of a secrecy system that still produces more than 6 million classified documents a year and that pokes and prods some 3 million individuals to certify their worthiness to be trusted with papers stamped Confidential, Secret, and Top Secret? It has been estimated (by Moynihan, in fact) that if every newspaper in the United States devoted its every page to printing the classified documents produced by the government on that day alone, there would be room for nothing else. "Dear Abby" would bite the dust, along with Doonesbury and the baseball scores.

How, Moynihan asks, has this pervasive system of secrecy affected America's efforts to protect its interests abroad and its democracy at home? And how can the country free itself from the Cold War legacy of a culture of secrecy that so obviously mocks any pretensions to self-government and an open society?

A manuscript does not often arrive in a bottle on the beach. Every book has its history, and the genesis of this one is particularly interesting.

Senator Moynihan's career in government could hardly have been better designed to equip him with the ideas and the experience he would need for this study. Most pertinent, of course, was his eight-year term (from February 1977 until January 1985) on the newly established Senate Select Committee on Intelligence, for the last four years as vice chairman. During those last years Moynihan was, along with committee chairman Barry Goldwater, among the few to whom Director of Central Intelligence William Casey was supposed to unveil his secrets. At one key moment during the Iran-Contra affair, Casey did not unveil, lied about mining the harbor of the Nicaraguan capital, and Moynihan resigned. (He returned when Casey apologized and promised to mend his ways.) On the gravity of the Iran-Contra crisis, as it darkened and deepened and spread, Moynihan agrees with Theodore Draper: "If ever the constitutional democracy of the United States is overthrown, we now have a better idea of how this is likely to be done."[1] It was a brush, almost a collision, with disaster, all brought on by the ability of the national security agencies (here the CIA and the National Security Council) to keep their activities secret—not from the enemy, which was well aware it was being mined, shot at, and otherwise discomforted, but from elected officials in the United States with the constitutional right and duty to know what was going on.

It is not to be thought that Moynihan entered (or left) the intelligence oversight committee an adversary of the secret agencies of national security. After his statutory term of eight years, he received the CIA's Agency Seal Medallion for having demonstrated, in the words of the award, "that effective oversight of intelligence can be realized in a democratic nation without risk to the intelligence process." Nevertheless, it can surely be said that Moynihan's term on the intelligence oversight committee deepened his already lively skepticism about the worth of secrecy in protecting national security and gave him an even livelier interest in the subject of secrecy as a problem in democratic government.

Moynihan recalls developing that skepticism during his days as ambassador to India (1973–75), when he was "incredulous at what the Soviets were getting away with in the 'developing' world."[2] In an article written for Norman Podhoretz's *Commentary* at about the same time, he argued that what was needed was less reliance on gathering secret information and more on telling the truth about the open realities of life in the Soviet Union and its client states. The American spokesman "should come to be feared in international forums for the truths he might tell."[3] Moynihan put that idea to work as permanent American representative to the United Nations (1975–76), when, as he says, he "got into all manner of disputes with the Soviets *which they started* but which we and the West generally had come to take for granted."[4]

Now it must be remembered that Moynihan (always) was the quintessential liberal anti-Communist. His commitment to that cause survived the Vietnam ordeal, which burnt away the anti-Communism of more than one of his liberal colleagues. (One of the most important connotations of the "neo" in "neoliberal" and "neoconservative"—and Moynihan has been called both—is anti-Communism.) Nevertheless, he had become increasingly skeptical about official Washington's assessments of the Soviet Union that warned of the Soviets' ever-increasing military, political, and economic strength. Moynihan was one of the first prominent Americans to point out that the Soviet empire had no clothes, not to mention no shoes, butter, meat, living space, heat, telephones, or toilet paper. In his view the Soviet Union was so weak economically, as well as so divided ethnically, that it could not long survive. That is just what he wrote in January 1975, though he then thought that the USSR might still "have considerable time left before ethnicity breaks it up."[5] Four years later, but still ten years before the Soviet bloc and the Soviet Union fell apart, he wrote in *Newsweek*: "The Soviet empire is coming under tremendous strain. It could blow up."[6]

It was data available to anyone who wanted to look for it, data that Moynihan examined with the eye of the professor he had once been, that gave him the confidence to make these startling predictions. The Soviets had indeed enjoyed a prodigious growth rate in the fifties, he conceded, but since then the "infrastructure of the Soviet state [had] sickened." From the 1950s to the 1970s the Soviet growth rate had halved, as had the volume of investment. The growth in the workforce was coming to an end, and productivity growth had halted. They were running out of oil. And there was something else thought impossible in modern societies, even in semimodern societies: the Soviet mortality rate was increasing and life expectancy was decreasing, probably because of epidemic alcoholism. Infant mortality was also climbing. And while the economy was collapsing, rising ethnic consciousness was turning the Soviet Union into a tinderbox of nationalisms.[7]

The Soviet Union, Moynihan argued, was dying, but he warned that its death throes could be dangerous. "So long as the [Soviet] economy was growing, the system could put up with the waste of armaments," he argued, "but that time is past." Its leaders might make a lunge for territory in the oil-producing regions "to reverse the decline at home and preserve national unity."[8]

In 1984 Moynihan told graduates of New York University that America "should be less obsessed with the Soviets," because "the Soviet idea is spent—history is moving away from it with astounding speed. . . . It is as if the whole Marxist-Leninist ethos is hurtling into a black hole in the universe. . . . The historical outcome is certain if we can keep the nuclear peace and attend to our own arrangements in a manner that they continue to improve. . . . Our grand strategy should be to wait out the Soviet Union—its time is spent. . . . When the time comes, it will be clear that in the end freedom did prevail."[9] He began to wonder if the end might not actually be at hand. He visited Alexander Solzhenitsyn at the Russian exile's Vermont farm and asked him, "Do you think you'll ever go back?" The novelist replied, "I had assumed I would be back by now."[10]

But, and this is the crucial "but," while Moynihan and

Solzhenitsyn could see that the Soviet Union was flat on its economic back, the men who shaped foreign policy in Washington could not. In the 1980s Moynihan was an observer at the START talks in Geneva. He would question the American negotiators about the Soviet Union's staying power: "When you are through with the mind-boggling details of this treaty with the USSR, what makes you think there will still be a USSR?" He drew blank stares.[11] In 1991 the chief negotiator, Max Kampelman, sent Moynihan an unsolicited letter recalling those exchanges. Kampelman wrote, "Whenever I am asked whether I had predicted the breakup of the Soviet Union or knew anybody who did, I have uniformly stated that the one person who had fully understood and made the correct analysis was you."[12] In 1992 Moynihan remarked within earshot of Henry Kissinger that the government "had failed to see the coming collapse of the Soviets, although some of us did argue it. So let's do better next time." Kissinger went into his "most sarcastic" mode and jeered, "I knew no one, at least I knew no one before this morning, who had predicted the evolution in the Soviet Union."[13] When Moynihan politely sent Kissinger documentation, he received a nice reply. Kissinger stood corrected: "Your crystal ball was better than mine."[14]

One factor that freed Moynihan to see what the policy-makers refused to notice may have been his anti-Communism. Moynihan had never believed in the stability of totalitarian states that tried to eradicate the human yearning for freedom. Anti-Communists like Moynihan believed that totalitarian regimes, because they were held together by brute force, were inherently unstable and destined to fall. This was the original rationale of the containment doctrine, although these first principles were forgotten as the Cold War settled into interminable routine. Thus Moynihan had no predisposition to reject evidence that seemed to show the Soviet Union as weak and getting weaker. It was just what he expected.

In contrast, American policy-makers after the 1960s, and perhaps even earlier, tended to be pragmatists who discounted the importance of hearts and minds and concentrated on the facts on the ground. (In the Vietnam era, this frame of mind reached tragically hubristic levels in Secretary of Defense Robert McNamara's use of body counts as an odometer during his drive toward the dark at the end of the tunnel—or was it the light?) Some pragmatic policy-makers were predisposed to believe that the Soviet Union was fundamentally strong: they assumed that centrally planned command economies, because they did not have to produce profits (which went down on the "waste" side of their ledger), were more rational than market economies, and that any setbacks must therefore be only temporary. Other policy-makers seem to have lacked any convictions at all about human nature or the good society, so they were impressed by the muscularity of regimes predicated on power. Or they may have been impressed by the superiority of a utilitarian regime (the greatest good for the greatest number) in harnessing social energies for social goals. For whatever reason, American policy-makers in the 1960s seemed to reject reflexively evidence that conflicted with their belief that the Soviet Union was fundamentally strong and destined to become only stronger.

Why did the presidents and their men get the Soviet economy so wrong, and why were they so confident that they were right? They supposedly had access to the best intelligence of all about the Soviets, that is, secret intelligence. The problem with this intelligence, Moynihan began to suspect, was precisely that it was secret.

Moynihan was onto something: secret information as a weakness in decision making. The CIA, the National Security Agency (NSA), and the other intelligence agencies relied on secret sources of information. Their assumptions, calculations, and ways of manipulating data were just as secret. How impressive. Surely their conclusions had to be more accurate than those of outsiders with no access to classified information. And thus when presidents, national security advisors, and secretaries of state announced that the Soviet economy was soon going to surpass ours, doubters had no opportunity to get their analytic meat hooks into the national security establishment's data and reasoning. Let it be mentioned that the president's Top Secret National Intelligence Estimate was claiming that the Soviet economy was more than 59 percent the size of America's, at a time when the true figure was closer to 33 percent.[15] That is an error of almost 100 percent. Or 50 percent, depending on how you look at it. In any case, as they say at the rifle range, not even on the paper.

Proceeding from these secret assessments of Soviet strength rather than from the openly available facts about the sorry state of the Soviet Union, the Carter and Reagan administrations went on history's greatest peacetime weapons spending spree, and in six years (1982–88) the United States transformed itself from the world's greatest creditor nation into the leading debtor. "While we're not disintegrating," Moynihan wrote in 1990, "we clearly blew an extraordinary economic lead."[16]

Why did American policy-makers make such monumental mistakes? Why did America, facing an adversary gasping out its last breaths, spend itself into debilitating debt, all the while expanding covert operations against Soviet client states until the secret wars recoiled upon us and precipitated a constitutional crisis? The culprit, Moynihan proposed, was secrecy itself. He wrote (in 1990):

> The national security state developed a vast secrecy system which basically hid from us our own miscalculations. The mistakes, you see, were secret, so they were not open to correction. My favorite is the presidential commission chaired by H. Rowen Gaither, a founder of the Rand Corporation, entitled "Deterrence and Survival in the Nuclear Age." It reached President Eisenhower a few weeks after

the launching of *Sputnik* in 1957. The report warned of a missile gap, concluded that the Soviets had surpassed the United States in terms of military effort, and projected a rate of growth for the Soviet economy which would have them passing the United States by 1993. (Their machine-tool production was asserted to be twice ours.) The document, replete with profound error, remained classified until 1973. This is what presidents in the grimmest years of the Cold War knew, and what they knew was mostly wrong.[17]

Like the rest of us, Moynihan likes to be proven right by events, but he could take scant pleasure in pointing out he had told us so: "We will be paying for those mistakes for a long while. We already are. Average weekly earnings in America today are lower than they were when Dwight D. Eisenhower was president. The least we can do is to start dismantling the system that got it so wrong. Dismantle the secrecy system; find honest work for the threat-analysis crowd. Pay a little heed to the needs of America."[18]

And so in January 1993, to find out how and why and at what cost America had moved so much of its government behind the curtain of secrecy, Moynihan introduced legislation for a bipartisan study of the problem. The result, on April 30, 1994, was Public Law 103–236, establishing the Commission on Protecting and Reducing Government Secrecy, with twelve members: half from government, half from private life, four each nominated by the president, the Senate, and the House. Moynihan was chairman of the commission, Representative Larry Combest of Texas, vice chairman.[19]

The commission held thirteen formal meetings and programs between January 10, 1995, and December 12, 1996. Members and staff made seventy-five visits and presentations where they gathered more information and spread the word about their study. They visited the Central Intelligence Agency, the National Security Agency, the Federal Bureau of

Investigation, the army, the air force, the Department of Defense Security Institute, the Department of State, the presidential libraries, the American Historical Association, and the national archives. They even interviewed convicted spies at the Lewisburg and Allenwood federal penitentiaries in Pennsylvania. All told, the commission interviewed more than ninety-six agencies, corporations, and organizations and more than three hundred individuals, among them some of the country's best-known historians, policy analysts, and journalists.

On March 3, 1997, the commission issued its report, endorsed by all its members. The commission had, it stated, fulfilled its statutory mandate, which was to propose reforms designed to reduce the volume of classified information, thereby strengthening the protection of information that had been legitimately classified, and to improve existing personnel security procedures. In designing these proposals it had sought to ensure both the guarding of information where there is a sound basis for its protection and the timely disclosure of the information where there is not, or where the cost of maintaining its secrecy outweighs the benefits.

The report declared, in its first sentence, "It is time for a new way of thinking about secrecy."[20] There followed, in the lively plain English that is supposed to be the standard in government documents but seldom is, a comprehensive analysis of the federal government's apparatus for designating documents as secret and providing security clearances for those authorized to read them. In large measure, the report was an institutional history of the security system: an analysis of the legislative acts and executive orders from which the security system evolved, the record of previous studies and commissions that had tried to reform the system, and an assessment of the effectiveness of the current system in its primary mission of protecting the nation's vital secrets.

The commission concluded that the government's security system was classifying far too many documents at every stage, at far too great a cost, and that vital secrets were not adequately protected because of the vast volume of needlessly classified materials. Secrecy also had intangible costs in the erosion of public confidence in government, because so much of the government secrecy served only to protect the careers and reputations of policy-makers, without any clear justification in terms of national security.

The report recommended that government classification and declassification programs be given, for the first time, a statutory basis that set up uniform classifying procedures across the government to weigh the public benefit gained by openness against any possible damage to national security. The commission also recommended that the current procedures for granting security clearances be brought up to date to reflect how American society has changed since the procedures were instituted and that those procedures be given a statutory basis to protect both the interests of government and the civil liberties of citizens. In short, the commission issued a plea for common sense in security matters by restricting secrecy to material that truly needed to be kept secret, while opening up all other government records to the public.

The commission made six formal recommendations.

- Information shall be classified only if there is a demonstrable need to protect the information in the interests of national security.
- The president shall establish procedures for the classification and declassification of information.
- In decisions about whether information should be classified, the benefit from public disclosure shall be weighed against the need for secrecy. Where there is significant doubt, the information shall not be classified.
- Information shall remain classified for no longer than ten years, unless the agency specifically recertifies the

need for continued secrecy. All information shall be declassified after thirty years, unless it is shown that demonstrable harm will result.

- There shall be no authority to withhold information from Congress.
- A national declassification center shall be established to coordinate, implement, and oversee declassification.[21]

While the commission was still gathering its materials and Moynihan was searching for the most effective way of presenting the commission's findings, he was asked to write an introduction to a new edition of *The Torment of Secrecy*, the McCarthy-era classic by sociologist Edward Shils.[22] While rereading Shils's outraged description of how the modern security system was imposed at the beginning of the Cold War, Moynihan discovered not only the theme of the commission's report but also the germ of the book you hold now in hand.

As Moynihan read Shils's work, he began to think as a social scientist about the problem of secrecy. Moynihan has a Ph.D. in government from the Fletcher School of Law and Diplomacy at Tufts University and has taught the social sciences at a number of universities, including Harvard. *Beyond the Melting Pot*, which he wrote with Nathan Glazer, is a classic study of American ethnicity and, among sociological studies of American culture, the tenth best-selling sociology book in American publishing history.[23]

Moynihan realized how social scientific theory could provide a unifying perspective to organize the commission's extremely disparate findings. Drawing on Max Weber and Emile Durkheim, he saw how he could discuss secrecy as a form of regulation (Weber) that could often take a ritualistic form (Durkheim) in order to stigmatize outsiders and critics (as distinguished from the functional secrecy that seeks simply to keep critical information from the enemy). The influence of these ideas is immediately felt in the commission's published report. In Moynihan's foreword to

Shils's book, he wrote, "I would hold that secrecy is best understood as a form of regulation."[24] The commission report, after calling for a new way of thinking about secrecy, suggests that the solution might be to consider secrecy "a form of government regulation."[25]

As we have seen, Moynihan had long been thinking about why American policy-makers had been so wrong in their evaluations of Soviet society and the Soviet economy. Shils's analysis of the impact of secrecy on science made him wonder if therein might lie the answer not only to that question but to many other Cold War puzzles.

Although Shils was a social scientist, when he examined the impact of secrecy on the sciences, for the most part he discussed only the physical sciences. Moynihan's attention was drawn to Shils's impatient and even irritated insistence that there really were no scientific secrets to be protected from the enemy, that the statement of a problem—the order to build a nuclear bomb, for example—is in itself for the engineer or the scientist a statement of the solution. More than that: because scientific progress depends on the open exchange of ideas, secrecy in science actually is a debilitating handicap to those enmeshed in its webs.

Moynihan realized that the most pressing intelligence problems of the Cold War had really been questions for the social scientist. How dynamic was the Soviet Union? What was the strength of its economy? How stable was its social order and its ethnic structure? Here secrecy was an even greater obstacle to research than it was in the physical sciences. In fact, secrecy made scientific investigation of these problems impossible, since, in order to be scientific, analysis requires that information be available to all for criticism and reevaluation. By this time Moynihan was accumulating more examples of how American policy-makers had relied on information that could have been exposed at the time as ludicrously wrong. In 1986 the CIA had claimed that the East Germans had a greater per capita production than did the West Germans. He found a Swedish economist who wrote

in 1988 that the CIA had been claiming that the Soviet Union's per capita national income was higher than Italy's: "Anyone who has visited both countries should be able to see for himself that such a statement is absurd."[26]

Moynihan's thinking about Shils shaped the commission's finding that "secrecy has significant consequences for the national interest when, as a result, policy-makers are not fully informed, government is not held accountable for its actions, and the public cannot engage in informed debate." Shils's essay also informed the committee's recommendation that the government should change its security procedures to weigh the benefits of openness against the needs of security: "Greater openness permits more public understanding of the government's actions and also makes it more possible for the government to respond to criticism and justify those actions. It makes free exchange of scientific information possible and encourages discoveries that foster economic growth. In addition, by allowing for a fuller understanding of the past, it provides opportunities to learn lessons from what has gone before—making it easier to resolve issues concerning the government's past actions and helping to prepare for the future."[27]

Many of the ideas that Moynihan developed while thinking about secrecy and the social sciences could be used to give shape and direction to the commission's work. Others clearly could not. He could now see, for example, that the government's security system and the top policy-makers' reliance on secret sources of information had made them the victims of bad science, the social scientific equivalent for Americans of the Lysenkoism that had made Stalin's biology a laughingstock. Moynihan was moving in the direction of a comprehensive study of official secrecy in America and its impact on modern American history, but this would have transcended the statutory purpose of the commission: to make concrete proposals to protect and reduce secrecy. And a narrative history of controversial events was not the sort of project often successfully accomplished by a committee, particularly a committee on its way, Moynihan hoped, to a unanimous report.

Shils had also started Moynihan thinking about another way secrecy had damaged the United States during the Cold War. Shils's book described and denounced America's exaggerated, even hysterical, reaction to postwar revelations about Soviet espionage. Shils analyzed McCarthyism and the loyalty programs of the Truman and Eisenhower administrations as populist, anti-intellectual rituals of symbolic secrecy. They were intended to stigmatize and silence an elite inconveniently skeptical about the threat of domestic Communism and opposed to the right-wing anti-Communist goal of repressing the radical Left. Moynihan, as a liberal anti-Communist, shared Shils's contempt for McCarthyism, but he also began to wonder about McCarthyism's flip side: the reaction against McCarthy that took the form of a modish anti-anti-Communism that considered impolite any discussion of the very real threat Communism posed to Western values and security. Might less secrecy have prevented the liberal overreaction to McCarthyism as well as McCarthyism itself?

For some time Moynihan had known about the Venona intercepts, the coded transmissions between Moscow and its espionage network in America during World War II, intercepted and decoded by the army's Signals Security Agency at Arlington Hall in northern Virginia. Moynihan had encouraged the CIA to release the intercepts, and he gave the speeches that opened and closed the 1996 conference marking the publication of the NSA-CIA history of the Venona project.[28]

The Venona intercepts contained overwhelming proof of the activities of the Soviet spy networks in America, complete with names, dates, places, and deeds. Moynihan thought about what might have happened after the war if the government had revealed all it knew about Soviet espionage and the complicity of the American Communist Party before the Communist issue degenerated into a controversy over civil liberties. Instead, the project had been kept secret to prevent the Russians from learning that we had broken their codes. (They already knew, thanks to a spy among the code-breakers and thanks also to Soviet spy Kim Philby, British intelligence's liaison to the American intelligence services, whom the proud code-breakers had invited to tour Arlington Hall.) "What if the American government had disclosed the Communist conspiracy when it first learned of it?" Moynihan asked. That might have "informed the legitimately patriotic American left that there was, indeed, a problem that the Federal Bureau of Investigation, for example, was legitimately trying to address. But this did not happen. Ignorant armies clashed by night."[29]

Here was something worth thinking about: how government secrecy had kept Americans from understanding the real (but limited) extent of Soviet espionage in America and had therefore left them at the mercy of charlatans like McCarthy, for whom ignorance was no impediment to passionate intensity. Add this to the previous question of how secrecy had kept us from recognizing the sorry state of Soviet society and its economy, beguiling us into a new and expensive arms race when watchful waiting would have accomplished the same end at much less cost: these were vital matters scarcely capable of being adequately discussed in a bipartisan committee report. And so Moynihan embarked on his own exploration of the origin and growth of the American secrecy system and its impact on Cold War America. The result was an eighty-six-page appendix to the commission report, "Secrecy: A Brief Account of the American Experience."

But that was not to be the end of the story. Moynihan's appendix to the commission report had given him a chance to trace the history of official secrecy from World War I to the end of the Cold War and how the secrecy system had had disastrous consequences for American society. But there were still unanswered questions. How much had the American government actually known about Soviet espionage at the outset of the Cold War? And why had President Truman not been informed about the Venona intercepts, when the information they contained might have kept him from ignoring the problem of Communist infiltration of the government and so handing the issue over to McCarthy and his gang? The answers were slow in coming from the FBI, but once they arrived, they were astounding. Moynihan now had all the pieces he needed to assemble the story of the American experience with secrecy in the twentieth century. This book is that story.

Secrecy and Memory

America's experience with secrecy during the Cold War was, as Moynihan amply demonstrates, catastrophic. Americans were needlessly diverted from responding sensibly to domestic and international challenges and were led into hysterical and profligate policies that tore the social fabric and the financial balance sheet. Secrecy ceded the issue of domestic Communism to demagogues, while presidents came to rely on estimates of Soviet strength cooked up by spooks protected by secrecy from skeptical questioning. But that story is part of a larger story. If official secrecy had a devastating impact on American history, its impact on Americans' understanding of that history was a collateral disaster.

People are fascinated by secrets. They always have been. Throughout history they have tried to nose out the secrets of the famous and the powerful, speculating that hidden patterns of dark conspiracies control the affairs of men and nations. Normally, these theories of secret conspiracies stay where they belong: on the pages of thrillers by writers with particularly extravagant imaginations; in the minds of individuals of paranoid disposition, usually solitary but sometimes organized into cultlike associations of like-minded confederates; or possibly in the remote regions of the lunatic fringe, where belief in conspiracy theories is expressed in mantralike chants blaming the chosen enemy for whatever ill winds blow.

The key word in the preceding paragraph is "normally." Moynihan has conjured up some of the abnormality of the twentieth century, when unprecedentedly dangerous totalitarianisms with universalistic ambitions provoked apocalyptic responses, responses that at times seemed more rational than the objections of those who protested that the sky was not falling down, at least not exactly or not quite yet.

During times like these, conspiracy theories of history, which feed on official secrecy, climb out of the vasty deeps of politics and jostle for attention like space aliens in the saloon in *Star Wars*. And because of official secrecy, historical writing about the Cold War, both popular and scholarly, came to be permeated with dark suspicions about secret forces concealed by official lies—suspicions that in more reasonable times would have led to challenges that the authors produce their evidence or hold their peace, to put up or shut up.

Moynihan and Shils both noticed how official secrecy during the Cold War took on the overtones of ritual, that is, a performance intended to demonstrate who was in and who was out, who could be trusted and who could not—in other words, who should have the power and who should be powerless. In the beginning the struggle had been along ethnic lines, and the fear was of German Americans and their possible disloyalty; then the fight took on an ideological dimension, as Soviet Russia's American sympathizers were suspected of even more dangerous disloyalties.

A remarkably charismatic triad of concepts—conspiracy, loyalty, and secrecy—had been invited into politics. Before they would be banished—if in fact they are banished, as Moynihan hopes—enormous harm was done to the soul of American politics and to Americans' understanding of their history.

Symbolic secrecy, in the ritualistic sense mentioned above, proclaims that there are those who can be trusted with secrets and those who cannot. As such, it is a powerful tool, enabling dominant groups in government to delegitimize their opponents. But because official secrecy is such an obvious affront to the democratic principle of open government, it takes no great rhetorical skill to turn the weapon of secrecy against those who use it and to insist that public leaders who conceal their deliberations can be up to no good—that they, and not their critics, are the real conspirators against the public weal.

In wartime there is normally no argument but that the enemy is dangerous. The enemy is, after all, shooting in our direction. But the Cold War *was* a cold war; it was possible to argue about how dangerous the enemy was—more or less than the government professed or perhaps not dangerous at all—or whether in fact the enemy was even an enemy. Did official secrets contain proof that the government was erring on the side of insouciance or of hysteria? Or had the government concocted the whole emergency for purposes carefully concealed from the nation?

Official secrecy with its rituals and symbols surged to the surface of American politics during the Cold War. On two momentous occasions, during the brief and deplorable reign of Senator Joseph McCarthy and during the Vietnam crisis, the issue of secrecy took control of political debate in America.

During the early Cold War years, the McCarthyite Right insisted that the government was deliberately concealing FBI files containing proof that Communists had in fact already infiltrated the federal government. McCarthyism would probably have been impossible except for the claim that official secrecy was keeping the American people from the truth about Communism. McCarthy's political demise, which had more to do with his personal character and irresponsible methods than his absurd ideas about conspiracies in high places, permanently discredited the right-wing conspiracy theory of Cold War history, at least within the political mainstream.

Secrecy surged onto the center stage of politics a second time during the late days of the Vietnam War and during the Watergate crisis. Politics in America is at times—maybe most times—a battle for public opinion, but that was particularly true at the height of the debate over the war in Southeast Asia. Secrecy—the insistence that the *real* explanation of events has been concealed from the public—raises the possibility of transforming public opinion by changing perceptions of reality, making the stone rejected (and hidden) by the builder the cornerstone of a new consensus. If the government has sold a policy to the public without disclosing all the policy-makers knew, particularly if what they knew contradicted what they said, then the public would have every reason to reject the official explanation of events and to embrace the alternative. And oh, yes, you may be sure there will be an alternative.

Here is where Cold War historiography came to be infected with the virus of secrecy. In an effort to overturn the official justifications of the Cold War, those protesting the Vietnam conflict produced new histories of the Cold War based not on the documentary history of the Soviet-American conflict, but on what the documents supposedly left out or, more precisely, based on documents kept secret by the security system. The fact of official secrecy became the central affidavit proving the government's guilty complicity in the Cold War. A hunt for official secrets now ensued, as tireless as a beagle's for a rabbit, and secrets became central to the "revisionist" history of the Cold War—the historical view that found Washington primarily responsible for the Cold War.

Moynihan has traced how the system of governmental secrecy developed during the twentieth century and how this secrecy blighted prudent policy making. The documents that he unearthed prove dramatically how secrecy changed the history of the Cold War, and changed it more lamentably than we had suspected.

How could official secrecy have exerted such power that

at key moments it shaped and even transformed American politics? Moynihan and Shils profitably suggest that secrecy's power has roots in the culture of secrecy, in the myths and symbols and rituals produced by decades of guerrilla warfare between conspiracy-minded groups contending on the outer margins of American politics. But there came a moment when the conspiracy theorists' obsession with secrets moved from the margins of politics to the center, and the mere fact that there were official secrets acquired the power to discredit those who made and kept the secrets of the Cold War. Americans began to view their history in a new and unhealthy light: official explanations of Cold War policies were rejected in the conviction that the real explanations were always secret, and secret policies were undemocratic and therefore illegitimate. Now the *revelation* of secrets became a ritual, and eventually this new ritual became as empty, meaningless, and banal as the old rituals of official secrecy.

But it is also a testament to the basic health of the American system that myths, symbols, and rituals will take you only so far. Sooner or later you must produce some facts. And eventually the facts *were* produced. In time, scholars began to examine the supposed secrets of the Cold War, to analyze their contents, instead of merely heaping them up as trophies in the victory of revisionism over Cold War orthodoxy. And when the secrets were unveiled, what surprises they revealed. But surprises should be unwrapped at the right time and the right place, and not before a writer has a chance to perpetuate a modest measure of suspense.

Patterns of Secrecy

Secrecy sells. If secrets aren't interesting, nothing is. Open a database on recently published books and search for titles that contain the word "secrets" or "secrecy," and you will find hundreds, even thousands. (In the interest of full disclosure: your present writer climbed on the secrecy bandwagon himself, with his biography of J. Edgar Hoover, *Secrecy and Power*. The mysterioso quality of the S-word probably accounted for whatever commercial success it enjoyed.)

The new power that secrecy acquired in the late twentieth century went far beyond its capacity to arouse and momentarily satisfy curiosity. Secrets took on a new significance. They came to be seen as the keys that unlocked the mysteries of history.

In order for secrets to attain such power there would have to be preexisting patterns of interpretation that could meld the individual secrets into a master theory of history. The half century of political strife that preceded secrecy's moment of power during the Cold War supplied those patterns.

The hunt for secret conspiracies to explain historical events is an American tradition of long standing. Readers can consult the writings of Richard Hofstadter, which Moynihan mentions, as well as the works of David Brion Davis.[30] To sample the real, bottled-in-bond article straight from the distiller, you can order a few samples from the John Birch Society backlist, available through a toll-free number. Modern conspiracy theorists are quite up to date, thriving on the Internet.

There had been a few instances before the twentieth century when conspiracies emerged as significant factors in American politics. During the Revolution, patriots worried that the British government was conspiring to abolish Americans' rights as Englishmen. During the anti-Catholic ferment over immigration in the 1840s, the Know-Nothings warned that Jesuits and nuns were planning to seize the government. Before the Civil War, the slave power conspiracy haunted the northern imagination; the South feared Yankees were contriving to encourage slaves to murder their masters in their sleep and to subject their mistresses to even worse fates in those same beds.

When the Communist Revolution swept Russia in November 1917, however, conspiracy theory entered a new phase. The patterns that began to develop prepared the way for secrecy's hold over the American imagination later in the century. It was enough to turn some patriots into paranoids when they learned that Germany had helped Lenin get to Russia and when they saw American radicals applaud as the Bolsheviks pulled Russia out of the war. When, in March 1919, Moscow set up the Communist International, an organization of Communist parties everywhere (the U.S. party included) that was dedicated to world revolution, some Americans decided that they knew then all they would ever need to know about the way the world worked. Anyone who tried to tip the American applecart must be following orders from Moscow.

Events during 1919 and 1920 crystallized the nebulous dread of worldwide revolution. Attorney General A. Mitchell Palmer responded to a wave of political bombings, including one that blasted his Washington, D.C., home, by appointing the twenty-four-year-old J. Edgar Hoover to head a new division at the Justice Department. Hoover's charge was to monitor and, where possible, prosecute political radicals.[31]

The industrious and ingenious Hoover, not content with simply rounding up Communists, organized a mass movement against them, issuing a blizzard of documents promoting the idea that the country faced the threat of a "Radical Network." This was supposed to be a secret conspiracy centering on the American Communist parties and the Bolsheviks' undercover operatives; they were allegedly linked to webs that entangled the entire American reform movement. Hoover reserved his special wrath for the "parlor pinks": wealthy individuals, among them some society ladies, who supposedly underwrote the costs of the revolution.

The grassroots anti-Communists began to produce imaginative charts—Red Webs—that diagrammed the radical movement, tracing the nefarious paths of Moscow's influence over the American Left.[32] But while the Comintern and the American Communists would have liked nothing more than to achieve the sort of power their enemies imagined, those Red Webs never existed except in the dreams and nightmares of Communists and anti-Communists. Nevertheless, the anti-Communists now had their theory and were convinced that government files held the secrets that would prove it. Thus the right wing's obsession with government secrecy.

The American Left simultaneously developed its own conspiracy theory. In the wake of Hoover's Red Scare raids, a group of prominent leftist, liberal, and civil libertarian lawyers associated with the National Civil Liberties Bureau (later the American Civil Liberties Union) published their *Report upon the Illegal Practices of the United States Department of Justice.* Citing the widespread and undeniable abuses of aliens' rights during the Red Scare raids, the lawyers charged that the Justice Department was the instrument of a conspiracy against the constitutional rights of all Americans.[33]

That document may be regarded as the blueprint for the Left's analog to the Red Web theory: that there existed a vast right-wing conspiracy against the Left, an unconstitutional, well-organized campaign that included big business, the police, the military, and right-wing civic groups, coordinated by J. Edgar Hoover and his antiradical division within the Justice Department. Because the Nazis would wear brown shirts, let us follow historian Leo Ribuffo and call it the Brown Web theory.[34]

When the ACLU persuaded Attorney General Harlan Stone in 1924 to order J. Edgar Hoover, now the newly appointed director of the Bureau of Investigation (after 1935 the FBI), to end surveillance of American Communists and radicals, right-wing countersubversives were convinced that the Red Web had extended its power into the White House and that the ACLU was the conspiracy's legal front.

During the 1930s historical events produced such rich fare for conspiracy theorists that they became almost giddy from too much food for thought, if such imaginings warrant the name of thought. First, the decade produced a political movement that looked to right-wing conspiracy theorists precisely like their image of the Red Web. After Hitler's triumph in Germany in 1933, followed by the liquidation of the German Communist Party (once the pride of the world movement), Stalin ordered Communist parties everywhere to ally themselves with anyone who would fight Hitler. The resulting Popular Front created an alliance between genuinely independent organizations in the arts, education, and the labor movement together with others claiming to be independent but actually controlled by the party.

Right-wing conspiracy theorists went gaga. Witness the fantastic Elizabeth Dilling's *The Red Network* and *The Roosevelt Red Record and Its Background* and J. B. Matthews's less fanciful but still extravagant *Odyssey of a Fellow Traveler*. The most authoritative evaluation of the Stalinist penetration of America was Eugene Lyons's *Red Decade*. Lyons's judgments about the considerable but not unlimited control that the party exerted over American culture and institutions during the 1930s were later extended, expanded, and confirmed by Daniel Aaron and William O'Neill.[35]

The Red Web theory was also promoted by the House Un-American Activities Committee (HUAC) under Texas congressman Martin Dies, Jr., whose hearings did provide some accurate information about Communist penetration of American institutions, but information so thoroughly mixed with the irresponsible maunderings of conspiracy theorists that the true and useful reports were discredited.

Whereas the Right uncritically absorbed the Dies committee's reports as incontrovertible evidence of Red Web conspiracies, HUAC's excesses caused other fair-minded Americans to regard any investigation of the Communist Party as Red-smearing intended to discredit progressive reform and the entire Roosevelt administration. Anti-Communism came in some quarters to be regarded as a fascist plot, the au courant term for the old Brown Web.

The Left's fear of fascist plots was fanned to a fever pitch after Hitler's invasion of Poland. President Roosevelt had Director Hoover announce that the FBI had once again begun to surveil Communists, Nazis, and other extremists. The Left snapped to attention: Hoover was on their trail again, the same Hoover who had indiscriminately Red-Webbed the entire Left during the Red Scare.

As Europe careened into world war and Americans debated whether the United States should come to the aid of Great Britain, the two conspiracy theories of the Red Web and the fascist plot chased each another like the gingham dog and the calico cat of the old nursery rhyme. Isolationists like Charles Lindbergh painted a menacing portrait: Jews, the British, and the Roosevelt administration were conspiring to pull America into the war. Interventionists, far more effectively, published "exposés," such as John Roy Carlson's *Undercover,* that construed contacts between isolationists and the Nazi propaganda machine as evidence that isolationism was a pro-Nazi, anti-Semitic conspiracy to turn America over to Hitler.[36]

Pearl Harbor did nothing to halt the conspiracy mongering. Isolationists attached themselves to the cause of Pearl Harbor commanders Admiral Husband E. Kimmel and General Walter C. Short, charging that Communists in the administration had maneuvered America into the war to rescue Stalin. The administration joined the interventionists in smearing critics of its war policies as Hitler sympathizers. In 1944 the Justice Department put a motley crew of prewar isolationists on trial for sedition, charging that they were part of an international Nazi conspiracy.[37]

As the Cold War began, then, two mirror-image conspiracy theories had sidled into American politics, the Red Web and the Brown, each with passionate adherents at the opposite extremes of the political spectrum. Informed opinion rejected them both as hallucinations induced by the sulfuric air of politics sealed off from the bracing oxygen of open debate, but these conspiracy theories lurked in the background of politics, awaiting political conditions when the public's attention would shift from the surface of government to its hidden secrets.

The first of these to reemerge was the Red Web. It was carried into the political mainstream by Senator Joseph McCarthy, whose brain was knocked so off kilter by the dazzling revelations of conspiracy theories that he could harangue an astounded Senate with the news that General George C. Marshall was a Communist traitor at the center of "a conspiracy so immense" as to dwarf any in history.

McCarthy would have been nothing without government secrecy. He was able to gain hearing for his fantastic charges only because he could claim that the evidence to support them was kept hidden by the executive branch. Every time he requested classified documents from the government and they turned out to discredit his charges, he simply moved on to new and even more fantastic allegations—the supply of secrets for him to exploit was inexhaustible.[38] Senator Moynihan has even suggested that McCarthyism might not have appeared had the security agencies revealed to the president, and the president to the country, the full and somewhat disappointing facts about the spy menace: that it existed, that it was small, that it had been thoroughly investigated by the FBI. A poignant thought.

McCarthy's run was brief but gaudy. His televised disgrace in 1954 permanently discredited the Red Web and its adherents. After McCarthy, right-wing conspiracy theories would lead a weird half life in American politics, kept alive by a few adherents on the lunatic fringe. In the future they would emerge into the public spotlight only when lugubriously dragged there by mainstream politicians intent on exploiting the public's fear of secret plots and conspiracies while posing as the public's moderate protectors against extremism.

Thus Senator Milton Young of North Dakota rose in 1961 to inform a startled nation that a mysterious figure named Robert Welch, head of an equally mysterious group called the John Birch Society, had written a bizarre biography of Dwight Eisenhower that contained an astounding charge: the war hero and president was a "conscious, dedicated agent of the Communist conspiracy."[39] In a flash the media threw itself into the sort of wild-eyed furor that would later be called a feeding frenzy. What kind of a menace was this maniac Welch? What kind of threat to the republic did this Birch Society represent? And how dangerous was this bizarre cult that, according to an investigation by the California attorney general, was made up of "wealthy businessmen, retired military officers, and little old ladies in tennis shoes"?[40] It certainly sounded bad.

Politicians now took advantage of the John Birch panic to launch an attack on extremism, by which they meant right-wing conspiracy theorists. The Kennedy and Johnson administrations argued that only moderates like themselves, not the conservative opposition (read "extremists"), should be trusted with nuclear weapons. Senator J. William Fulbright pressured Secretary of Defense Robert McNamara to abolish the military's anti-Communist indoctrination programs, which Fulbright charged were producing an army of extremists. Walter Reuther wrote a memo that appealed to the president for a government attack on the extremist Right.[41]

Hollywood pitched in with films like *Seven Days in May* and *Dr. Strangelove* (both 1964) that exploited the liberal nightmare of a nation helpless before malevolent right-wing extremists with a power base in the military. President Eisenhower's valedictory warning about the military-industrial complex, originally meant to caution against the weapons industry's undue influence in politics and culture, was reinterpreted as a revelation of a conspiracy by the military and the big industrialists to subvert democracy.

The fear of right-wing conspiracies was used with devastating effect against Barry Goldwater during his 1964 presidential campaign. Goldwater's opponents for the Republic nomination portrayed him as a tool of the extremists. Nelson Rockefeller called him a dupe and a puppet of sinister right-wing forces. When Goldwater vacationed in Germany before the Republican convention, CBS correspondent Daniel Schorr claimed that Goldwater was making a spiritual pilgrimage to "Hitler's onetime stamping ground" and that the "American and German right-wings are joining up." CBS News ran a documentary on Goldwater that called him the candidate of "the John Birch Society, the Minute Men, and other extremists."[42]

By the time the Johnson administration began to escalate the Vietnam War, many Americans, particularly liberals, had developed a vague dread of a danger on the Right—conspiracies and plots by powerful secret forces at the highest echelons of industry and the military. The moment had come when the rituals of secrecy could move into the center of political life.

The Moment of Secrecy

That moment arrived early Sunday morning, June 13, 1971, when the first in an explosive series of stories by Neil Sheehan appeared on the front page of the *New York Times*.[43]

In 1967 Secretary of Defense Robert McNamara had commissioned an official history of the Vietnam involvement, a massive project that would become known as the Pentagon Papers. The project was completed by members of the Pentagon's in-house task force, one of whom was a Harvard-educated former marine named Daniel Ellsberg. An enthusiastic supporter of the war during his tour of Vietnam in 1965 and 1966 as a State Department official serving with the legendary General Edward T. Lansdale, Ellsberg had undergone a conversion into an antiwar activist.

While working on the "Top Secret–Sensitive" Pentagon Papers, Ellsberg became convinced that the record of the government's actual policy making in Vietnam was so greatly at variance with the government's stated rationale that, if the public had a chance to read the Papers, it would demand an end to the war. Ellsberg made an unauthorized copy for himself and began to shop the Papers around to antiwar politicians in Washington.

Then Ellsberg learned that Sheehan, whom he had known in Vietnam, was writing a *New York Times* essay that reviewed thirty books about the war. The title was to be "Should We Have a War Crime Trial?" That got Ellsberg's attention. He brought the Papers to Sheehan. Since Sheehan was convinced the war was a crime, there had to be criminals somewhere. Now he had a massive collection of secret government documents that detailed the decisions leading to that criminal war. Logically, then, these documents should constitute the evidence of official crimes.

The *Times* realized that it had one of the greatest scoops in journalism history. Maintaining absolute secrecy, the newspaper's reporters and editors barricaded themselves in a hotel and began to digest and summarize the huge bulk of documents that Ellsberg had handed over. These were the stories that began to appear in daily installments in the *Times* that Sunday. Government secrets—not what they revealed, but the mere existence of government secrets—would now prove to have the power to change the public's mind about the most controversial political issue of the day.

How did secrets acquire that power? Certainly it was sensational for a major newspaper—or any newspaper—to publish classified documents. It was the height of the Vietnam War, and the secret information that they contained was certainly of enormous interest to the country. Americans could now read a behind-the-scenes, day-by-day account of how the nation's leaders had evaluated conflicting reports from the field, guessed at the best response to confusing battlefield situations, and then urged their policies on the country with a confidence that none of them felt in private. At a minimum, the Pentagon Papers dramatized the old saw that every political decision is a 51–49 proposition but has to be sold as 100 percent certainty.

But as controversy over the war reached a boiling point, minimal interpretations were not on the table. Sheehan's introduction to the edition of the Papers that the *Times* published as a book claimed, "To read the Pentagon Papers in their vast detail, is to step through the looking glass into a new and different world. This world has a set of values, a dynamic, a language, and a perspective quite distinct from the public world of the ordinary citizen and of the two other branches of the Republic—Congress and the judiciary."[44]

Sheehan described the war as something hatched by plotters in deepest secrecy: "The guarded world of the government insider and the public world are like two intersecting circles." Within the secret circle of power, the public and Congress are seen as "elements to be influenced" rather than as participants having a legitimate interest in knowing what the government is planning: "The Papers also make clear the deep-felt need of the government insider for secrecy in order to keep the machinery of state functioning smoothly and to maintain maximum ability to affect the public world."[45] Vietnam policies were made in secret and had to be kept secret from a public that might have questioned, even rejected, them.

Senator Mike Gravel of Alaska, in the introduction to his edition of the Papers, went even further: "The Pentagon Papers tell of the purposeful withholding and distortion of facts. . . . The Pentagon Papers show that we have created, in the last quarter-century, a new culture, a national security culture, protected from the influences of American life by the shield of secrecy."[46]

In a matter of days the Pentagon Papers became the touchstone for a new view of American history: the decisions that shaped the Cold War were secret, and secrecy had protected these policies from a (virtuous) public that would have struck down the miscreants had the truth been known.

This remarkable transformation in popular attitudes, let it be remembered, was caused by a work of forty-seven volumes (the original length of the classified report) that almost no one had read (then or later). This massive government study was then abridged and published first in the lengthy newspaper series, which, again, few people read from beginning to end; then in a 677-page book, the *New York Times* paperback, which almost nobody read in its entirety; and then, finally, in a six-volume set, published by the Government Printing Office, which it would be remarkable if anyone has ever read from cover to cover.

Was there ever a greater illustration of the medium (secrecy) being the message (conspiracy)? Almost none of the minds changed by the Pentagon Papers ever came into contact with the words that supposedly constituted the proof of the conspiracy. Amazing.

Such a miraculous conversion of so many Americans from skeptics about conspiracies to believers in them could have happened only if they were predisposed to be so converted and only if the conversion conferred immediate benefits, if only of the psychological variety. Namely, if they went along with the interpretation of the Pentagon Papers urged by Ellsberg and Sheehan, readers and nonreaders alike could claim that they were not involved in the Vietnam disaster, were not complicit, because they had been kept from full awareness of the facts by government secrecy.

The impact of the Pentagon Papers on the popular mind was reinforced by the Nixon administration's ham-handed effort to keep them secret. Nixon's immediate instinct had been to let the *Times* publish and be damned, since the misdeeds that the Papers revealed, if misdeeds they were, were the work of Democrats. But Henry Kissinger was engaged in negotiations with the Chinese and is said to have persuaded the president that the Chinese wouldn't continue their secret parleys if they saw that Washington couldn't keep *its* secrets.

The government's effort to suppress the Papers seemed to prove that Sheehan and Ellsberg were right: that the Papers revealed guilty secrets about a government conspiracy to lead the country into Vietnam, because otherwise the government would not have tried to stop their publication. Ellsberg was put on trial for illegally possessing and copying classified documents, but the case was dismissed when the White House "plumbers" broke into the office of Ellsberg's psychiatrist and rummaged around for incriminating information. The collapse of the case seemed equivalent to a guilty verdict against the government.

Ironically, it had been liberals like those in the Kennedy and Johnson administrations that had taught the public to fear militarists secretly conspiring to drag the country into apocalyptic military adventures. Now this propaganda recoiled on the liberal architects of the Vietnam War. The Pentagon Papers launched the theory that the war in Southeast Asia (and perhaps the entire Cold War) had been a conspiracy hatched in private by liberal cold warriors who had used governmental secrecy to hide their decisions from the public and to avoid constitutional checks and balances. In their political strategy of posing as the public's defenders against the danger on the Right, "moderates" had built a trap for "extremists" and had stumbled into it themselves.

Opponents of the war, many of them involved from the beginning in the Cold War containment policies that had led finally to Vietnam, now could absolve themselves of guilt: it had not been the constitutional government that had led the country into war, they could now say; it was the secret work of the hidden government. The public had been out of the loop. And so was born a new history of the Cold War. It had been a secret history, and secrecy had brought it into the open.

The Power of Secrecy

Secrecy could achieve such a powerful hold on the American imagination because it became part of a ritual that reapportioned blame for Vietnam and Watergate, absolving some while condemning others. In Washington and in the culture as a whole, there was a political tendency—perhaps a movement—that had an investment in revelations of gov-

ernmental secrets. Its political power was based on the belief that the secret files concealed guilty secrets that explained the Vietnam disaster and perhaps even the entire
course of the Cold War.

An interpretive pattern now existed that could fit isolated secrets into a grand—and chilling—vision of a covert
government hiding behind official secrecy, manipulating
policy, with nothing but contempt for the will of the electorate and the rules of the Constitution. Revelations of the
government's secret activities during the Cold War now fell
like hammer blows against the schoolbook image of a constitutional, representative American government. An obvious point, but one worth repeating: we fit facts to our assumptions more than we fit our assumptions to the facts. As
American society disintegrated during the final stages of the
Vietnam War and the government splintered during the Watergate crisis, secrecy came into its own as a judgment on
America's role in the Cold War.

As the revelations proceeded, they became self-inter-
preting—the simple fact of government secrecy was seen as
proof that the government was steered behind the scenes by
unknown conspirators. And more revelations that seemed
to confirm the conspiracies of a secret government were not
long in coming.

On March 8, 1971, a group of antiwar activists (probably the Catholic East Coast Conspiracy to Save Lives) raided
the FBI resident agency in Media, Pennsylvania, and made
away with the agency's domestic security files. At the end of
the month an eighty-two-page extract was printed in the
pacifist-socialist journal *WIN*. The files revealed a wide range
of FBI activities against the antiwar movement. Hoover's
aide Mark Felt said that the raid was "the turning point in
the FBI's image," because release of the files justified the New
Left's "paranoid fear of the FBI, which it hysterically equated
with the Soviet secret police"—a view, he added, that now
"seeped into the press and found growing expression among

the more bewitched and bothered opinion makers." Even so, the FBI probably could have ridden out the storm if one of the files had not carried the hitherto unknown caption "COINTELPRO." This caught the eye of NBC correspondent Carl Stern, who used the Freedom of Information Act (FOIA) to sue the FBI for all documents dealing with COINTELPRO.[47]

On December 6, 1973, Stern received those documents. He now had evidence of the FBI's most deeply buried secrets: its operations modeled on counterintelligence programs (hence the acronym, from COUNTERINTELLIGENCE PROGRAMS) that used unusual, invasive, and possibly illegal tactics to disrupt first the Communist Party; then the Ku Klux Klan, the Black Panther Party, and the Socialist Worker Party; and, finally, the antiwar movement, with special focus on the Students for a Democratic Society.

Each of these groups could now argue convincingly that its constitutional rights had been violated by the bureau and, less logically but still plausibly (at least to some), that democratic debate had been aborted because their voices had been stifled. In other words, dissent had been defeated, not because its arguments lacked merit, but because of secret and illegal government plots.

Further proof of the new power of secrecy as a force in history came with Richard Nixon's resignation from the presidency. The ultimate political prize had been wrested from the disgraced president because he had been unable to prevent the press and the Congress from exposing the "White House horrors" to public gaze.

The Watergate era saw the normal political process partially eclipsed by a frenzied search for political secrets that, properly handled, could destroy the opposition. The congressional elections of 1974 and 1976 and Jimmy Carter's victory over Gerald Ford in 1976—one of his campaign promises was the vow "never to lie to you"—brought to power politicians who owed their success to the pursuit of secrets and to the public's readiness to interpret secrecy as a pattern of illegal, conspiratorial activity. The hunt for secrets made national heroes and Hollywood stars out of the investigative reporters who dug out those secrets.

In 1975 both houses of Congress lent their authority to investigations based on the thesis that a secret government had been directing the affairs of state during the Cold War. The Senate and House each appointed select committees (under Senator Frank Church and Congressman Otis Pike) to investigate, in the words of the Senate resolution, "the conduct of domestic intelligence or counterintelligence operations against United States citizens" to see whether they threatened "the rights of citizens."[48]

Both committees, armed with the ultimate weapon of the congressional subpoena, tunneled through the files of the FBI, the CIA, and the other national security agencies. The Pike committee, the more aggressive of the two, stirred up so much controversy that its report was suppressed. The Church committee's report was published, however, and it placed an official stamp of legitimacy on the conspiracy theorist's history of the Cold War. The investigators wove together examples of illegal (or at least unsavory) malfeasance by the intelligence agencies, producing a narrative in which the historical context of the security agencies' sins receded and sank below the historical horizon, while the misdeeds themselves were pilloried in isolated ignominy as self-motivated, self-indicting, and self-condemning. The purpose of domestic anti-Communism, it could be said (and was said), was simply to attack the rights of anyone who stood in the way of the government's power elite and its clients. By extension, the purpose of the Cold War abroad was to obliterate those unlucky enough to stand in the way of that elite's global power.

The Church committee made the Vietnam era's antiwar movement represent all dissenting movements of the past. Just as government repression had contributed to the Vietnam disaster, the committee suggested, the repression of earlier dissent had probably contributed to the country's misguided Cold War policies. Arguing backward, the committee held that if the FBI's repression of Vietnam-era dissent was unnecessary and wrong, then so were the bureau's earlier domestic intelligence campaigns. The Church committee complained that "from today's perspective it is harder to understand the nature of the domestic threats to security which, along with foreign espionage, were the reasons for establishing the FBI's intelligence program in the 1930s."[49]

The committee devoted most of its energy to exposing the FBI's COINTELPROS. Dismissing bureau attempts to justify the programs, the select committee flatly stated that COINTELPRO was a "sophisticated vigilante program aimed squarely at preventing the exercise of First Amendment rights of speech and association, on the theory that preventing the growth of dangerous groups and the propagation of dangerous ideas would protect the national security and deter violence." The committee was able to produce ample evidence that Hoover had labored hard to keep these activities secret, and in the post-Watergate era, which saw a cover-up as an admission of guilt, that proved that they were wrong.[50]

The House committee located a disaffected ex-agent who provided the exactly the conclusion the new view of secrecy was driving toward: "The FBI now constitutes a degenerative dictatorship in which the structure still remains but from which public support is rapidly being withdrawn. I further submit that such a dictatorship is incompatible with the constitutional concepts upon which this Nation is founded. I feel that this can be historically paralleled with the ascension of other dictatorships throughout the world."[51] Years later, the definitive study of the Church and Pike committees would be titled *Challenging the Secret Government*.[52]

The CIA also contributed its share of guilty secrets to the cauldron of boiling paranoia. Reporter Daniel Schorr broke the story of CIA assassination plots against foreign leaders, among them Patrice Lumumba of the Congo. Throughout 1975 the *New York Times* and other newspapers followed up with more details on the assassination story: the targets included, besides Lumumba, Ngo Dinh Diem of Vietnam and Rafael Trujillo Molina of the Dominican Republic. There were rumors of plots against Sukarno of Indonesia and Duvalier of Haiti, along with reports on the CIA's involvement with the Mafia in plots against Castro. In none of these cases did proof emerge that the CIA's plans had gone beyond the contingency phase, but the stories indelibly imprinted on the public mind an image of the CIA as a secret murder squad.

In 1973 retired Air Force colonel Fletcher Prouty (Oliver Stone's model for Colonel X in the film *JFK*) published *The Secret Team: The CIA and Its Allies in Control of the United States and the World*. One of his charges was that Allen Dulles had "positioned CIA personnel and agency oriented disciples inconspicuously throughout the Government." Schorr put Prouty on the air to charge that Nixon aide Alexander Butterfield had been the CIA's spy in the White House. The story fell apart when Butterfield convincingly refuted the allegations, but again there seemed to be another glimpse into the secret government.[53]

The power and prestige of the secret as the key to understanding the history of the Cold War now created a new receptivity for Cold War studies that blamed America for the whole ungodly mess. A brilliant group of revisionist historians associated with the so-called Wisconsin school of William Appleman Williams had been charging that the United States had been the guilty party in the breakdown of the wartime alliance with the Soviet Union. Williams's own *Tragedy of American Diplomacy* (1959) had argued that American diplomacy was dominated by the search for commercial markets for American produce and products. Other revisionists followed Williams in discovering that motives far less lofty than altruistic Wilsonianism lay behind American policies at the beginning of the Cold War. Denna Fleming, in *The Cold War and Its Origins* (1961), argued that anti-Communists in the Roosevelt and Truman administrations had sabotaged Roosevelt's plan for friendly relations with the Soviet Union. Gabriel Kolko's *Politics of War: The World and United States Foreign Policy, 1943–1945* made America's anti-Soviet policies during World War II largely responsible for the breakdown of the Soviet-American alliance and the beginning of the Cold War. Lloyd C. Gardner's *Architects of Illusion: Men and Ideas in American Foreign Policy, 1941–1949* concluded that "responsibility for the way in which the Cold War developed, at least, belongs more to the United States." Gar Alperovitz's *Atomic Diplomacy: Hiroshima and Potsdam, the Use of the Atomic Bomb, and the American Confrontation with Soviet Power* argued that the bomb had been dropped on Japan to warn Stalin against interfering with American plans for world empire.[54]

David Horowitz, whose *Free World Colossus: A Critique of American Foreign Policy in the Cold War* (1965) turned the revisionist thesis into a blistering anti-Vietnam polemic, later explained that his book had become standard reading in college history courses because Vietnam had created a hunger for works that discredited the historical justifications for Vietnam. "Cold War revisionism," he said, "that is, accounts of post-war history significantly at variance with the State Department line, was still illegitimate [before 1965]: it had no status as serious scholarship inside or outside the university." But Vietnam and Watergate created an opportunity for "secret histories" of the Cold War to undermine the old Cold War verities by denying the reality of the Soviet threat and questioning the motives behind the containment doctrine.[55]

Anti-Communists mounted a furious attack on the revisionists, questioning their selection of sources and their assumptions about Stalin's intentions. In particular, they noted a "proof by lack of evidence" as a characteristic methodology in revisionist Cold War history.[56] In other words, the revisionists discounted the policy-makers' explanations of events as insincere and dishonest, while deriving their revisionist views from the assumption that the real design of American foreign policy was so discreditable that, if it appeared on paper at all, it did so only on documents kept secret from the American people.

The revisionist historians certainly believed in what they were saying, and they were often researchers who spent their lives combing archives for evidence to support their arguments. In retrospect, however, it can be seen that acceptance of their ideas was the unforeseen (but, naturally, welcome) consequence of the public's general rejection of official explanations around the time of the Pentagon Papers. Revisionism's thesis was hardly sustainable without the assumption that the real explanation of events is always hidden behind a wall of official secrecy.

It was more because of these circumstances than the intrinsic force of their arguments that the revisionists' critique of American policy emerged in the 1970s first as an alternative and then as the dominant view of the Cold War's origins. Anti-Communists were demoralized to see what they had always held to be unassailable truths—the evil and danger of Communism—were now scorned and rejected by some of the brightest, most idealistic minds of the rising generation.

Congress itself avidly pursued more secrets. Bella Abzug of New York hectored the late J. Edgar Hoover's aged secretary, trying to wring from her an admission that the files she destroyed after the director's death were Hoover's long-rumored secret blackmail files. In 1976 the House established the Select Committee on Assassinations. After two years and nearly $5.8 million, the committee was on the verge of concluding that the Warren commission had been basically correct about President Kennedy's assassination, when it received an acoustic interpretation of police radio transmission recordings seeming to indicate that a second gunman had fired shots near the grassy knoll. Chief Counsel G. Robert Blakey, a specialist on organized crime who later achieved fame as the father of the RICO statute, suggested that the assassination was a mob hit and speculated that Santo Traficante of Tampa or Carlos Marcello of New

Orleans, or both, were involved. This was as close as any official body has ever come to endorsing a conspiracy theory on the JFK assassination, but it was soon discovered that the recording was made after the shooting, so that whatever the sounds were, they were not of gunfire.[57]

By the late 1970s a veritable industry had been built on acquiring secret FBI files via the Freedom of Information and Privacy Act and interpreting them as revelations of a secret government in charge of the national destiny. To scholars like Athan Theoharis, who served on the staff of the House Select Committee on Intelligence, we owe much of what we know about the FBI's behind-the-scenes activities under Hoover. But like the Spanish explorers whose geographical discoveries were an unintended consequence of their quest for the chimerical city of El Dorado, the scholars who intended to map the activities of a secret government advanced our historical knowledge without ever locating that secret government. Most of their time was spent digging through the debris left by bureaucrats and politicians reluctant to let the public in on discussions that would have been highly embarrassing if discovered by political enemies.

In some quarters, and they included some influential precincts in the government, the universities, and the media, secrecy became the explanation for almost everything that ailed America: had it not been for their ability to keep their machinations secret, the powers of darkness would not have enjoyed so long a reign. Full disclosure would produce, if not lemonade springs, then at least a golden age of good government devoted to progressive causes, with the swords of the cold warriors morphed into plowshares designed for ecologically sustainable development. Ah, if things were only that simple.

The Banality of Secrecy

Things were not that simple. The election of 1980 brought an unabashed anti-Communist to the White House. The

Cold War was revived and then resolved in one of the most peculiar endgames in history. To extract an analogy from Senator Moynihan's analysis, it was as though two chess grand masters had pursued an interminable and highly sophisticated strategy of feint and counterfeint, not noticing that, for the past forty or fifty moves, one side not only has been in checkmate but has had his queen, rooks, bishops, and knights all taken from the board. Of course, one not inconsiderable detail—that both sides had nuclear weapons—kept the game from being completely boring.

And the secrecy industry rumbled on. The Freedom of Information Act allowed failed and forgotten political activists to validate their identities. The FBI had always been the far Left's excuse for its political failures. Now the FBI provided old radicals with one final service: supplying files that proved a radical movement had actually existed, present appearances to the contrary. They must have had some importance if the FBI had kept tabs on them. The FBI's FOIA office was transformed into a genealogy service for the old Left, and the bureau had to devote major resources to processing files for release. Individuals bragged that they had filed hundreds, thousands, tens of thousands of requests. Every few weeks the media breathlessly revealed that the FBI had been keeping a file on a leftist writer or artist or Hollywood star. Or an FOIA request had revealed that a conservative or sometimes a liberal celebrity had furnished information to the FBI. Horrors!

But the unending revelations of government secrets was beginning to seem forced, clichéd, even a bit pointless. True, we live in an age of hype, but the hype for the latest revelations of government secrets had soared far beyond anything that could be supported by what the files revealed. A collection of the FBI's files on American writers carried the subtitle *The FBI's War on Freedom of Expression,* although the book was a themeless hodgepodge of investigative files, clipping files, cross-reference files, and files established because writers were named during a related or unrelated investigation. Missing was any proof that the FBI had ever established files on writers simply because they were writers. William F. Buckley, Jr., in fact, was moved to protest mildly, "Some of us will stop short of saying that the FBI was engaged in a war against freedom of expression, while agreeing that if that had been Mr. Hoover's intention, he was off to an appropriate start."[58]

Another collection of FBI files on American writers was billed as a shocking account of "the fifty-year espionage campaign waged by the CIA, FBI, and other intelligence agencies against . . . famed American writers." That shock was undercut by the content of the dossiers, which included newspaper clippings lodged in files for want of anywhere else to put them. The documents were less dangerous than ineffectual and a little silly, particularly because for the most part nothing came of them. Most Americans today would deplore the bureau's having accumulated these files. But it is easy after the fact to discount the security agencies' worries about the pro-Soviet sympathies of American artists and intellectuals. At the time, the Soviet Union had been able to mobilize much of the world's intellectual and artistic community against the United States' efforts to contain Stalin, when the success of those efforts was very much in doubt. But even if no allowances are made for the historical emergency that caused the files to be gathered, the dossiers hardly constitute evidence of the claim made in the aforementioned book's subtitle: *The Secret War Against America's Greatest Authors*. Some war. Some secrets.[59]

The ritual of secrecy was running out of steam. The new revelations were falling short of spectacular because the historical crisis (Watergate and Vietnam) was now receding into the past. Because the times no longer provided the public with a way of interpreting secrets, the political significance intended to be drawn from them had to be explicitly provided, and that interpretation had an embarrassing resemblance to the old "fascist plot" conspiracy theory.

A collection of interviews with radicals of the 1930s and

1940s was titled *It Did Happen Here*. "It" was fascism, an allusion to Sinclair Lewis's antifascist novel *It Can't Happen Here*, implying that the Cold War had turned the United States into a fascist country and that this fascist repression had defeated the Left. The Left did not simply lose out in the marketplace of ideas because of the weight of its own errors or because of the affluence of the American working class. "It" could not have simply been that Americans understood and rejected the politics of the interviewees. The title of another oral history of the Cold War, *Memories of the American Inquisition*, insinuated the same charge: the Cold War was simply a pretext for eliminating radicals from American politics, a view echoed in the title of *J. Edgar Hoover and the American Inquisition*. A documentary history of the domestic Cold War was called *The Age of McCarthyism*, thus eliminating the possibility that America's response to Communism was anything except its worst excesses.[60]

Desperation seemed to push some writers into disclosing that their obsessive laceration of Cold War orthodoxy was motivated less by logical reason than by something approaching religious fervor. A history of the Cold War was titled *Losing Our Souls*, although it was pretty clear that by "our souls" the author meant "your souls," that is, the souls of the policy-makers he attacked: "Our Cold War policy, for all its success in dissolving the USSR, was so grievously flawed that the United States may never fully recover from its effects upon our values, our freedoms, our politics, our security, the conditions of our material life, the quality of our productive plant, and the very air we breathe."[61]

Now when headlines (in gradually diminishing type sizes) announced that an FOIA request had revealed that the FBI had maintained a file on someone famous, the press had a vague sense that such things ought to be newsworthy, but it was no longer sure exactly why. Flipping to the more yellowed cards in their Rolodexes, reporters had to depend on aging radicals to vent the appropriate outrage and tie the new revelation into a sweeping indictment of the FBI, the Cold War, or the whole damn country.

By the late 1980s it was becoming difficult to get a hearing for the old fascist-plot theory without hyping it up by linking it to the grand tradition of conspiracy theory. A 1988 edition of I. F. Stone's *Hidden History of the Korean War* strained to justify its republication by placing Stone in the context of conspiracy-minded Roman historians. Stone was praised for connecting secret events into a pattern of the "arcana imperii [imperial secrets]—empire and its method as a hidden thing, shrouded above all from the people it ruled." Stone, the foreword claimed, "described a war in which 'an ephemeral elective occupant' at home [Truman] jousted with an 'ambitious proconsular Caesar abroad' [MacArthur], already plotting to turn against the capital the armies with which he had been supplied to hold distant marches against barbarian hordes."[62] The ad writers for *Star Wars* could hardly have done better.

Secrecy was beginning to evolve from a theme in historical analysis to the status of an aesthetic formula and plot convention in popular entertainment. Most viewers and reviewers scoffed at Oliver Stone's pretensions as a historian, but few could resist the melodramatic excitement that Stone (I. F. Stone's namesake and spiritual heir) drew from the revisionist history of the Cold War. In *JFK* (1991) and *Nixon* (1995), the major events of the century are explained as the results of "black ops": covert operations by hidden conspirators so highly placed that they amount to a secret government that wielded the real power in the Republic, a secret government that Stone calls "the Beast."

JFK wove the Kennedy assassination into the venerable conspiracy theory of the Cold War as an American plot. Stone based his film on New Orleans district attorney Jim Garrison's *On the Trail of the Assassins,* in which Garrison raved: "What happened at Dealey Plaza in Dallas on November 22, 1963, was a coup d'état. I believe that it was instigated and planned long in advance by fanatical anti-Communists in the United States intelligence community . . . and that its purpose was to stop Kennedy from seeking détente with the Soviet Union and Cuba and ending the Cold War."[63] For Stone, the Kennedy assassination was part of a century-long plot to use the threat of Communism to protect the interests of America's ruling class. American anti-Communism was fascism, and it had been secretly running the country since World War II.

As the original political intent behind the search for government secrets slipped from memory, what survived of the politically rooted plot convention might be called postmodern secrecy mongering. Balzac said that the fundamental principle of popular writing is that behind every great fortune lies a great crime. Postmodern popular culture holds that behind every great political career lies a great scandal— a formula that provides the catharsis of discrediting the powerful, thereby vicariously empowering everyone else.

By way of example, there is television's wildly successful program *The X-Files*, which sends FBI special agents Fox Mulder (David Duchovny) and Dana Scully (Gillian Anderson) to hunt for government secrets about the extraterrestrial and the paranormal; their mottoes are "The truth is out there" and "Trust no one." The FBI in *The X-Files* is an organization suffused with paranoia and riven by plots and counterplots to frustrate Mulder and Scully from learning what is concealed in the bureau's X-Files, bureauspeak for cases too disturbing to be revealed to the public (unless they are concocted for the purpose of distracting the public from more important government conspiracies—sometimes the show's writers can't make up their minds).

The show's main plot device, a war between an FBI intent on concealing its guilty secrets and a citizenry determined to learn the truth, recalls the Church committee's portrayal of FBI director Hoover as the master blackmailer of American history who used secret files to promote his extremist political agenda. The series also draws on the faith of the era of the Pentagon Papers and the Nixon White House tapes: that the release of government secrets has the power to redeem American history and save the national soul.

The transformation of governmental secrecy and the historical theories based on it into popular entertainment formulas can also be seen in big-budget thrillers like *The Rock* (1996). Nicholas Cage plays an FBI agent–scientist at the bureau's laboratory in Washington; he is sent to San Francisco when terrorists take over the prison at Alcatraz and threaten to poison San Francisco Bay. But in postmodern FBI entertainment, it is no longer enough for the special agent–superhero to defend the nation against underworld conspiracies. *The Rock* also serves up a conspiracy *within* the bureau. Sean Connery plays a British operative held in a federal prison for stealing microfilms documenting the government's involvement in covering up UFO landings, planning the Kennedy assassination, and so on—all the standard fixtures of modern paranoia; the FBI's demented director plans to have Connery killed leading an assault on the island. But the characters played by Cage and Connery liberate the island, capture the terrorists, kill the director, and, as the picture ends, are about to release the microfilmed secrets that will save the world. Almost too much for one movie.

Postmodern secrecy mongering is part of what might be called postmodern paranoia, an aesthetic preference for "alternative" modes of thought that leads to a playful interest in conspiracy theories about government secrecy just for the hell of it. On the Internet, one site (www.conspire.com) is a spin-off from a book entitled *The Sixty Greatest Conspiracies of All Time*. Other, often ephemeral sites are named "Conspiracies, Cover-Ups, and Crimes"; "Secret No More," which posts FBI files obtained through the FOIA; and "Skeleton Closet," which tracks presidential hopefuls and reports "all the dirt on all the candidates—because character *does* matter." As I write this, the A&E Television Network is advertising a special program on conspiracies, a survey of the "hidden truths" of the great events of our time. As Art Linkletter liked to say, "People are funny." Maybe the culture of openness that Senator Moynihan proposes will finally let us laugh political paranoia out of American politics. It's a nice thought, but perhaps a trifle optimistic.

And as the original political motivation for the pursuit of government secrets devolves into the apolitical exploitation of scandal, earnest conspiracy theorists of the old school scold the popular culture for its obsession with the sex lives of the rich and powerful. When Anthony Summers described J. Edgar Hoover's supposed transvestism (in his biography *Official and Confidential*), some of Hoover's old enemies complained not just that the exposé was probably bogus, but that interest in the salacious side of the FBI would distract the public from the more serious political conspiracy theories about the bureau.[64] And while most historians noted that Seymour Hersh's revelations, in *The Dark Side of Camelot*, about JFK's sexual hijinks were unlikely to alter our evaluation of the Kennedy presidency, one reviewer, while contributing a few tidbits of his own, speculated darkly that the hubbub surrounding the book's publication amounted to an establishment plot to distract the public from the real Kennedy scandal: the media's complicity in the national security state's defeat of popular government.[65]

The history of secrecy has finally reached a point where people choose to believe in conspiracy theories—and even concoct their own—to satisfy aesthetic criteria, to purge themselves of personal demons, or just to have something to think and talk about. Some undertake their hunts for government secrets in order to resurrect lost causes, to vindicate positions taken during the Cold War, or to validate their status as certified victims of American fascism. Others simply cash in on secrecy because it once paid off and probably always will.

Sic transit gloria arcanorum.

The Irony of Secrecy

As political conspiracy theories about governmental secrecy devolved into the banality of commercial entertainment formulas, the accelerating declassification of Cold War secrets, often over the determined objection of the security agencies themselves, was taking an ironic—and, to some, an unwelcome—turn.

Over the years the Left had turned the Hiss and Rosenberg trials into case studies of its argument that the domestic Cold War had been a right-wing plot to repress radical reform and create an American empire. Central to this attack on Cold War orthodoxy was the claim that both Alger Hiss and the Rosenbergs had been put on trial, framed, and then unjustly punished to create hysterical public support for the Truman administration's containment strategy. These cases went to the heart of Washington's Cold War policies, both at home and around the world, because if the defendants were guilty as charged, it meant that the Soviet Union, far from being a friendly ally of the United States, had engaged in aggressive, hostile espionage against its American partner; that the American Communist Party was the willing and essential accomplice in Soviet espionage; that American Communism was not twentieth-century Americanism, as its 1930s slogan claimed, but a new form of treason. But if the charges were false, so were the government's justifications for the Cold War.

When historian Allen Weinstein began his study of the Hiss case in 1969, his position was that Hiss may have lied about not knowing Chambers but that Chambers "had falsely accused Hiss of Communist ties and espionage."[66] When Weinstein was denied the classified documents that he needed to test this hypothesis, he sued the FBI under the Freedom of Information Act. After three years of legal wrangling, he obtained more than thirty thousand pages of FBI files on Hiss and Chambers. Weinstein supplemented these with documents from archives in the United States and abroad, and he interviewed American and foreign members of Soviet espionage rings living in the Soviet bloc.

While Weinstein was pursuing this research, the Watergate crisis erupted. In an illogical but psychologically compelling association, some saw the Hiss case and Watergate as enmeshed: since Watergate refuted the patriotic belief that "the government would not lie, that law enforcement agencies would not fabricate evidence," the reasoning ran, "how much further would the Bureau have moved into illegality and fabrication when the spy mania was at its height and J. Edgar Hoover was in total control?" Since the point of raising the issue of secrecy was to prove a pattern of secret conspiracy, all government secrecy must be part of the pattern. Hiss's son recalled that there was "talk going around Washington . . . that all the recent political trials, beginning with the 'Hiss case,' were fixed."[67]

But at the end of his meticulously researched and argued study of the case, which finally appeared in 1978, Weinstein concluded that "the body of available evidence proves that [Hiss] did in fact perjure himself when describing his secret dealings with Chambers, so that the jurors in the second trial made no mistake in finding Alger Hiss guilty as charged."[68]

In some quarters this was the worst sort of bombshell, because it was friendly fire, and so the rage against Weinstein pulsed with a sense of betrayal. One historian wrote that Weinstein's sin was that he had demolished the fondest hopes of those who had used the Hiss case as their point of attack against the Cold War establishment: the belief among old and new leftists that establishing the innocence of Alger Hiss would redeem their history.[69]

In 1983, secret documents dealt an even more devastating blow to the revisionist position that government secrecy was evidence of anti-Communist plots. Like Weinstein, Ronald Radosh and Joyce Milton began their research for *The Rosenberg File* convinced that the government's secret documents must contain proof of the Rosenbergs' innocence. Radosh recalled that demonstrating against the Rosenbergs' executions was the beginning of his political education—it was "simply . . . an article of faith, an axiom, that Julius and Ethel Rosenberg were the victims of a government-sponsored conspiracy."[70]

But when Radosh gained access to the more than 200,000 pages of FBI, CIA, and navy documents released to the Rosenberg children in settlement of their FOIA lawsuit, he was amazed to find just the opposite. After dogged investigations and surprising discoveries that make their book the equal of the best true-crime reporting, Radosh and Milton concluded that the Rosenbergs, though unjustly executed, were guilty as charged: Julius had been a principal and Ethel his accomplice in one of the most important of Russia's espionage networks, and they had delivered valuable information about nuclear weapons to the Soviet Union.[71]

Radosh and Milton naively believed that their book would be salutary for the Left: "If the Rosenberg case has an ultimate moral, it is precisely to point up the dangers of adhering to an unexamined political myth." They did not expect bouquets, but they were unprepared for the rhetorical violence that greeted their book's publication. "To some veterans of the Old Left, merely to say in print that the Rosenbergs were involved in espionage," Radosh discovered, "was tantamount to calling for the resurrection of McCarthyism." During a public debate, their book was called the "fraud of the century," their scholarship "garbage in, garbage out."[72]

Since then, a wealth of evidence has accumulated to reinforce Radosh and Milton's conclusions, including documents from Soviet and American archives and information from new interviews with American spies who escaped prosecution by fleeing to the Soviet Union. Soviet case officer Aleksandr Feklisov of the KGB, for example, who formally signed up Rosenberg and directed him in his activities, has now confirmed Rosenberg's espionage activities. All this corroborates what Radosh and Milton wrote years ago, and in a new edition of their book they say: "If there is anything we have established, it is that the Rosenberg case resulted from a genuine effort to combat Soviet espionage; it was not a witch-hunt. It was not Julius Rosenberg's civil liberties that were being jeopardized but his espionage activities."[73]

It had been governmental secrecy that had allowed critics of the Rosenberg and Hiss cases to construct their elaborate theories about frame-ups and cover-ups. For years the Rosenbergs' defenders had demanded that the government reveal its secrets about the case, probably never dreaming that someday the files would land with a thump on their doorsteps. When the government gave in and released the documents, the secrets made the government's case even stronger. "Over the years," Radosh scoffs, "the Rosenbergs' defenders have loudly demanded the release of government documents on the case, only to deny the documents' significance once they are made public."[74] As the secret archives of the Cold War are released, the original case made against Soviet espionage in this country has received ever more conclusive corroboration. Secrecy raised doubts about the great internal-security cases of the Cold War; ending that secrecy has resolved them.

The release of secret Soviet documents after the collapse of the Soviet Union has also provided conclusive evidence of the American party's disloyalty, thus demolishing the theory that domestic anti-Communism was simply a conspiracy against the Left. In 1992 Harvey Klehr of Emory University traveled to Moscow to study the Russian archives on the Communist Party of the United States (CPUSA). On subsequent trips he was joined by John Earl Haynes of the Library of Congress. They collaborated with Fridrikh Igorevich Firsov of the Comintern archive at the Russian Center for the Preservation and Study of Documents of Recent History to produce *The Secret World of American Communism* (1995), part of Yale University Press's Annals of Communism series. Klehr, Haynes, and Firsov reprinted documents from

the Russian archives that proved beyond doubt that the Soviet Union had heavily subsidized the CPUSA throughout its
history, that prominent American radicals had laundered
money for the Comintern, that the American party had
maintained a secret espionage network in the United States
with direct ties to Russian intelligence, that the testimony of
former Communists like Whittaker Chambers and Elizabeth Bentley with regard to underground activity in the
United States had been accurate in substance and in detail,
that American Communists in government agencies had
stolen secret documents and passed them to the American
party, which forwarded them to the Soviet Union—and
much more.

"It is no longer possible," Klehr, Haynes, and Firsov conclude, "to maintain that the Soviet Union did not fund the
American party, that the CPUSA did not maintain a covert apparatus, and that key leaders and cadres were innocent of
connection with Soviet espionage operations. Nowhere in
the massive Comintern archives or in the American party's
own records did the authors find documents indicating that
Soviet or CPUSA officials objected to American Communists
cooperating with Soviet intelligence or even having second
thoughts about their relationship. Both the Soviet Union
and the American Communist leadership regarded these activities as normal and proper. Their only concern was that
they not become public."[75]

The most dramatic release of secret files from the Cold
War, the publication of the Venona intercepts between July
1995 and August 1996, was another devastating blow to revisionist theories that minimized or dismissed the threat of
Soviet espionage and the treasonous activities of American
Communist spies. As noted earlier, "Venona" was the code
name for one of the greatest cryptanalytical achievements in
the history of espionage and counterespionage. Between
1940 and 1948, army code-breakers managed to decipher
more than 2,900 messages between the Soviet Union and the
United States, messages detailing the activities of the Soviet

espionage networks in this country. A fantastic achievement, given the fiendishly difficult nature of the codes used.

As Moynihan notes, these intercepts provided a limited number of security professionals, including J. Edgar Hoover and his top associates, with fine-gauge descriptions of the activities of precisely the same Soviet spies who were named by defecting Soviet agents Alexander Orlov, Walter Krivitsky, Whittaker Chambers, and Elizabeth Bentley. In these coded messages the spies' identities were concealed beneath aliases, but by comparing the known movements of the agents with the corresponding activities described in the intercepts, the FBI and the code-breakers were able to match the aliases with the actual spies. Thus Julius and Ethel Rosenberg, Harry Dexter White, Klaus Fuchs, David Greenglass, and Theodore Alvin Hall were dragged, like moles from their tunnels, blinking in the bright light of history.

The prosecutors in the internal-security cases of the 1940s had not known, nor, until Venona, had we, that they had not been given all or even the best government evidence against the Rosenbergs et alia. The Venona materials would have been conclusive in establishing the cast of characters in the Soviet spy networks. But the documents were not handed over to the prosecutors to keep the Russians from learning that their codes had been broken. All in vain. As mentioned earlier, the Soviets had already found out, through the efforts of English spy Kim Philby. Thus information that could have corroborated the testimony of Whittaker Chambers and Elizabeth Bentley was denied not only to the government prosecutors and the American people but to the president himself. How, though not yet why, Harry S. Truman was denied this desperately needed information has been revealed for the first time in FBI documents obtained by Senator Moynihan in his research for this volume.

Not only have newly released secret documents undercut the charge that the government concocted the threat of Soviet espionage, but they have also discredited the claim that Washington deliberately (or unwittingly) misled the public about the Soviet threat to the United States, Europe, and Asia. John Lewis Gaddis, who is the Robert A. Lovett Professor of Military and Naval History at Yale University and is generally considered the most authoritative historian of the Cold War, has surveyed what can now be said about the history of this conflict. His book's title, *We Now Know*, refers to the fact that, whatever new information about the Cold War surfaces in the future, we now know *how* that war ended—the critical fact not known by writers of earlier Cold War histories.

It does Gaddis no favor to summarize his nuanced discussion in a few sentences, even if the sentences are his own. His main conclusion is that "the 'new' history [of the Cold War] is bringing us back to an old answer: that *as long as Stalin was running the Soviet Union a Cold War was inevitable*" (emphasis in original). Moreover, the conditions that made the Cold War inevitable did not end with Stalin's death, because Stalin "built a system sufficiently durable to survive not only his own demise but his successors' fitful and half-hearted efforts at 'de-Stalinization.'"[76]

"Who then was responsible [for the Cold War]?" Gaddis asks. "The answer, I think, is authoritarianism in general, and Stalin in particular." Gaddis drives home his point: "Did Stalin therefore seek a Cold War?" His answer: "Does a fish seek water?"[77]

Gaddis shows in case after case how the latest information from American and foreign archives tends to support the original explanations that Washington offered for its policies. Archival documents relating to "the hidden history of the Korean War," to use I. F. Stone's term, now show that the war was fully premeditated by North Korea and that the plans were approved by Stalin himself.[78] There is no documentary support for Stone's thesis that the Korean War was the result of a secret power struggle in Washington; instead, everything refutes it.

There is, moreover, no documentary evidence for the

most fundamental thesis of all Cold War revisionism—that the United States deliberately embarked on the conflict simply to increase its economic and political power. Not only do the recently released secret archives of the Cold War fail to support the revisionists, but the documentary evidence refutes them. Gaddis points to the crucial difference between what the revisionists call the American "empire" and Stalin's: Stalin forcibly constructed an empire with a brutality that ensured its instability, whereas the Europeans voluntarily sought refuge within an American empire. We now know that the savage behavior of the Red Army in Eastern Europe eliminated any possibility that the Russians could construct an empire by consent similar to that which evolved in the West. In the Soviet empire "there were few people left apart—from the party and official bureaucracies who ran it—who believed that they had anything to gain from living within a Soviet sphere of influence." In the American zone, "Europeans were meanwhile convincing themselves that they had little to lose from living within an American sphere of influence."[79]

The Soviet archives and the testimony of Soviet diplomats and agents also undercut the revisionists' fallback position: that even if Stalin and later Soviet leaders seemed to act aggressively, they were merely behaving in a manner customary to world powers, who all try to expand their influence and carve out spheres of influence. Far from relinquishing Lenin's goal of world revolution, Stalin's innovation was to view the Soviet Union as the center from which socialism would spread and eventually defeat capitalism: "The effect was to switch as the principal instrument for advancing revolution from Marx's idea of a historically determined class struggle to a process of territorial acquisition Stalin could control."[80] Soviet memoirs and archives furnish ample proof that what Gaddis calls Soviet leaders' "romantic" attachment to the world revolution continued to guide their actions. A paramount example of that continued attachment to revolutionary ideology was Khrushchev's dangerous and provocative support for Castro, which in turn led to the missile crisis.

In assigning responsibility for the Cold War to Stalin, Gaddis is careful not to say the United States and the West were blameless in their responses. "This argument by no means absolves the United States and its allies of a considerable responsibility for how the Cold War was fought," he writes. "Nor is it to deny the feckless stupidity with which the Americans fell into peripheral conflicts like Vietnam, or their exorbitant expenditures on unusable weaponry: these certainly caused the Cold War to cost much more in money and lives than it otherwise might have. Nor is it to claim moral superiority for western statesmen. None was as bad as Stalin—or Mao—but the Cold War left no leader uncorrupted: the wielding of great power, even in the best of times, rarely does."[81]

The irony of secrecy's impact on Cold War historiography is that, as documents from the Soviet archives and newly declassified materials from American agencies become available, there may be developing a historical consensus that will once again resemble the original justification for containment offered by Truman, Marshall, Kennan, Acheson, Nitze, and the other policy-makers. Once dubbed by revisionists the architects of illusion, these leaders are coming to be seen as having acted sensibly and responsibly in light of the knowledge available to them, and that knowledge now seems to have been accurate in view of what is now known about the intentions, character, and personality of Joseph Stalin and the system he created.

The End of Secrecy?

This seems to be the final irony of government secrecy in the Cold War: originally imposed largely as a ritual to delegitimize critics of Cold War policies, secrecy was transformed by revisionists into a counter-ritual to discredit America's role in the Cold War—only to end, when the secrets were finally revealed, as a vindication of the original architects of the war. The door swings both ways. It swings open. And it swings closed.

It would be too much to say that there the matter rests, because so much in Cold War history touches on basic human questions that will forever be disputed. But it would not be too rash to say that the inordinate role of secrecy in setting the terms of the historical debate is over. Throughout much of the Cold War, conjecture about secrets produced an adversarial alternative to the official explanation of American government policies. The end of secrecy has returned our view of Cold War history to facts instead of speculations about what is not known. The debate will go on, but it will be more honest.

Yet if the end of secrecy has confirmed that the substance of American Cold War policies was sound, it has confirmed just as strongly how wrong our leaders were to rely on secrecy in order to achieve their goals. The irony of secrecy is that it cut most deeply those who used it to stifle opposition to their policies. In the short term, secrecy may have made it easier for Washington to mobilize the country during the postwar crisis with Stalin. But the government's reliance on secrecy raised doubts about the wisdom and morality of policies that might well have been more solidly supported had the issues been fully aired in debate. What secrecy grants in the short run—public support for government policies—in the long run it takes away, as official secrecy gives rise to fantasies that corrode belief in the possibilities of democratic government. All because of secrets locked away foolishly and in the end, it would seem, needlessly. Secrecy is a losing proposition. It is, as Senator Moynihan has told us, for losers.

CHAPTER ONE

Secrecy as Regulation

ecrecy is a form of regulation. There are many such forms, but a general division can be made between those dealing with domestic affairs and those dealing with foreign affairs. In the first category, it is generally the case that government prescribes what the citizen may do. In the second category, it is generally the case that government prescribes what the citizen may know.

In the United States, secrecy is an institution of the administrative state that developed during the great conflicts of the twentieth century. It is distinctive primarily in that it is all but unexamined. There is a formidable literature on regulation of the public mode, virtually none on secrecy. Rather, there *is* a considerable literature, but it is mostly secret. Indeed, the modes of secrecy remain for the most part—well, secret. On inquiry there are regularities: patterns that fit well enough with what we have learned about other forms of regulation. But there has been so little inquiry that the actors involved seem hardly to know the set roles they play. Most important, they seem never to know the damage they can do. This is something more than inconveniencing to the citizen. At times, in the name of national security, secrecy has put that very security in harm's way.

How did secrecy and bureaucracy become so entwined—a vast secrecy system almost wholly hidden from view? What has it cost (no less than what it has achieved)? A clearer picture is emerging.

The Foreign Relations Authorization Act for Fiscal Years 1994 and 1995 created the Commission on Protecting and Reducing Government Secrecy to conduct "an investigation into all matters in any way related to any legislation, executive order, regulation, practice, or procedure relating to classified information or granting security clearances."[1] In truth, apart from atomic energy matters, there was only one such general statute—the Espionage Act of 1917 at the outset of World War I. As for inquiry, there had been but one other commission, the Commission on Government Security, created in 1955. This, of course, came in the aftermath of the Communists-in-government issue which convulsed American politics following World War II. The first commission, however, added nothing to our knowledge of that subject, and many of the issues were still out there. It seemed a good place for the new commission to begin.

It happened that the National Security Agency, our signals outfit—successor to the Army Signals Intelligence Service and the army security agency and under the leadership of its deputy director, William P. Crowell—was beginning to think it time to reveal some of the things that the army had learned about Soviet espionage in those years. After all, the Soviet Union had disappeared, and the code-breakers who had decrypted the secret messages were in their late years, still unacknowledged. And now there was this new commission. In short order it was determined to turn the Venona decryptions, as they were called, over to the commission. ("Venona" is a made-up word designating a Soviet code.)

In July 1995 the first set of documents was released at a

ceremony at the Central Intelligence Agency's headquarters in Langley, Virginia, and the story began to unfold. On February 1, 1943, the Signals Intelligence Service had begun transcribing Soviet cables (mostly KGB)* sent between Moscow and the United States (mainly to and from contacts in New York and Washington). The cables were both coded and enciphered, and it remains a marvel that any were ever broken. Not many were: only about 2,900 in all, a fraction of the many thousands intercepted. The arduous decoding work began in 1943 and was done at Arlington Hall, a former girls' school in Virginia; the setup resembled that of the Ultra project at Bletchley Park in wartime Britain, where German signals were intercepted and decoded.

But unlike the British team, which had a smuggled copy of the encoding machine used by the Germans, the American team had only the coded cables themselves. Led by Meredith Knox Gardner, the code-breakers put in much hard work during World War II, but they broke nothing. In the summer of 1946, however, Gardner managed to extract a phrase in a KGB message sent from New York to Moscow on August 10, 1944. Next was a report on the presidential election of 1944. Then, on December 20, 1946, a cable sent to Moscow two years earlier. It contained a list of the scientists working on the Manhattan Project, the secret U.S. government project that developed the first atomic bombs.

This decoded cable and the ones that followed were a revelation. As the monograph accompanying the 1995 release of the documents puts it, "The Venona decrypts were . . . to show the accuracy of Chambers' and Bentley's disclosures"—that is, the accuracy of the information about Soviet espionage that Whittaker Chambers (beginning in 1939) and Elizabeth Bentley (beginning in 1945) had provided to the American government. As more cables were decoded,

* For the sake of clarity, in this book the acronym KGB refers not only to the Komitet Gosudarstvennoi Bezopasnosti, or the Committee of State Security, which was established in the Soviet Union in 1954, but also to its predecessor organizations.

General Carter W. Clarke of army intelligence informed the FBI liaison officer that "the Army had begun to break into Soviet intelligence service traffic, and that traffic indicated a massive Soviet espionage effort in the U.S."[2]

"Massive" is a relative term. In all, the Venona decryptions came up with some two hundred names or code names of Americans who were passing secret information to Soviet agents. There were neighborhoods in New York City in which this number would have seemed surprisingly small, such were the politics of that time and place. (Possibly the most important of the atomic spies was a nineteen-year-old from the West Side of Manhattan, Theodore Alvin Hall, who betrayed his country's secrets quite on his own initiative. Indeed, he had to go looking for a Soviet agent to give the secrets to.) On the other hand, two hundred Communist spies might have seemed chilling to someone living in Kansas City, Missouri. Given that not a few Republicans were then attacking the New Deal as being soft on Communism, the charge could easily have been dismissed as domestic politics. Perhaps especially by the president of the United States, a Democrat from Missouri.

National politics and national security are always to some extent interrelated, but in the years of the Truman presidency the relationship became problematic. Trust leeched out of the political system, loyalties waned, betrayal became common. Communism—as an indigenous force, as yet another manifestation of diaspora politics, or as an instrument of Soviet policy—achieved astonishing influence not in its own right, much less on its own behalf, but as an agent for poisoning American politics. The effects were felt for a generation or more; the reverberations are felt even today, after the collapse of the Soviet Union. Government secrecy, as the commission was discovering, played a large role in all this.

Begin with the Federal Bureau of Investigation and its director, J. Edgar Hoover. At that time a prudent operative reported every hint of danger, and did so immediately. Consider Hoover's letter of May 29, 1946, sent to the director of what was then a powerful federal agency and meant to be shared with Truman; the commission retrieved the document, until now unpublished, from the Harry S. Truman Library.

Federal Bureau of Investigation
United States Department of Justice
Washington 25, D.C.
May 29, 1946

PERSONAL AND CONFIDENTIAL
BY SPECIAL MESSENGER

Honorable George E. Allen
Director
Reconstruction Finance Corporation
Washington, D.C.

Dear George:

I thought the President and you would be interested in the following information with respect to certain high Government officials operating an alleged espionage network in Washington, D.C., on behalf of the Soviet Government.

Information has been furnished to this Bureau through a source believed to be reliable that there is an enormous Soviet espionage ring in Washington operating with the view of obtaining all information possible with reference to atomic energy, its specific use as an instrument of war, and the commercial aspects of the energy in peacetime, and that a number of high Government officials whose identities will be set out hereinafter are involved. It has been alleged that the following departments and agencies of the United States Government handle the problem and current development of atomic energy and among these departments and agencies, the United States secret of atomic energy is held in trust. The names of the individuals in each department or agency who control such matters have been furnished as follows:

State Department—Under Secretary of State <u>Dean
Acheson</u>
    Assistant to the Under Secretary of State
    <u>Herbert Marks</u>
    Former Assistant Secretary of War <u>John J.
    McCloy</u>

War Department—Assistant Secretary of War
<u>Howard C. Peterson</u>

Commerce Department—Secretary of Commerce
<u>Henry A. Wallace</u>

Bureau of the Budget—<u>Paul H. Appleby</u>
    <u>George Schwartzwalder</u>

Bureau of Standards—<u>Dr. Edward U. Condon</u>

United Nations Organization—<u>Alger Hiss</u>
    <u>Abe Feller</u>
    <u>Paul Appleby</u> (who is being considered for trans-
    fer from the Bureau of the Budget to the United
    Nations Organization)

Office of War Mobilization and Reconversion—
<u>James R. Newman</u>

Advisors to the Congressional Committee on Atomic
Energy—<u>James R. Newman</u>
    <u>Dr. Edward U. Condon</u>

The individual who furnished this information has reported that all of <u>the above individuals mentioned are
noted for their pro-Soviet leanings, mentioning specifically Alger Hiss of the United Nations Organization, Paul
Appleby and George Schwartzwalder of the Bureau of the
Budget, Dr. Condon of the Bureau of Standards, and John
J. McCloy of the State Department.</u>

The informant has stated that the McMahon Committee headed by Senator Brien McMahon of Connecticut is charged with formulating the policy concerning atomic energy[,] and serving as advisors to the Committee are <u>Dr. Condon of the Bureau of Standards, who, the informant states, is nothing more or less than an espionage agent in disguise, and James R. Newman, an employee of the Office of War Mobilization and Reconversion who is known to the informant to be a personal friend of Nathan Gregory Silvermaster,</u> who, you may recall, is one of the principal individuals known to have operated as an agent of the Soviet Government in U.S. Government offices for a considerable time until December, 1944. <u>It is known that Silvermaster obtained information through his associates in a Russian espionage network and such information was turned over to the Soviet Government.</u> The informant has indicated that Newman is also a friend of the news commentator <u>Raymond Gram Swing and columnist Marquis Childs. Newman is also reported to be the so-called ringleader of this particular Soviet espionage network</u> and through his employment with the Office of War Mobilization and Reconversion, he had access to material flowing from the <u>White House.</u> The informant stated that through Dr. Edward Condon at the Bureau of Standards, Newman has access to technical data concerning atomic energy. The informant further stated that Secretary of Commerce Henry A. Wallace knows of the background of Dr. Condon but condones his further employment in this highly strategic and important position.

<u>James Newman allegedly obtains from the War Department through the cooperation of Assistant Secretary of War Peterson highly technical information on the atomic bomb itself</u> and all matters relating generally to atomic energy. According to the informant, Newman has a direct line to Assistant Secretary Peterson's office.

With reference to the State Department, it was reported that Newman is in personal and daily contact with Dean Acheson, Herbert Marks, and on some occasions with John J. McCloy, and therefore, any knowledge of atomic energy and international relations with reference to it are immediately known to him. In so far as the international picture is concerned with respect to atomic energy, it was reported that Newman is in a position to obtain this information from Alger Hiss of the State Department who holds the position of advisor to Mr. Stettinius,* the American Representative to the United Nations Organization.

Concerning the Bureau of the Budget, the informant reported that Paul Appleby and sometimes George Schwartzwalder pass upon the recommendations of the Office of War Mobilization and Reconversion which are made to the President concerning the necessary appropriations to carry on experimental operations concerning atomic energy and particularly its relative position to that of a large Army and Navy. It was pointed out that in almost all cases the final decision at the Bureau of the Budget on such matters is passed upon by Paul Appleby.

The informant has drawn the conclusion that the entire setup of the McMahon Committee to investigate and recommend legislation on atomic energy and its use is a scheme to make available information concerning the atomic bomb and atomic energy, and that it all amounts to Soviet espionage in this country directed toward the obtaining for the Soviet Union the knowledge possessed by the United States concerning atomic energy and specifically the atomic bomb.

The informant stated that technical and exacting information which Newman desires to pass on to Russian principals is made available to Mr. Silvermaster, or, in those matters of a highly technical nature, Dr. Edward Condon of the Bureau of Standards contacts Silvermaster directly. The news commentator Raymond Gram Swing, according to the informant, is utilized for subtle propa-

* Edward R. Stettinius, Jr., served as U.S. secretary of state (1944–45) and as the first U.S. delegate to the United Nations (1945–46).

ganda with reference to agitation for release of atomic energy to the Allied Powers and that the same use is made of Marquis Childs, a feature Washington newspaper writer.

The informant is of the opinion that <u>the entire setup has a use other than that of espionage</u> for the Soviet Government, namely, <u>the promotion of pro-Soviet propaganda,</u> which, when reduced to its simplest form, advances the argument <u>"why keep a large Army and Navy when the use of atomic energy eliminates the necessity for such a large force."</u> In Government circles and among those handling the question of atomic energy, the unanimous argument of all and especially of those mentioned above is in agreement that a large Army and Navy are not necessary to the United States as the United States has exclusive knowledge and the "know how" of the atomic bomb.

<u>It is known to this Bureau that Dr. Condon is a personal friend of Nathan Gregory Silvermaster, and although Silvermaster is presently under investigation by this Bureau, no information has been developed to substantiate the fact that Condon has turned over any information of a confidential nature to Silvermaster.</u> It has also been made known to this Bureau through various sources in the past that the political views of Under Secretary of State Dean Acheson, Assistant Secretary of War Howard C. Peterson, and Secretary of Commerce Henry Wallace have been pro-Russian in nature, and therefore, it is not beyond the realm of conjecture that they would fit into a scheme as set out above. Alger Hiss of the United Nations Organization has been reported to this Bureau as a former member of the Communist underground organization operating within the Government in Washington, D.C.

Since James R. Newman has been described as the ringleader of this alleged espionage network and, further, since Herbert S. Marks is in close touch with information dealing with relations between the United States and Russia at the State Department in the office of Dean Acheson, investigations are being conducted by this Bureau concerning the activities of these two individuals. You may be assured that you will be kept advised of all developments in connection with the above allegations.

Sincerely yours,
Edgar[3]

This was baseless corridor talk. There were scraps of truth here, but in the main it was fantasy and dismissed as such. Both fantasies *and* truth.

We now know how it came about in those surreal times. John E. Haynes of the Library of Congress has unearthed the document that led to Hoover's bizarre compendium of May 29. The day before, the director had received a memorandum from D. Milton ("Mickey") Ladd, head of the FBI's security division. Ladd, the son of Senator Edwin Freemont Ladd of North Dakota, appears to have been an exemplary agent, later becoming assistant to the director. And he cleared his desk. The subject of Ladd's memorandum, which the director had requested, was Alger Hiss. Page after page laid out what was known about Hiss (including the fact that his wife, Priscilla, may have been a member of the League of Women Shoppers). Mostly atmospherics, but then, many a mafioso got in trouble for less. The serious charges were those leveled by Whittaker Chambers, who insisted that Alger Hiss was a member of "the underground organization of the Communist Party in Washington, D.C., as early as 1933." In New York no shortage of people knew what Chambers had been; now Washington was catching on. Ladd's memorandum was for the most part an admirable summation, but then it included this extraordinary claim:

> Mr. Joseph A. Panuch, Deputy to Assistant Secretary of State Russell, has reported to the Bureau that Alger Hiss together with Dean Acheson, Under Secretary of State; Herbert Marks, Assistant to the Under Secretary of State; John J. McCloy, former Assistant Secretary of War; Assistant Secretary of War Howard Peterson; Henry A. Wallace, Secretary of Commerce; Paul H. Appleby and George Schwartzwalder of the Budget Bureau; Dr. Edward U. Con-

don of the Bureau of Standards and the Senate Committee on Atomic Energy; James Newman of the Office of War Mobilization and Reconversion and also an advisor on the Committee on Atomic Energy and Abe Fuller of the Budget Bureau and UNO [United Nations Organization] are operating as an enormous espionage ring in Washington with the ultimate objective of obtaining all information concerning atomic energy, its specific use as an instrument of war and commercial aspects thereof in peacetime for the purpose of making such information available to the Soviet Union.[4]

Here Ladd grew a little careless. For starters, he didn't have the name of their source quite right. It was J. Anthony Panuch (pronounced "panic"), then deputy to the assistant secretary of state for administration, Donald S. Russell. Panuch was born in Prague, emigrated to the United States early, and graduated from Fordham University and Columbia University School of Law. Afterward he had a wide-ranging career, but he was evidently not welcomed at the higher reaches of the State Department. ("I knew him before he was nobody," recalls one contemporary.) His charges were loony, but the director of the FBI passed this lunacy on to the president of the United States the very next day.

Except there *was* the matter of Alger Hiss.

When the Commission on Protecting and Reducing Government Secrecy acquired the first Venona decryptions and a number of further releases now available in *Venona: Soviet Espionage and the American Response, 1939–1957*, the fine volume by Robert Louis Benson and Michael Warner, we were prompted to ask a simple, urgent, central question. As the Venona documents showed, by 1947 the United States was acquiring solid evidence of Communist espionage. The FBI knew all about this, for it fell to them, specifically to their brilliant agent, Robert Lamphere, to break the code names in the KGB cables. (Elizabeth Bentley, for instance, was "Good Girl.") Now then, did the director of the FBI, who had been quite prepared the year before to rush to the president a report of an all but fictional "enormous Soviet espionage ring in Washington," inform the president of the possibly less than enormous but *real* Communist spying when *real* evidence became available?

This seemed a simple matter to sort out. Surely the FBI's archives contained documents that would answer the question one way or another. The commission decided to ask the current director of the FBI, Louis J. Freeh, for help. This was done, and agents were immediately placed at the commission's disposal. Or rather, the agents came round one morning, professed not to know much about the matter, but promised to look into it. They were never heard from again.

Bureau "property," the commission members surmised. After the commission report was completed and published, I wrote, as chairman, to Director Freeh, recounting what had happened, or rather had not happened, expressing a measure of disappointment. Freeh was quietly indignant; a statutory commission had made a legitimate request for information and been stonewalled, as it were, by his own agents. He ordered his personal staff to sweep the basement. In short order they produced a loose-leaf binder of Top Secret files: some thirty-six documents, now at last available.

And we have our answer. President Truman was never told of the Venona decryptions.

It gives one pause to think now that all Truman ever "learned" about Communist espionage came from the hearings of the House Un-American Activities Committee, the speeches of Senator Joseph R. McCarthy, and the like. But, as the commission discovered, the decision not to tell the president was made not by J. Edgar Hoover, who hated Truman. It was made by Omar Nelson Bradley, chairman of the Joint Chiefs of Staff, who admired Truman in a most personal way and served him with the highest professional standards. The proof was in the binder. On October 18, 1949, an FBI agent, Howard B. Fletcher, sent to Ladd a memorandum describing a recent conference with General Carter W. Clarke, then chief of the army security agency, "regarding the dissemination of [Venona] material to the Central Intelligence Agency" (Figure 1).

> General Clarke stated that when Admiral Stone* took over in charge of all cryptanalytical work he was very much disturbed to learn of the progress made by the Army Security Agency in reading [Venona] material. Admiral Stone took the attitude that the President and Admiral Hillenkoetter† should be advised as to the contents of all of these messages. General Clarke stated that he vehemently disagreed with Admiral Stone and advised the Admiral that he believed the only people entitled to know anything about this source were [deleted] and the FBI. He stated that the disagreement between Admiral Stone and himself culminated in a conference with General Bradley. General Bradley, according to General Clarke, agreed with the stand taken by General Clarke and stated that he would personally assume the responsibility of advising the President or anyone else in authority if the contents of any of this material so demanded. General Bradley adopted the attitude and agreed with General Clarke that all of the material should be made available to [deleted] and the FBI.
>
> General Clarke stated the reason that he recently called upon you was for the purpose of informing you as to the difference of opinion between himself and Admiral Stone and to acquaint you with the opinion of General Bradley. He stated that he wanted to be certain that the Bureau was aware of this and to make sure that the Bureau does not handle the material in such a way that Admiral Hillenkoetter or anyone else outside the Army Security Agency, [deleted,] and the Bureau are aware of the contents of these messages and the activity being conducted at Arlington Hall.[5]

Army "property." And so Truman was never told.

* Admiral Earl E. Stone was the head of the newly created Armed Forces Security Agency, which in 1952 became the National Security Agency.

† Admiral Roscoe H. Hillenkoetter was the first director of Central Intelligence (1947–50).

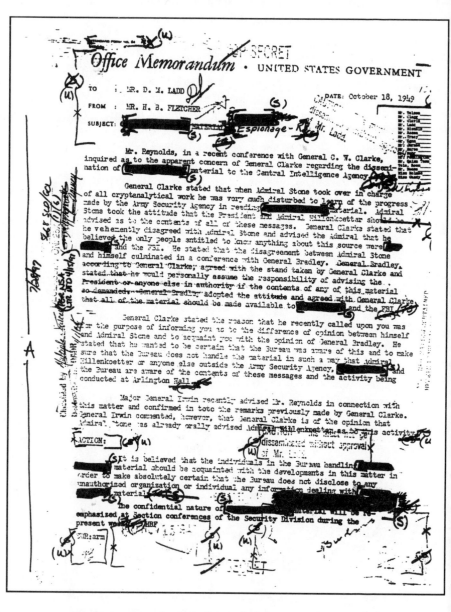

Figure 1. The October 18, 1949, memorandum reporting Omar Bradley's decision not to inform President Truman of the Venona decryptions. *Source:* Federal Bureau of Investigation, Washington, D.C.

Here we have government secrecy in its essence. Departments and agencies hoard information, and the government becomes a kind of market. Secrets become organizational assets, never to be shared save in exchange for another organization's assets. Sometimes the exchange is in kind: I exchange my secret for your secret. Sometimes the exchange resembles barter: I trade my willingness to share certain secrets for your help in accomplishing my purposes. But whatever the coinage, the system costs can be enormous. In the void created by absent or withheld information, decisions are either made poorly or not made at all. What decisions would Truman have made had the information in the Venona intercepts *not* been withheld from him?

The question tantalizes, for the president was hardly a passive figure. Claude D. Pepper would tell a story about Truman from the days when they were fellow senators; it now seems to suggest how different things might have been. One midday in the late 1980s, I was walking with the former senator from Florida back from the Senate to the House, he having returned to Congress as a member of the House of Representatives. We left the Senate chamber by the west entrance, turned left, and were soon passing S-224, one of those nameless rooms in the Capitol where members assemble for assorted activities (one of which, in an earlier time, was a morning tumbler of bourbon). "See that room?" Pepper remarked. "I was walking just where we are now one morning in 1940, when Harry Truman came out. 'Claude,' he said to me, 'don't you think we ought to get up a committee to look into the profits all these defense industries are making these days out of the Army and Navy? If we don't, the Republicans will!'"

By March 1, 1941, the year after this exchange, the Truman committee, formally known as the Committee to Investigate the National Defense Program, was created. It wasn't that many years later that Truman became president. It is surely logical to suppose that such a man would sense the political peril of a Communist espionage ring operating within his own government. If only he had known this—known for real, that is, from the likes of Bradley. If only political liberals had known. If only those in the universities had known. Seymour Martin Lipset has observed that at the height of the McCarthy era, an academic would be in worse trouble with his peers if he believed Chambers than if he believed Hiss. The Hiss perjury trial was a defining political event, as Richard Gid Powers observes in his Introduction. Allen Weinstein, in *Perjury: The Hiss-Chambers Case*, notes that even before Hiss went to prison, Hiss and Chambers and their "supporting casts" had achieved "the status of icons in the demonologies and hagiographies of the opposing camps." The result was a kind of unconscious obscurantism: "Contemporary arguments by politicians and intellectuals alike over the 'meaning' of the Hiss case, more than the evidence itself, set the direction and limits of subsequent historical investigation."[6] Affairs need not have been so misdirected. Secrecy ensured that they were.

And secrecy continues to flourish even now, with the Cold War ended and military outlays beginning, or in some instances continuing, to decline. Current projections for the year 2002 call for the number of military personnel to be reduced by one-third and military procurement, in constant dollars, to be reduced by one-half compared to 1985 levels.[7] Even today there are considerably fewer military officers and fewer "classification authorities" (or "original classifiers"), that is, individuals designated "in writing, either by the president or by selected agency heads, to classify information in the first instance." The 1996 report of the Information Security Oversight Office—part of the National Archives and Records Administration, which keeps track of classified information—summarized the year's trends as follows.

- The number of original classification authorities decreased by 959 to 4,420.
- Reported original classification decisions decreased by more than 62,000 to 105,163.

The numbers are declining, as one would expect in the post–Cold War era. But then the report summarizes the year's "derivative" (as opposed to original) classification decisions—documents classified because they incorporated, paraphrased, restated, or otherwise referred to classified information—and the year's total for all classifications, original and derivative. Here there is an increase.

- Reported derivative classification decisions increased by 2.2 million to 5,684,462.
- The total of all classification actions reported for fiscal year 1996 increased by 62 percent to 5,789,625.[8]

The CIA accounted for 52 percent of all classification decisions, the Department of Defense for 44 percent. It is hard to see how fewer military officers and fewer classification authorities could result in a stunning 62 percent *increase* in new secret documents—almost 6 million in all, and all of them deemed threats to national security if ever disclosed. Such is the grip of secrecy entwined with bureaucracy.[9]

Bureaucratic boundaries have also proliferated, although occasionally they have been surmounted by public servants of rare quality. In the case of the CIA and the FBI in the 1990s, John M. Deutch as director of the CIA, Jamie S. Gorelick as deputy attorney general, and Louis J. Freeh as director of the FBI have developed guidelines for sharing intelligence information and thereby have successfully reduced tensions between these two rivals. At the top, at all events. In the vaults and tunnels, however, the secret wars have gone on as before.

A notable example of this continuing conflict occurred in Berlin in the early 1990s, after the wall fell and East Germany reunited with West Germany. The CIA station in Berlin had begun obtaining files from the now defunct East German Stasi (domestic intelligence) and HVA* (foreign intelligence). The FBI, for its part, was just then beginning the mole

* The HVA, or Hauptverwaltung Augklärung (Main Department of Reconnaissance), was part of the Ministry of State Security.

hunt that would lead in 1994 to the arrest of Aldrich Ames (quite the most spectacular infiltrator in our nation's history and to all appearances completely apolitical; the traitors, at least, knew when the Cold War was over). But the CIA station chief in Berlin, dubbed by FBI agents "the Poison Dwarf," or so it was reported in the press, refused to provide access to the files.[10]

There was no misfeasance in this; the culture of the intelligence community was to develop sources and keep them in place, as was that of the law enforcement community. But this time the matter grew so contentious that the head of the Department of Justice's Office of Intelligence Policy and Review suggested that the FBI begin investigating whether the chief of the CIA Berlin station ought to be indicted by the U.S. government for obstruction of justice. In the end, the station chief retired and matters were resolved, but it seemed that some things had not changed since 1949.

Indeed, although the Central Intelligence Agency had been created only in 1947, in fairly short order it had acquired most of the institutional trappings of the military and diplomatic agencies it lived with. An "iron triangle" of sorts developed. In 1966, the Office of Legislative Counsel was established, with a staff of six for handling congressional relations. A decade later, after the House and Senate had established select committees on intelligence (one under Senator Frank Church, the other under Congressman Otis Pike), the staff was increased to thirty-two. Later renamed the Office of Congressional Affairs, it now has a staff of forty-five. The intelligence budget remained secret—Article 1, section 9, to the contrary—until 1997, when a gross number, $26.6 billion, was made known.[11]

But by that time, as Evan Thomas remarked on reading the Church committee reports, it seemed that the public knew more about the inner workings of the Central Intelligence Agency's Clandestine Service than it did about the Department of Health and Human Services.[12] Established in the mid-1970s, the CIA's Center for the Study of Intelligence had been at work. As described in its Web site (www.odci.gov/csi), the center conducts research on intelligence; publishes classified and unclassified editions of the journal *Studies in Intelligence*, as well as books, monographs, and a quarterly newsletter; hosts conferences and symposia on military, intelligence, and political history; manages the systematic declassification review of historically valuable CIA records; and coordinates a number of academic outreach programs.

Much of the vigor of this scholarly endeavor is the work and legacy of Sherman Kent, a Yale historian who joined the Office of Strategic Services during World War II and had moved on to the CIA. In 1955, in the first issue of *Studies in Intelligence*, Kent observed that "intelligence today is not merely a profession, but like most professions it has taken on the aspects of a discipline": a methodology, a vocabulary, a body of theory and doctrine, a set of refined techniques, a large professional following. But the intelligence community did not have its own literature. Kent set forth the ambitious but reasoned goal of establishing a literature on intelligence. "The most important service that such a literature performs is the permanent recording of our new ideas and experiences," he added. "When we record we not only make possible easier and wider communication of thought, we also take a rudimentary step towards making our findings cumulative."[13]

In 1992, the editors of *Studies in Intelligence* wrote that, in the nearly forty years since Kent had underscored the need for it, "a vast literature" on intelligence had been built up. They allowed that until just then much of the material had been unavailable to the public. Fair enough. Yet surely any attempt at a cumulative literature on intelligence must have circulated within the intelligence community itself. To little effect, it would seem. For all the daunting achievements of American statecraft during these years, the unstinting support of massive intelligence budgets, and the startling technological and scientific achievements, the overall quality of American intelligence may well have declined over time. Two statements, one anecdotal, the other analytic, argue the point.

First is Jeffrey Smith's account of the experience of General George Lee Butler, commander of U.S. Strategic Command (STRATCOM) from 1990 to 1994. As the one responsible for drafting the overall U.S. strategy for nuclear war, Butler had studied the Soviet Union with an intensity and a level of detail matched by few others in the West. He had studied the footage of the military parades and the Kremlin, had scrutinized the deployments of Soviet missiles and other armaments: "In all, he thought of the Soviet Union as a fearsome garrison state seeking global domination and preparing for certain conflict with the West. The only reasonable posture for the United States, he told colleagues, was to keep thousands of American nuclear weapons at the ready so that if war broke out, Washington could destroy as much of the Soviet nuclear arsenal as possible. It was the harrowing but hallowed logic of nuclear deterrence." But Butler began having doubts about this picture, upon which so much of U.S. foreign policy was based, by the time of his first visit to the Soviet Union, on December 4, 1988. When he landed at Sheremetyevo Airport, on the outskirts of Moscow, he thought at first that the uneven, pockmarked runway was an open field. The taxiways were still covered with snow from a storm two days earlier, and dozens of the runway lights were broken. Riding into downtown Moscow in an official motorcade, Butler noticed that the roads were ragged, the massive government buildings crumbling. He was astonished when the gearshift in his car snapped off in his driver's hand. After poring over thousands of satellite photos and thirty years' worth of classified reports, Butler had expected to find a modern, functional industrialized country; what he found instead was "severe economic deprivation." Even more telling was "the sense of defeat in the eyes of the people," Butler told Smith. "It all came crashing home to me that I really had been dealing with a caricature all those years."[14]

The second statement is by Admiral Stansfield Turner, director of the CIA from 1977 to 1981. In an article in *Foreign Affairs* in 1991, well after Butler's doubts had been confirmed by the collapse of the Soviet Union, Turner averred: "We should not gloss over the enormity of this failure to forecast the magnitude of the Soviet crisis. We know now that there were many Soviet academics, economists and political thinkers, other than those officially presented to us by the Soviet government, who understood long before 1980 that the Soviet economic system was broken and that it was only a matter of time before someone had to try to repair it, as had Khrushchev. Yet I never heard a suggestion from the CIA, or the intelligence arms of the departments of defense or state, that numerous Soviets recognized a growing, systemic economic problem." Turner acknowledged the "revisionist rumblings" claiming that the CIA had in fact seen the collapse coming, but he dismissed them: "If some individual CIA analysts were more prescient than the corporate view, their ideas were filtered out in the bureaucratic process; and it is the corporate view that counts because that is what reaches the president and his advisers. On this one, the corporate view missed by a mile. Why were so many of us insensitive to the inevitable?"[15]

The answer has to be, at least in part, that too much of the information was secret, not sufficiently open to critique by persons outside government. Within the confines of the intelligence community, too great attention was paid to hoarding information, defending boundaries, securing budgets, and other matters of corporate survival. Too little attention was paid to ethnic issues, both domestic and foreign. The Soviet Union, after all, broke up along ethnic lines. And *much* too little attention was paid to the decline of Marxist-Leninist belief, both here and abroad. The Red Scare was far less fearsome than many would have had us believe.

Government regulations dealing with domestic affairs derive from statute. Congress makes a law, entrusting its enforcement to a bureaucracy that issues rules and rulings to carry out the law. Since 1936 these regulations have been published in the *Federal Register*, there for all to see. But as for secrecy in foreign affairs, the statutory basis is slim—as noted, a handful of limited measures enacted in 1917 and 1947. Yet around these have developed an enormous intelligence bureaucracy, almost a secret government of its own, operating largely out of public view.

As new information about the Cold War emerges from the archives of the former Soviet Union and from American files, we can more easily trace the history of how secrecy and bureaucracy became enmeshed. We can see how, as the secrecy system took hold, it prevented American government from accurately assessing the enemy and then dealing rationally with them during this and other critical periods. Always excepting—the reader may take this as a personal bias—the scientists. They had little use for secrecy, but they put up with it. Among other things, in 1960 they put up the Corona reconnaissance satellite that enabled us, more or less literally, to keep track of every tank in the Soviet empire. If the Soviets had ever decided to launch an invasion through the celebrated Fulda Gap, we would have known about it weeks in advance, and it would not have succeeded. The first camera operated until 1972. Possibly, nay, probably, it was declassified and put on display as the commission proceeded with its work. That was a secret worth protecting—for a time—and that, too, is a theme of this study.

CHAPTER TWO

The Experience of
World War I

hen Woodrow Wilson was inaugurated as president in 1913, he inherited a system of government that valued openness over secrecy. To be sure, the American Constitution—which had been drafted in closed, or, if you like, secret, sessions—presumes the need for secrecy in some matters. Article 1, section 5, provides that "each House shall keep a Journal of its Proceedings, . . . excepting in such Parts as may in their Judgment require Secrecy." (Not without a measure of prescience, Anti-Federalists argued that senators and representatives, who were given the power to fix their own salaries [Article 1, section 6], would do so in secret.)[1] The practice of closed deliberations was nothing unusual for the age, but it quickly lost its luster in the United States. Although Senate sessions were closed at first, in 1794 a resolution was adopted creating public galleries that were to remain open "so long as the Senate shall be engaged in their legislative capacity, unless in such cases as may, in the opinion of the Senate, require secrecy, after which the said galleries shall be closed."[2]

Openness in deliberation and not least in diplomacy came to be seen as something of a democratic virtue, even an aspect of national character. In 1860, one of Andrew Jackson's early biographers reported an anecdote that cast the general as the very embodiment of this virtue. When Jackson was told that one Augustus, a servant with the run of the White House, might be smuggling presidential papers to the general's opponents, Jackson responded: "They are welcome, sir, to anything they can get out of my papers. They will find there, among other things, false grammar and bad spelling; but they are welcome to it all, grammar and spelling included. Let them make the most of it. Our government, sir, is founded upon the intelligence of the people; it has no other basis; upon their capacity to arrive at right conclusions in regard to measures and in regard to men; and I am not afraid of their failing to do so from any use that can be made of any thing that can be got out of my papers."[3]

Apocryphal or not, the anecdote bespeaks what appears to have been a widely shared sentiment. Then with the onset of the Civil War we observe the surely unprecedented notion of openness as an instrument of foreign policy. On December 3, 1861, at the beginning of the second session of the Thirty-Seventh Congress, Abraham Lincoln accompanied his State of the Union message with 410 pages, all promptly printed, of dispatches to American ministers abroad. The dispatches dealt with the Confederate states' efforts to obtain recognition from foreign powers, notably Spain, France, and Great Britain. It was a fateful enterprise in which assertive openness was considered the most effective policy, and there is reason to judge that this proved to be the case. Openness communicated our threats as well as our entreaties, and it did so, in the case of Britain, not only to Whitehall but also to an increasingly literate and volatile public. The United States was dealing with insurrection at home; did Her Majesty's Government, did the British people, consider that this same misfortune might befall England? Or Ireland?*

This is not to say that American diplomacy of the Civil War was without its secret missions, messages, and the like. Even so, the American government began to espouse the concept of openness. One outcome of this policy was that the Department of State began publishing annual compilations of correspondence and similar material, in a series that became known as *Foreign Relations of the United States*. Something new under the sun. Hewing to a publishing schedule of one volume per year, the anonymous editors from the 1870s through the 1890s were surprisingly aboveboard when selecting and editing the documents at hand. The occasional coded communication was paraphrased. Portions of other communications were omitted in order to protect relations with a particular country or the sensitivity of ongoing matters, especially litigation. Otherwise, writes State Department historian William Z. Slany, "the immediateness of the publication confirmed the Department's lack of concern about issues of sensitivity or possible impact upon cur-

---

* Secretary of State William H. Seward could be subtle indeed in such matters. On June 19, 1861, he concluded a dispatch to Charles Francis Adams, the minister to Great Britain, with "a single remark" by way of persuading the British government to leave the United States to manage its "domestic controversy" on its own. "The fountains of discontent in any society are many, and some lie much deeper than others," Seward observed. "Thus far this unhappy controversy has disturbed only those which are nearest the surface. There are others which lie still deeper that may yet remain, as we hope, long undisturbed. If they should be reached, no one can tell how or when they could be closed. It was foreign intervention that opened and that alone could open similar fountains in the memorable French revolution" (*Executive Documents Submitted to the Senate*, 37th Cong., 2d sess. [Washington, D.C.: Government Printing Office, 1861–62], 1:109). The allusion to the fountains of discontent in Ireland was unspoken, but it was there. Seward, of Auburn, New York, was a vocal supporter of Irish freedom and would not have failed to note that the Fenian Brotherhood, an American support organization for revolutionary Irish nationalists, had been founded in his own state four years earlier. The brotherhood supported several attempts at insurrection in Ireland and several invasions of Upper Canada, the Niagara frontier well within Seward's regional sphere (for all that he would be remembered only for the purchase of Alaska).

rent negotiations. . . . The question of secrecy appears rarely to have arisen in the editing of published documents."[4]

Openness in foreign relations had clearly become an American theme. On January 8, 1918, in an address to Congress, Woodrow Wilson set forth the Fourteen Points to be used as a guide for a peace settlement. His first point stated the goal: "open covenants of peace, openly arrived at, after which there shall be no private international understandings of any kind but diplomacy shall proceed always frankly and in the public view."[5]

Wilson surely believed this, and he surely was believed. Yet as the twentieth century advanced, secrecy and conspiracy were to become primary instruments of statecraft even as states themselves attained unprecedented authority and presumption. Wilson's sixth point concerned Russia, which he assured "a sincere welcome into the society of free nations under institutions of her own choosing."[6] But Lenin had already seized power in what would become Leningrad. The United States was already at war, and it would continue to be at war in one form or another for most of the rest of the century. Amid the pressures of protecting national security, secrecy was to become pervasive within the American state.

Indeed, much of the structure of secrecy now in place in the U.S. government took shape in just under eleven weeks in the spring of 1917, while the Espionage Act was debated and signed into law. The Espionage Act had an antecedent in the Alien and Sedition Acts of 1798—three statutes dealing with aliens and one with sedition. These bills were passed by a Federalist Congress in order to silence opposition to war with France, which then seemed inevitable. (Neither country had declared war, but French and American ships had fought battles.) One measure required an alien to live in the United States for fourteen years before he could become a citizen; at the time, immigrants were mostly French and Irish natives who supported the Democratic-Republicans, who in turn tended to support France. Thomas Jefferson and James Madison both challenged the constitutionality of the acts, and the laws were a prominent issue in the 1800 election, which Jefferson ultimately won. Thereafter the acts expired, were repealed, or were amended out of existence.[7] It was the nation's first experience with how war or the threat of war changed the balance between private liberty versus public order, an instability that was eerily reenacted 119 years later.

It would be an exaggeration to state that from the outset of hostilities in 1914 the Democratic administration of Woodrow Wilson expected war with Germany. But its sympathies lay with Great Britain, as would those of the administration of Franklin D. Roosevelt, a spare two decades later. The plain fact is that the American governing classes have always—with the exception of an occasional Roosevelt, one Eisenhower, and one Kennedy—been ethnically English, Scottish, or Scotch-Irish. In 1861, when Secretary of State William H. Seward was doing his diplomatic best to ensure that Great Britain did not interfere with the civil crisis in the United States, he observed, "It would be a hazardous day for both the branches of the British race when they should determine to try how much harm each could do the other." This was a threat of war. But because the threat was between two "branches" of the same "race," war was surely unthinkable.[8]

Thus the pattern was established well before Wilson took office: the perception of civil order as subject to both external and internal threats, with the two connected primarily through ethnicity. At the outset of this century the United States had a considerable foreign-born population, concentrated mostly in a few urban centers; in 1910 about 40 percent of the populace of New York City were immigrants.[9] Many of these folks were caught up in diaspora politics, much of it difficult for natives to follow. (Fenians? Yes, that was a given. But Mensheviks?) Nor was this merely a first-generation preoccupation with the politics of the "old country." There came a figurative time, which W. S. Gilbert would have recognized, when "every boy and every gal" born in the Bronx was either a little Stalinist or else a little Trot-skyite or Lovestonite or Shachtmanite.[10] Nathan Glazer has described his being *"socialist by descent"* (his emphasis) in the Bronx in the 1930s: "I was what would be called today a social democrat. Again, it was a matter of descent. My father . . . was strongly anticommunist. He was a member of the International Ladies Garment Workers Union and, after the fierce battle over control of the union in the 1920s, communists had as bad a reputation among ILGWU members as among middle Americans. Had he been a member of the Fur Workers Union, my politics by descent would very likely have been communist."[11] American socialism was by now respectable enough. For the rest, much of it was concealed, or partly concealed, behind language barriers and ghetto walls. And more.

One comment, however digressive, does seem in order here. Our conduct as a society has grown better, not worse, in a civil libertarian sense. The persecution of German Americans in World War I was atrocious and for the most part groundless. That of Japanese Americans, Italian Americans, and again German Americans in World War II was offensive but not uniformly hysterical. During and after World War II, a fair number of first- or second-generation Russian Jews were involved with Soviet espionage, but little was made of the ethnic (or, if you like, religious) dimension of this fact: Communism was the issue, and the ideological focus seemed all the clearer because there were, we may be thankful, a sufficient number of Protestant and even Catholic Marxists. More recently, Arab Americans have found themselves under suspicion as potential terrorists, but not by those whom we may call the authorities. There has been a learning process.*

* After Islamic terrorists bombed the World Trade Center in 1993, some in the American public and media lashed out at Arab Americans and Muslims. But on August 5, 1997, following the arrest of several Palestinians who allegedly planned to bomb crowded sites in New York City, Clyde Haberman of the *New York Times* recorded an atmosphere quite different from

In all this it helps to recall the tentativeness that attended much of American civic life during and after the Civil War. There was the war itself, of course—the fiercest in human history. When the war finally ended, the president was assassinated, his death part of a plot that extended to his secretary of state. (Seward, who was stabbed and pistol-whipped in his Washington home on the same evening that Lincoln was shot, was badly hurt but did survive.) Woodrow Wilson was born in Virginia in 1856, growing up amid secession and this aftermath. Another president was assassinated: William McKinley, slain in 1901 by a Polish anarchist, Leon F. Czolgosz, who thought all rulers deserving of death. Anarchism was a real enough threat, and its roots were foreign.

By contrast, the Industrial Workers of the World (IWW), the radical labor organization whose members were known as Wobblies, was very much an American movement, founded in Chicago in 1905. But industrial agitation inevitably involved foreign-born workers, and these were frequently in conflict with native workers. This was remarkably apparent at the strike in the silk mills of Paterson, New Jersey, in 1913, an event that aroused all manner of emotion across the nation. Even the famously radical Elizabeth Gurley Flynn, the "Rebel Girl," was struck by Paterson's "tenacious ethnic divisions," and John Reed, who was then a reporter covering the strike for the socialist newspaper *The Masses*, carried away from the city the same impressions. As historian Melvyn Dubofsky relates the encounter, Reed once asked a young Jew which nationalities were united in the

---

that following the 1993 attack. Haberman interviewed Hamed Nabawy, a Brooklyn grocer and a naturalized American from Egypt, who had endured "verbal violence" not only after the World Trade Center incident but also after others, like the Oklahoma City bombing, that had no known connection to the Middle East. But when the 1997 bomb plot was uncovered, Nabawy said, fewer people seemed ready to heap collective blame on Arab Americans: "Maybe we are a little less quick these days to point accusing fingers at an entire ethnic or religious group when something bad happens."

strike, and received the following reply: "'T'ree great nations stick togedder like dis.' He made a fist. 'T'ree great nations—Italians, Hebrews, and Germans.'" How about Americans? Reed inquired. But "the Jew shrugged his shoulders, grinned scornfully, and answered: 'English peoples not go on picket line. Mericans no lika fight!'" Reed concluded: "It is the English-speaking contingent that remains passive at Paterson, . . . while the 'wops,' the 'kikes,' the 'hunkies'—the 'degraded and ignorant races from Southern Europe'—go out and get clubbed on the picket-line and gaily take the medicine in Paterson jail."[12]

Compounding the ethnic divisions within the iww was the iww's division from the rest of the country. Of this period, Dubofsky writes: "From 1909 to 1919 a legend enveloped the iww. Many Americans, especially during World War I and the postwar Red Scare, became convinced that the Wobblies were 'cut-throat, pro-German, or . . . bolshevik, desperadoes who burn harvest-fields, drive iron spikes into fine timber and ruin sawmills, devise bomb plots, who obstruct the war and sabotage the manufacture of munitions—veritable supermen, with a superhuman power for evil, omnipresent and almost omnipotent.' The hobo Wobbly had replaced the bearded, bomb-carrying anarchist as a bogeyman in the middle-class American's fevered imagination."[13]

Imperial Germany blundered here as elsewhere. In the face of proclaimed American neutrality, it set upon a campaign of espionage aimed at curtailing the American supply of armaments for the Allies, enlisting American ethnic elements for the purpose—typically Germans and Irish but also a new cadre, Indians from the subcontinent (mainly Punjabis) opposed to British rule in India. Thus it came about, on November 20, 1915, that Wilson's secretary of state, Robert Lansing, the most moderate of men (who before the outbreak of war had negotiated international arbitral tribunals that promised an era in which disputes between nations could be settled by law rather than by arms), urged the president to include in his forthcoming State of the Union address "some suggestion as to legislation covering foreign intrigues in our internal affairs such as conspiracies to blow up factories, to encourage strikes, to interfere with industrial operations, to gather information of this government's secrets, etc., etc."[14]

More than six months earlier, Wilson, the embodiment of the academic in politics (thoughtful, careful, devoted to reason), had told a Philadelphia audience, "There is such a thing as a man being too proud to fight."[15] Now, on December 7, 1915, in his State of the Union message to Congress, Wilson observed, speaking of the war in Europe, "We have stood apart, studiously neutral." But unprecedented events abroad called for unprecedented actions at home, and Wilson made a plea that astonishes still, as much for its passion as for what it proposes.

> There are citizens of the United States, I blush to admit, born under other flags but welcomed under our generous naturalization laws to the full freedom and opportunity of America, who have poured the poison of disloyalty into the very arteries of our national life; who have sought to bring the authority and good name of our Government into contempt, to destroy our industries wherever they thought it effective for their vindictive purposes to strike at them, and to debase our politics to the uses of foreign intrigue. . . . A little while ago such a thing would have seemed incredible. Because it was incredible we made no preparation for it. We would have been almost ashamed to prepare for it, as if we were suspicious of ourselves, our own comrades and neighbors! But the ugly and incredible thing has actually come about and we are without adequate federal laws to deal with it. I urge you to enact such laws at the earliest possible moment and feel that in doing so I am urging you to do nothing less than save the honor and self-respect of the nation. Such creatures of passion, disloyalty, and anarchy must be crushed out.[16]

No president had ever spoken like that before; none has since. Even during a half century of Cold War, when there were indeed persons of foreign birth living in the United States and actively involved in seditious activities on behalf of the Soviet Union, no president spoke like that. Others in public life did; many others in private life did, including not a few who knew what they were talking about. But the telling fact is that the intensity of fear and, yes, loathing of those years was never equaled later.

With war's arrival, securing loyalty and unearthing treason had never seemed more important. The first statute enacted by the First Congress had prescribed the oath of allegiance to be taken by officers of the American government. It was simply an oath to support the Constitution of the United States. In 1861, four months into the Civil War, it was amended: it was now an oath to "support, protect, and defend the Constitution and Government of the United States against all enemies, whether *domestic or foreign*" (emphasis added).[17] Note that the designation "domestic" comes first. The linkage never thereafter dissolved.

Assistant Attorney General Charles Warren was assigned the task of drafting the laws that Wilson had called for. And on June 3, 1916, seventeen separate bills were sent to Congress.[18] On February 3, 1917, Germany resumed unrestricted submarine warfare, and the United States broke diplomatic relations. On February 20, the Senate combined thirteen of the seventeen bills and passed that measure, but the House did not act. At a cabinet meeting on March 20, Attorney General Thomas W. Gregory asserted that "German intrigues" were afoot but complained of the "helplessness of his Department under existing laws."[19] In his address asking for a declaration of war, Wilson cited spying as an example of the hostile intent of the "Prussian autocracy": "From the very outset of the present war it has filled our unsuspecting communities and even our offices of government with spies and set criminal intrigues everywhere afoot against our national unity of counsel, our peace within and without, our industries and our commerce. Indeed it is now evident that its spies were here even before the war began."[20]

Following the procedure prescribed by the Constitution, President Wilson called a special session of the Sixty-Fifth Congress on April 2, 1917, asking a joint session for a declaration of war against Germany. On that same day, the chairman of the House Judiciary Committee, Edwin Y. Webb, Democrat of North Carolina, introduced H.R. 291, *A Bill to Punish Acts of Interference with the Foreign Relations, the Neutrality, and the Foreign Commerce of the United States, to Punish Espionage and Better to Enforce the Criminal Laws of the United States*. On April 3, Senator Charles A. Culberson, Democrat of Texas and chairman of the Committee on the Judiciary, introduced a similar bill in the Senate (S. 2). On April 4, the Senate adopted a Declaration of War. On April 5, the U.S. Civil Service Commission provided the president with a choice of executive orders for "excluding from the Government service any person of whose loyalty to the Government there is reasonable doubt."[21]

On April 6, the House declared war. On April 7, the president signed a confidential executive order concerning the loyalty of government employees. The debate on the Espionage Act continued through the spring. These bills were based on the legislation proposed by the attorney general the previous year. Both provided for press censorship. The Senate bill, chapter 2, section 2(c), read:

> Whoever, in time of war, in violation of regulations to be prescribed by the President, . . . shall collect, record, *publish*, or communicate . . . information relating to the public defense calculated to be, or which might be, useful to the enemy, shall be punished by a fine of not more than $10,000 or by imprisonment for not more than 10 years, or by both such fine and imprisonment: Provided, That nothing in this section shall be construed to limit or restrict, nor shall any regulation herein provided for limit or restrict, any discussion, comment, or criticism of the Government or its representatives, or the publication of the same: Pro-

vided, That no discussion, comment, or criticism shall convey information prohibited under the provisions of this section.[22] (Emphasis added.)

Section 4 of the House bill similarly provided that during wartime the president could, "by proclamation, prohibit the publishing or communicating of or the attempting to publish or communicate any information relating to the national defense which, in his judgment, is of such character that it is or might be useful to the enemy."[23]

To repeat, in the Sixty-Fourth Congress, the Senate had passed espionage legislation, including the press censorship provision, largely as proposed by the attorney general, but the House had not taken action when Congress adjourned on March 3. By April 2, then, the measure had been around for a few months, and now opposition appeared. In a definitive article for the *Columbia Law Review,* Harold Edgar and Benno C. Schmidt, Jr., sum up the objections to section 2(c): "First, opponents claimed that the provision would establish a system of prior restraint censoring newspaper publications of news about the war. Second, the provision was challenged as delegating unlimited power to the President to decide what information should be published. Third, objection was again made to the lack of a specific culpability standard."[24]

The Encyclopedia of the United States Congress records that the censorship portion of the Espionage Act "set off a storm of Congressional controversy," with House Speaker James Beauchamp (Champ) Clark declaring that censorship of the press was "in flat contradiction of the Constitution."[25] The issue was intermittently debated, and with some intensity, during a seven-week period in which much else was going on. The most important debate took place in the Senate, which had of course already passed the measure but now had the opportunity to reconsider.

A sample of the debate can be found in the *Congressional Record* of April 18, when Charles S. Thomas, Democrat of Colorado, spoke with some force against the measure: "Mr. President, that is not justice; that is not law; that is not liberty; that is the suppression of every field of legitimate inquiry in time of war. . . . Surely an expression of that kind should not go into a statute, and especially now, when we are acting upon a subject of far-reaching importance, without due deliberation." Thomas noted that although the law was one of the most important ever considered by the Senate, fewer than twenty or so senators were on hand to reconsider its consequences: "It strikes directly at the freedom of the press, at the constitutional exemption from unreasonable search and seizure, not to mention other provisions so sacred . . . that they should not be modified or imperiled, however great the exigency, except upon the most serious, far-reaching, and extended consideration. Yet we are going ahead with this as a war measure, although when enacted it will be permanent in its operation; and I very much fear that with the best of intention we may place upon the statute books something that will rise to plague us."[26]

Jacob Harold Gallinger of New Hampshire, chairman of the Republican caucus, interrupted to say he had been "somewhat disturbed in glancing over this bill" and was very interested in what the senator from Colorado had been saying. Gallinger then asked Thomas to yield so that he might ask for a quorum, as "more Senators ought to be here." Thomas replied that Gallinger knew as well as he did that when a quorum call is placed, "the Senators will simply come in and answer to their names and go out again." (At that time there was no watching of the debates on television.) Even so, it was agreed: a quorum was called, and the debate drifted on. Thomas offered an amendment to strike the provision; it failed.

On May 14, John Knight Shields, Democrat of Tennessee, offered a long legal brief on the First Amendment and the constitutionality of the administration proposal. Shields cited Henry Campbell Black's *Handbook on American Constitutional Law* (commonly known as *Black's Constitutional Law*) and Judge Joseph Story's great work upon the Constitution, where the nineteenth-century jurist declares that the language of the First Amendment "imports no more than every man shall have a right to speak, write, and print his opinions upon any subject whatsoever, *without any prior restraint,* so always that he does not injure any other person in his rights, person, property, or reputation, and so always that he does not thereby disturb the public peace or attempt to subvert the Government" (emphasis added). Shields also cited the Supreme Court of Ohio, which had defined the parallel between the private citizen and the press: "The liberty of the press, properly understood, is not inconsistent with the protection due to private character. It has been well defined as consisting in the right to publish with impunity the truth, with good motives and for justifiable ends, whether it respects government, magistracy, or individuals." Black writes, "It is now thoroughly understood that freedom of the press includes not only exemption from previous censorship but also immunity from punishment or sequestration after the publication, provided that the comments made keep within the limits of truth and decency and are not treasonable." Lest his point not seem forceful enough, he returns to the words of Judge Story: "In the United States no censorship of the press has ever been attempted or would for a moment be tolerated. It is clearly and indubitably prohibited by the constitutional provisions under consideration."[27]

William E. Borah, Republican of Idaho, was the stormiest in his opposition, and he had his history down. He began with the Sedition Act of 1798.

> Once before in the history of the Government we undertook to establish something in the nature of an abridgment of speech and of the press. It was a complete and ignominious failure. It did not serve the objects and purposes of those who fathered it. It accomplished nothing in the way of that which they desired to accomplish. That was in 1798. Then during the Civil War we undertook again, in an indirect way, to establish a censorship by suppressing cer-

tain publications and to prevent the distribution of certain printed material coming supposedly, and in fact at that time conceded to be, from those who were in sympathy with the southern side of the contention. That was an ignominious failure, conceded to be such. It served no purpose whatever and accomplished no good whatever. The historians writing upon the subject and some of the men who enforced it, even, before they died conceded and acknowledged that their attempt to suppress these publications served no benefit and in no way aided the Government in its work.[28]

Clearly the press had its defenders in this debate, but it also had its critics. The incorrigibility of journalists and publishers drew some attention. Senator Thomas James Walsh of Montana recalled that General Robert E. Lee was driven to distraction when his campaign plans were reported in the Richmond newspapers.[29]

On May 12, the Senate voted thirty-nine to thirty-eight in favor of a motion by Hiram W. Johnson, Republican of California, to strike the censorship provision.* A margin of one vote.

But opinion had shifted. A parliamentary move was made to salvage some part of the measure when Senator Lee Slater Overman, Democrat of North Carolina, introduced an amendment that had originally been submitted by opponents of the censorship provision in order to soften its effects but that had been defeated in a vote on April 20. Henry Cabot Lodge, Republican of Massachusetts, who two days before had opposed the Johnson amendment to strike the provision and who had earlier supported the language proposed by Senator Overman, reversed himself in a short statement on May 14: "I have come to the conclusion very distinctly that it would be far better not to have any legislation of this sort than to permit [the Bureau of Information] to exclude, as

* As for party affiliation, the vote was fifteen Democrats and twenty-four Republicans in favor, twenty-seven Democrats and eleven Republicans opposed. Not voting were twelve Democrats and seven Republicans.

they will have the power to exclude, practically anything from the newspapers of the country."30*

A complex conference with the House followed. President Wilson sent a letter to Edwin Yates Webb of North Carolina, the Democratic chairman of the House conferees, and reiterated the administration's position: "Authority to exercise censorship over the press to the extent that that censorship is embodied in the recent action of the House of Representatives is absolutely necessary to the public safety." Most newspapers would observe a "patriotic reticence" about publishing anything that could be injurious to national security, Wilson admitted, "but in every country there are some persons in a position to do mischief in this field who can not be relied upon, and whose interests or desires will lead to actions . . . highly dangerous to the Nation in the midst of a war." Wilson was adamant: "I want to say again that it seems to me imperative that powers of this sort should be granted."31

But despite Wilson's last-minute lobbying, the Espionage Act did not contain the censorship provision. The law was signed on June 15, 1917, and it remains the law. The two main provisions cover the unlawful obtaining of national defense information and the unlawful disclosure of such information to a foreign government or its agents. The criminal penalties are more severe for the second offense and

* Lodge's reference to a Bureau of Information, "if that is its name," as he put it in his May 14 statement, was surely to the Committee on Public Information, which Wilson had established by executive order a few weeks earlier. The committee had been proposed to Wilson on April 14 by Secretary of State Lansing, Secretary of War Newton Diehl Baker, and Secretary of the Navy Josephus Daniels, who had written of their concern about "premature or ill-advised announcements of policies" and the need to "safeguard all information of value to an enemy" (Lansing, Baker, and Daniels to Wilson, April 14, 1917, in *The Papers of Woodrow Wilson*, edited by Arthur S. Link [Princeton: Princeton University Press, 1984–92], 42:55). It would come to be known as the Creel committee for its chairman, George Creel, a newspaperman from the Midwest, and as an agency that promoted the administration's war aims, but it narrowly missed becoming the Bureau of Censorship. It was the age of burgeoning bureaus.

harsher in times of war than at other times. It did include a provision punishing certain "seditious or disloyal acts or words in time of war," but this did not satisfy the Wilson administration, or at all events Attorney General Gregory. The next year, accordingly, new provisions, known collectively as the Sedition Act of 1918, were added to the basic statute and signed into law by the president on May 16, 1918.

Whereas the 1917 act focused on different forms of conduct—obtaining, communicating, or publishing designated information, for example—the 1918 act focused on speech itself, making criminal an extensive variety of listed "utterances." It defined eight specific offenses punishable by up to twenty years' imprisonment and a ten-thousand-dollar fine, making it a crime to "utter, print, write, or publish any disloyal, profane, scurrilous, or abusive language about the form of government of the United States, or the Constitution of the United States." Another stricture, which prohibited those who would "urge, incite, or advocate any curtailment of production in this country of any thing . . . necessary or essential to the prosecution of the war," was aimed at left-wing labor unions. When Congress grew increasingly concerned that the 1918 amendment was too strenuous in its restrictions on speech, the Sedition Act was repealed in March 1921.[32]

The 1917 act was amended again in 1933 to prohibit government employees from publishing any foreign code or anything transmitted in such a code; this was a narrow provision that followed publication, by a former top signals intelligence official, of what became a popular book about the State Department's code-breaking activities against Japan. A 1938 amendment added two new sections to prohibit the taking and disseminating of photographs of military installations and equipment designated by the president.

In 1950 Congress added a new subsection to specifically cover the unauthorized possession of national defense information by persons *outside* the government. This amendment has proven confusing, primarily because it does not include any culpability requirement. The degree of "scienter," or guilty knowledge, required for behavior to be covered under the 1917 act had long been a source of controversy; now Congress appeared to be avoiding the issue entirely. Little wonder that Edgar and Schmidt judge the Senate report on the 1950 legislation "inexplicit" on this issue and the House report "inexplicable."[33] The statute has been amended several more times since 1950, but these instances have amounted to either technical updates of the list of protected information (such as adding spacecraft, satellite systems, and other advanced technologies) or modifications of penalties for those who violate the statute (such as adding a provision allowing forfeiture of their property).

In 1986 Samuel L. Morison, a civilian analyst with the Office of Naval Intelligence, was convicted of supplying photographs of a Soviet nuclear-powered aircraft carrier, then under construction, to *Jane's Defence Weekly* (July 1984). Morison was the first individual convicted under the 1917 Espionage Act for unauthorized disclosure of information to the press. No one has been convicted since.

The Atomic Energy Act of 1954 was a narrowly defined statute concerning nuclear data and its communication or disclosure "with intent to injure the United States" or "with reason to believe such data will be utilized to injure the United States or to secure an advantage to any foreign nation."[34] Penalties were prescribed for doing so. By contrast, the National Security Act of 1947, which created the Central Intelligence Agency, provided that the Director of Central Intelligence would be responsible for protecting intelligence sources and methods from unauthorized disclosure. But there are no penalties for not doing so. If there were, half of our national security advisors would have spent time in jail.

And so the modern age began. Three new institutions had entered American life: Conspiracy, Loyalty, Secrecy. Each had antecedents, but now there was a difference. Each had become institutional; bureaucracies were established to attend to each. In time there would be a Federal Bureau of Investigation to keep track of conspiracy at home, a Central Intelligence Agency to keep tabs abroad, an espionage statute and loyalty boards to root out disloyalty or subversion. And all of this would be maintained, and the national security would be secured, through elaborate regimes of secrecy. Eighty years later, at the close of the century, these institutions continue in place. To many they now seem permanent, perhaps even preordained; few consider that they were once new.

What is more, we began this age by trampling on liberty. And we did so at the behest of the most learned and liberal of presidents, who in short order was to become the world's standard-bearer for the right of all peoples to freedom under law. A president who envisioned a world league of nations governed by law. A president who could state with chilly precision what would be the alternative. Wilson sketched just such a scenario once, in 1919, when he was in St. Louis campaigning for the League of Nations and someone asked him what would happen if the treaty establishing the league were not ratified.

> Very well, then, if we must stand apart and be the hostile rivals of the rest of the world, then we must do something else. We must be physically ready for anything to come. We must have a great standing army. We must see to it that every man in America is trained to arms. We must see to it that there are munitions and guns enough for an army that means a mobilized nation; that they are not only laid up in store, but that they are kept up to date; that they are ready to use tomorrow; that we are a nation in arms; because you can't be unfriendly to everybody without being ready that everybody shall be unfriendly to you. . . .
>
> You have got to think of the President of the United States, not as the chief counselor of the Nation, elected for a little while, but as the man meant constantly and every

day to be commander in chief of the armies and navy of the United States, ready to order it to any part of the world where the threat of war is a menace to his own people. And you can't do that under free debate. You can't do that under public counsel. Plans must be kept secret. Knowledge must be accumulated by a system which we have condemned, because we have called it a spying system. The more polite call it a system of intelligence and you can't watch other nations with your unassisted eye. You have got to watch them by secret agencies planted everywhere. Let me testify to this, my fellow citizens. I not only did not know it until we got into this war, but I did not believe it when I was told that it was true, that Germany was not the only country that maintained a secret service. Every country in Europe maintained it, because they had to be ready for Germany's spring upon them, and the only difference between the German secret service and the other secret services was that the German secret service found out more than the others did. And therefore Germany sprang upon the other nations unawares, and they were not ready for it.

And you know what the effect of a military nation is upon social questions. You know how impossible it is to effect social reform if everybody must be under orders from the government. You know how impossible it is, in short, to have a free nation if it is a military nation and under military orders.[35]

As it turned out, it *was* possible. Not that the United States ever became a military nation, but for the longest while we have been a nation on constant military alert. Each of Wilson's successors has been followed everywhere by a man carrying "the football," that is, the black briefcase containing the nuclear missile launch codes. And as for spying and intelligence and secrets . . . well.

But the larger and more important development was of just the opposite character. Now a civil liberties movement that imposed a kind of prior restraint on government also entered American life. Gradually, over time, American government became careful about liberties. Due process appeared in our calculation of such matters as loyalty, and this in turn steadily eroded the base of radical rejection of American society. It was slow in coming, too slow. But it came, and in the process American democracy not only survived but prevailed. One could date this development from May 14, 1917, when Henry Cabot Lodge switched his vote on the issue of press censorship. In 1876 Lodge had been awarded the first Ph.D. in political science conferred by Harvard University; later he taught there. He was an authority on Alexander Hamilton and the age of American independence. And he likely would have known of Madison's letter to Jefferson of May 13, 1798: "Perhaps it is a universal truth that the loss of liberty at home is to be charged to provisions against danger, real or pretended, from abroad."[36]

In the meantime, though, there was a war to be won against Germany.

Then as now, the United States had a large population of Americans of German ancestry. German culture was widely admired, the German language was taught in public schools, and German political traditions were viewed as essentially democratic. Germany was arguably the most advanced culture in Europe. Early in the war, the Berlin government set out to use these attachments and attractions in order to strengthen opposition to entering the war. When war began in August 1914, the German ambassador arrived in the United States with $150 million in German treasury notes ($2.2 billion in current dollars) to pursue a propaganda campaign, purchase munitions for Germany, and conduct an espionage campaign aimed at denying war matériel to the Allies.[37] This last task was the province of the military attaché, Captain Franz von Papen.

In a fateful manner, while the British made friends, the Germans made enemies. Early on the morning of July 30, 1916, German agents, probably assisted by Irish nationalists, blew up a munitions dump at the Black Tom railroad

THE WEATHER
Partly cloudy and warmer Monday;
partly cloudy, with probable
showers Tuesday; moderate
southwest winds.

The New York Times.

NEW YORK, MONDAY, JULY 31, 1916.—EIGHTEEN PAGES.

ONE CENT

STRIKE TIES UP 3D AV. SYSTEM AND MAY EXTEND

General Manager Hedley Gets Police Protection for N. Y. City Railways' Cars.

ORGANIZING SUBWAY MEN

From Battery to Westchester, Including Crosstown and Belt Lines, No Red Cars Move.

SERVICE IS PROMISED TODAY

System Carries 250,000 Passengers Daily—Union Officials Busy in All Five Boroughs.

MUNITION EXPLOSIONS CAUSE LOSS OF $20,000,000; 2 KNOWN TO BE DEAD, MANY MISSING, 35 HURT; THE HARBOR RAKED BY SHRAPNEL FOR HOURS

View of the Wreck of the National Storage Company's Plant on Black Tom Island.

FIRST EXPLOSION TERRIFIC

Earth Torn Away and Great Hole Filled with Blazing Debris.

TWO MEN UNDER ARREST

Barge of High Explosive Alleged to Have Been Moored Against Orders.

87 CARS OF SHELLS FIRED

Heavy Damage in Manhattan and Brooklyn—Statue of Liberty Hit.

Detailed Estimates of the $20,000,000 Loss by the Fire and Explosion in Jersey City

Glass Damage Exceeds a Million; Few Downtown Buildings Escape

Insurance Companies Prepare to Pay Heavy Losses, While Small Property Owners Who Are Uninsured Suffer Heavily—Strange Freaks of Blast Are Seen.

Ellis Island Like War-Swept Town; Damage Estimated at $75,000

Only Six of 607 Persons at Bureau Receive Injuries—Immigrants Taken to Battery Till Danger Is Past—Hospital Roof Caves In.

Figure 2. A bomb explodes at the National Storage Company's plant on Black Tom Island, Jersey City, July 30, 1916. The next day, the front page of the *New York Times* carried a photograph of the sabotage at New York Harbor. Reprinted courtesy of the *New York Times*.

yard and adjoining warehouses at New York Harbor (Figure 2). (The site is now Liberty State Park, the debarkation point for boats carrying tourists to the Statue of Liberty.) It was a stunning event in both magnitude and consequence. The first and most powerful blast, at 2:08 A.M., shook houses along the New Jersey shore, rocked skyscrapers in Manhattan, shattered windows from Brooklyn to Hoboken, and threw people from their beds miles away. The noise of the explosion was heard as far away as Maryland and Connecticut, and on both sides of the Hudson, people in their pajamas rushed to the streets to watch the sky glow red from the flames as more explosions thundered from the harbor.[38] Sabotage became a national issue.

Captain von Papen also provided support for the Ghadar movement (*ghadar* is Urdu for mutiny), which was composed mostly of Punjabi Indians seeking independence from British rule. It was based principally in California, to which Punjabi agricultural workers had migrated from Canada. Once the United States declared war on Germany, the government indicted 105 people of various nationalities for participating in the conspiracy. From the start, the "Hindoo conspiracy" was viewed as an "offshoot of the German neutrality plots": according to the *San Francisco Chronicle*, the complaint charged that those arrested had "conspired to 'Cripple, hinder and obstruct, the military operations of Great Britain' by sending Hindoos to India to stir up a revolt, and to help Germany by forcing Great Britain to withdraw troops from Europe for service in India to quell the revolt."[39] At the trial, the conspiracy was described as one that "permeated and encircled the whole globe."[40] Twenty-nine defendants were found guilty: fifteen Indians and fourteen German Americans or Germans, including Franz von Bopp, the German consul in San Francisco. The "Hindoo conspiracy" entered the national imagery.[41]

For all the energy and expenditure that these events represented, it is not clear what Berlin had to show for its elaborate and extensive espionage activity. At this time the United

States possessed only one genuine defense secret: that the American military was in no sense prepared for a major war with powerful adversaries. The U.S. Army was so underequipped that when it arrived in France it had to borrow French artillery. But even this was an open secret, and in that regard the Espionage Act can be said to have accomplished little or nothing. German espionage (whether real or imagined) did, however, do great damage to German Americans and thereby to the American people at large.

As war approached, Wilson delivered a mordant forecast, one recorded by Frank Irving Cobb: "'Once lead this people into war,' he said, 'and they'll forget there ever was such a thing as tolerance. To fight you must be brutal and ruthless, and the spirit of ruthless brutality will enter into the very fibre of our national life, infecting Congress, the courts, the policeman on the beat, the man in the street.' Conformity would be the only virtue, said the President, and every man who refused to conform would have to pay the penalty."[42] Wilson seems not to have noticed his own excess, a failing not unknown in presidents. Remember, he had alerted Congress to the intrigues of the foreign-born pouring poison into "the very arteries of our national life." Whether he realized it or not, Wilson was forever showering civil liberties on Germans in Germany while taking them away from American citizens of German descent. In his message to Congress asking for a declaration of war, he was emphatic: "We have no quarrel with the German people. We have no feeling towards them but one of sympathy and friendship."[43] Throughout the war, he pressed a policy of "war on the German government, peace with the German people."[44] Save, it appears, such Germans as might have migrated to Milwaukee.

Never before, never since, has the American government been so aroused by the fear of subversion, the compromise of secrets, the danger within. In *The Growth of the American Republic*, Samuel Eliot Morison, Henry Steele Commager, and William E. Leuchtenburg write: "In

1917–19 the people of the United States abandoned themselves to a hysteria of fear of German conspiracies and of Communist subversion, and the government indulged in greater excesses than at any previous crisis of our history."[45] Again we see the linkage of ethnic identity and political radicalism, a connection that had been present in Wilson's 1915 message to Congress and his reference to "creatures of passion, disloyalty, and anarchy" who "must be crushed." Now it all broke out. As the historians note: "The war offered a great opportunity to bring patriotism to the aid of personal grudges and neighborhood feuds. The independent-minded sort of citizen who was known to his conforming neighbors as a 'Tory' in the Revolution, a 'Jacobin' in 1798, and a 'Copperhead' in the Civil War became a 'pro-German traitor' in 1917 and a 'Bolshevik' in 1918 and was lucky if he did not have garbled scraps of his conversation sent in to the Department of Justice or flashes from his shaving mirror reported as signals to German submarines." Even though no one had any reason to suspect the vast majority of German Americans, libraries withdrew German books from circulation, schools dropped German from their curricula, and some universities not only abolished their German departments but also revoked degrees conferred upon distinguished Germans. A number of German publications, feeling the pressure, went under cover. The governor of Iowa declared an English-only policy for conversations conducted in public places or even over the telephone, and the mayor of Jersey City refused to allow the Austrian-born violinist Fritz Kreisler to appear in concert.[46]

The last word, as it were, was left to former president Theodore Roosevelt in an address at Kansas City on October 1, 1917: "The men who oppose the war; who fail to support the government in every measure which really tends to the efficient prosecution of the war; and above all who in any shape or way champion the cause and the actions of Germany, show themselves to be the Huns within our own gates and the allies of the men whom our sons and brothers are crossing the ocean to fight."[47] It is well that Dwight D. Eisenhower graduated from West Point in 1915; had he been younger and had the war hysteria gone on much longer, an Eisenhower might not have been admitted to the U.S. Military Academy.

Back in Washington, Congress made some attempts to restrain the executive, although it might be more accurate to say that Congress simply lagged. Postmaster General Albert S. Burleson and Attorney General Gregory vied with each another in cracking down on those who were deemed to have made treasonable utterances, and soon the president proposed amendments to extend the Espionage Act to cover "profane, scurrilous, or abusive language about the form of government, . . . the Constitution, . . . or the flag of the United States, or the uniform of the Army and Navy." Thus it was that the Sedition Act became law on May 16, 1918. Although Congress allowed the law to expire in 1921, during the three years that the act was in force, pro-German newspapers, German speakers, and, more often, socialists and other antiwar radicals were suppressed or punished.[48]

Under the combined force of the Espionage Act and the Sedition Act, the government also instituted a widespread program of supervision and censorship of the press; prohibited two socialist newspapers from the mails; quashed the circulation of *The Public*, a tax journal that advocated using taxes to bear more of the costs of the war; and banned Thorstein Veblen's *Imperial Germany and the Industrial Revolution*. A film producer received a jail sentence of ten years for making *The Spirit of Seventy-Six*, a film whose subject, the American Revolution, was thought to inflame anti-British sentiments. A Vermont minister received a sentence of fifteen years for citing Jesus as an exemplar of pacifism.[49]

At this now considerable distance, it is difficult to appreciate the force of pacifism as a political movement of the late nineteenth and early twentieth centuries. It was international, based on creed, and given to association with socialism and other such commitments. There was nothing notably exotic in its doctrine, certainly not in the age of The Hague Peace Conferences—which were convened in Holland in 1899 and 1907 by the czar of Russia and which established the Permanent Court of Arbitration and fifteen other conventions on the customs and laws of war—and The Hague Peace Palace, the gift of Andrew Carnegie, built there between 1907 and 1913.

William Jennings Bryan, Wilson's first secretary of state, was a pacifist—in the words of his biographer, a "pacifist committed, with remarkably few reservations, to nonviolence in dealings between the nations." To this end, Bryan had set about negotiating some nineteen "cooling-off" treaties providing for international commissions to conciliate disputes when ordinary diplomatic methods failed.[50] (In the Hoover administration, Secretary of State Frank B. Kellogg would negotiate another nineteen such treaties.) Bryan resigned, gracefully, over the tone of Wilson's response after the Germans torpedoed the passenger ship SS *Lusitania* in 1915. Arthur Link observes that what Bryan could not accept was not so much what the president said as what he did not say about American neutrality: he did not say that the United States would do everything possible to avoid "even the possibility of war."[51] Josephus Daniels, Wilson's secretary of the navy, was a Bryan supporter and was certainly thought to be a pacifist; even his obituary noted as such.[52] When Wilson appointed Newton Diehl Baker as secretary of war, the *New York Times* ran an article with a rather pointed subtitle: "He Is Known as an Ardent Pacifist."[53]

Nonviolence had been advocated by Quakers in America since the seventeenth century. Of a sudden, such views became subversive and "foreign" and a penal offense. The United States grew reckless in its infringement of liberty. Consider the matter of Eugene V. Debs, who had run for president as the candidate of the Socialist Party of America in 1912. He had received 900,369 votes, 6 percent of all votes cast. (Wilson received only 41.9 percent.) On June 16, 1918, Debs delivered an antiwar speech in Canton, Ohio, expressing solidarity with three men—Wagenknecht, Baker, and Ruthenberg—who had been convicted of failing to register for the draft. He also condemned the conviction of Kate Richards O'Hare, who had been charged with obstructing the draft. Because such speech was now forbidden under the Espionage Act, Debs was tried, convicted, and sentenced to ten years' imprisonment on each of three counts, to be served concurrently.

The Supreme Court did not consider the constitutionality of the Espionage Act of 1917 and the Sedition Act of 1918 until after World War I. The enduring legal precedent established by the Court in its consideration of these acts comes from *Schenck v. United States*. In writing the opinion on behalf of the Court, Justice Oliver Wendell Holmes articulated the test of "clear and present danger." The ruling affirmed that Congress has a right to limit speech in an attempt to limit certain "evils." Holmes explained: "The most stringent protection of free speech would not protect a man in falsely shouting fire in a theatre and causing a panic. It does not even protect a man from an injunction against uttering words that may have all the effect of force . . . . The question in every case is whether the words used are used in such circumstances and are of such a nature as to create a clear and present danger that they will bring about the substantive evils that Congress has a right to prevent."[54] Subsequent to *Schenck*, Justice Holmes also wrote the opinion, for a unanimous court, upholding Debs's conviction on March 10, 1919.[55]

The American presidency, with the cooperation of Congress and the courts, was obstructing democracy to an unprecedented extent, and doing so in the name of defending it.

Democracy was not obstructed altogether, of course. In 1920, Debs was once again the presidential candidate of the Socialist Party of America, this time running from a penitentiary in Atlanta. He received more votes, 915,940, than in 1912, but a lower proportion of the electorate, 3.4 percent.

On Christmas Day 1921, President Warren G. Harding commuted Debs's sentence, and he was provided a railroad ticket from Atlanta to Washington. On December 26, Debs called first on Attorney General Harry M. Daugherty and then had a half-hour visit with President Harding at the White House. In the 1920 election, Harding had promised a return to normalcy, and he did his best. Just before Harding took office, on Wilson's last day as president, Congress had repealed the Sedition Act, the 1918 amendment to the Espionage Act. But nothing would be quite the same again.

CHAPTER THREE

The Encounter with Communism

Loyalty to country had appeared as a force in American affairs. The day after the declaration of war in 1917, Wilson had issued an executive order that in effect required government employees to support government policy, both in conduct and in sympathy. The order read: "The head of a department or independent office may forthwith remove any employee when he has ground for believing that the retention of such employee would be inimical to the public welfare by reason of his conduct, sympathies, or utterances, or because of other reasons growing out of the war. Such removal may be made without other formality than that the reasons shall be made a matter of confidential record, subject, however, to inspection by the Civil Service Commission." The order was intended to be in effect only temporarily—"this order is issued solely because of the present international situation, and will be withdrawn when the emergency is passed"—but in the manner of bureaucracies, the "emergency" lingered. The Civil Service Commission debarred persons from examinations for reasons relating to loyalty as late as 1921, years after the war had ended.[1]

Part of the reason for this lingering caution was that loyalty had become enmeshed with a kind of bureaucratic hoarding instinct. All bureaucrats have this instinct, and it intensifies during times of crisis. Moreover, as the concept of loyalty adopted in 1917 implied, the various federal departments and agencies did possess a great deal of information that could be used to injure the government or the national interest if revealed by disloyal persons with ties to hostile nations or to internal elements hostile to the American way of life.

Among these internal elements were impassioned anarchists, who believed that any form of regulation or government was immoral and who had formed an international movement in the nineteenth century.[2] In their terrorist mode, they had set about blowing up czars and such. After the assassination of President McKinley, the United States adopted a statute barring anarchists from entering the country. The arrest, imprisonment, and deportation to Russia of Russian-born American anarchist Emma Goldman was a celebrated case of the later Wilson years. Although no doubt idealists, the anarchists were also frequently violent and so threatened the necessary state monopoly on violence. Even so, there does not appear to have been any systematic search for anarchists at the federal level until passage of the Espionage Act of 1917. But shortly thereafter, bureaucracies were compiling dossiers and government officials were classifying information by various degrees of secrecy. It appears that the American military borrowed today's three-tier gradation in classifying documents—Confidential, Secret, and Top Secret (at that time, For Official Use Only, Confidential, and Secret)—from the system used by British forces in France.[3] Again, it all begins in 1917.

If 1917 was an eventful year in the United States, it was a momentous one in Russia. In a cabinet meeting on March 20, called after German submarines sank three American merchant vessels, President Wilson spoke of summoning Congress and, by implication, asking for a declaration of war. Secretary of State Lansing recorded that the president spoke of the situation in the belligerent countries, "particularly in Russia where the revolution against the autocracy had been successful."[4] Lansing took up the point to argue that "the revolution in Russia, which appeared to be successful, had removed the one objection to affirming that the European War was a war between Democracy and Absolutism"; further, American entry into the war "would have a great moral influence in Russia."[5] A moment all but erased from history by the events that followed.

That autumn, the Bolsheviks seized power and created the world's first totalitarian regime. On October 26 (in the Russian calendar), the day after the storming of the Winter Palace in St. Petersburg, Lenin pronounced in *Pravda* that the "dictatorship of the proletariat" had commenced. If hardly a democratic society, czarist Russia had been a reasonably open one (*Pravda* itself had been freely circulated since beginning publication on May 5, 1912). All this was now supplanted by terror, violence, and, above all, secrecy. If something like the Soviet regime had been envisioned, both by those who had great hopes for it and by those who instinctively feared it, no one seems to have anticipated that secrecy would be its most distinctive feature. Everything that went on in government was closed to public view. Civil society ceased to exist. Only the nameless masses and the reclusive leaders remained.

Soviet secrecy in domestic affairs carried over into foreign affairs. The new regime was both threatened and threatening. Early on, American, British, and French expeditionary forces were sent to overturn the new Bolshevik government and somehow keep Russia in the war. (It could be fairly remarked that the United States took this intervention rather too offhandedly. Nothing came of it, and we may be said to have assumed that it did not affect Soviet attitudes and conduct later on. As it was, the United States did not recognize the Soviet government and exchange ambassadors until 1933.)

Even while under attack, however, the Soviets began recruiting secret agents in foreign countries. They saw themselves as leaders of a worldwide movement—the red flag, symbol of universal brotherhood—and anticipated early success as other regimes began to collapse at the close of World War II. Some agents were under cover, some quite public, some both.

John Reed, a Harvard graduate of the class of 1910, was of the hybrid sort. In 1913, he joined the staff of *The Masses*, a socialist journal published in New York. (Its fame today is largely accounted for by its illustrations, created by John Sloan and other artists of the Ashcan school.) In August 1917, Reed published an antiwar article, "Knit a Strait-Jacket for Your Soldier Boy." This brought upon him prosecution for sedition under the Espionage Act and, with his acquittal, a measure of fame in his own circles.[6] But the great event was Reed's trip to Russia, where he witnessed the Bolshevik coup. His account of the revolution, *Ten Days That Shook the World*, appeared in 1919 (soon after his acquittal in *The Masses* trial) and proved a master work of what would come to be called agitprop. He also attended the All-Russian Soviet convention in January 1918. In the summer of 1919 he was expelled from the Socialist Party at its convention in Chicago and thereupon helped to found the Communist Labor Party. That same year, the Bolsheviks founded the Communist International, or Comintern, an association of national Communist parties that in theory were equals but in practice were always dominated by the Soviet party; Reed promptly returned to the Soviet Union to seek the Comintern's recognition of his new Communist Labor Party as *the* Communist party in the United States. He died of typhus in Moscow in October 1920 and was buried beside the Kremlin wall. Lenin, who had become Reed's close friend, wrote an introduction to one edition of Reed's book, although he did not live to see the movie (*Reds*, 1981).

Reed was a Soviet agent. On January 22, 1920, the Comintern gave him gold, jewels, and other valuables worth

1,008,000 rubles for party work in the United States.[7] The U.S. government did not know this, nor much else besides; it has only recently been discovered in the archives of the former Soviet Union. We now know that for the next seven decades the U.S. government would be the object of a sustained Soviet campaign of infiltration and subversion. In the United States the Soviets were to have a measure of success among elites, as they did in Great Britain (Kim Philby was, properly speaking, Harold Adrian Russell Philby), but in the pattern already seen, an ethnic factor—the workings of diaspora politics—was to be the most prominent.

In the beginning, most American Communists were Russians. The Communist Party of the United States of America (CPUSA) was organized at Moscow's behest in 1921, merging Reed's Communist Labor Party with the Communist Party of America, which had been organized by a former socialist, midwesterner Charles Emil Ruthenberg. The membership was not large and was overwhelmingly of foreign birth: Theodore Draper, in *The Roots of American Communism*, estimates that but 10 percent of the members spoke English.[8] Harvey Klehr, John Earl Haynes, and Fridrikh Igorevich Firsov, in *The Secret World of American Communism*, place that estimate at about 12 percent for the two parties that merged in 1921.[9] Draper comments that the American Communist movement began as a "predominantly Slavic movement," as immigrants brought their politics with them or responded sympathetically to political changes in their homelands.[10] This situation changed somewhat as "Americans" and "other nationalities" joined the movement.[11] But the ethnic dimension of American Communism never ceased, although at times it seems to have been overshadowed by the likes of Reed.

Perhaps a quarter of a million persons passed through the Communist Party between 1919 and 1960—with the emphasis on passing through.[12] Nathan Glazer estimates that at the peak of the movement's popularity there were "considerably fewer than 100,000 Communists."[13] Nor did the party, or parties in the first instance, have an auspicious beginning. Fear of radical revolutions got out of hand in 1919–20. There was a good deal of disorder and no small amount of criminal behavior. On May Day 1919, thirty-six bombs were mailed to prominent politicians, judges, and other "enemies of the Left." The *New York Times* wrote of a "nationwide bomb conspiracy." As noted, the Washington home of Attorney General A. Mitchell Palmer was damaged by a bomb that went off prematurely and blew up the bomber.[14]

All this would appear to have been a last surge of anarchism, but it was generally taken for Bolshevism. "Russian Reds Are Busy Here," ran a headline from the *Times*. Palmer, the "Fighting Quaker," responded with major cross-country raids—the Palmer Raids—on radical organizations, including the New York–based Union of Russian Workers, on November 7–8, 1919, the second anniversary of the Bolshevik Revolution. On January 2, 1920, federal agents in thirty-three cities arrested more than four thousand Communists as undesirable aliens deserving of deportation. The *Washington Post* warned, "There is not time to waste on hair-splitting over infringement of liberty." J. Edgar Hoover, then a twenty-five-year-old Justice Department official, located a U.S. Army transport, nicknamed the "Soviet Ark," and sent a shipload of radicals home, inviting members of Congress to see them off at Ellis Island. Hoover now emerged as a national figure, while his superior, the attorney general, began making plans to run for president and warning of likely strikes, bombings, and other terror on May Day.[15]

The unrest did not last. May Day 1920 passed without incident, damaging Palmer's credibility. His raids came to be seen as excessive, and his presidential aspirations faded. Most Americans had begun to agree with Warren G. Harding, who, while running for president against Democrat James Cox, had commented, "Too much has been said about

Bolshevism in America."[16] The Democratic administration, leaderless following Wilson's stroke on October 2, 1919, had become undisciplined and erratic.

Such intervals would recur, with both parties involved, but now a sense of civic order returned. Draper observes: "Ironically, the Palmer raids came as a blessing in disguise to the foreign-language federations. More than ever they were able to imagine themselves Russian Bolsheviks in America. Had not the Russian Revolution been forced to work illegally almost to the very eve of the seizure of power? Was there any fundamental difference between Palmer's prisons and the Czar's dungeons? . . . If the Russian road to the revolution was right, then the postwar repression in the United States merely offered additional proof that the American revolution was really approaching. The underground character of the movement became the supreme test of its revolutionary integrity."[17]

And now the new rulers of Russia turned their acolytes into agents. Klehr, Haynes, and Firsov write: "Soviet intelligence was able to make use of the Comintern and its operatives because, from its foundation, the Communist International had encouraged Communist parties to maintain both a legal political organization and an illegal or underground apparatus. Among the twenty-one conditions required for admission to its ranks, the Comintern in 1920 stipulated that all Communist parties create an illegal 'organizational apparatus which, at the decisive moment, can assist the Party to do its duty to the revolution.'"[18]

Intended both to protect the parties from police repression and to promote secret political subversion, these underground apparatuses conducted operations that were as inventive as they were extensive. Comintern representatives traveled with false passports, and they elaborated clandestine courier services, mail drops, and various codes and cryptographic systems for communicating with foreign Communist parties, which were urged to form secret units and to have safe houses and fake identification documents at the ready. And the Comintern representatives were pre-pared to assist these foreign Communist parties with cash and valuables. Before the United States officially recognized the USSR in 1933, Soviet money for American Communists was sent by way of secret couriers. The subsidy of valuables sent to Reed has already been mentioned; the document from the Soviet archives that mentions Reed's payment also details others sent to three other Communists in the United States in 1919–20, for a total subvention worth 2,728,000 rubles. As Klehr, Haynes, and Firsov comment, "This ac-count reveals that in this period the Comintern supplied the tiny American Communist movement with the equivalent of several million dollars in valuables [that is, gold, silver, or jewels], an enormous sum in the 1920s."[19] In time the size of the subsidies fell off, but even so, they continued for decades afterward.[20]

American Communists were relatively isolated. Apart from circles in New York and a very few other metropolitan centers, and apart from elements in the American labor movement, Communists were almost unknown. Among in-tellectuals and especially within the labor movement, the en-counter with Communism produced an often fierce anti-Communist response. (For the duration of the Cold War, the American Federation of Labor was unmatched in its under-standing of Communism and its antagonism to it.) In time, an opposition appeared in the form of ex-Communists who had broken with the party. With a sure sense of things to come, Ignazio Silone predicted that "the final battle would be between Communists and ex-Communists," so great were the insight and loathing of the disillusioned.[21]

But because a measure of social distance separated most ex-Communists from the rest of the nation in these years, their tales, when told, often seemed too exotic to be true. They were easily dismissed as fantasists or worse. Such was the experience of Benjamin Gitlow, who had worked with Reed in founding the Communist Labor Party but who was expelled from the CPUSA in 1929, during one of the recurrent purges that followed Stalin's exile of Trotsky. In 1939 Gitlow testified before a congressional committee that the fledgling party in America had received Soviet subsidies, frequently in the form of diamonds and jewelry that it could convert to cash with the aid of sympathetic businessmen. But Gitlow, like other ex-Communists, was often seen as an unreliable witness. His testimony was discounted.[22]

Trotsky was an emblematic figure. He was living in Manhattan when the Bolsheviks came to power in St. Petersburg, whereupon he rushed home, became foreign minister, commanded armies, might have succeeded Lenin, was exiled by Stalin, and in time was assassinated in Mexico City. Sidney Hook, a professor at New York University and a onetime fellow traveler who, with many a New Yorker, followed Trotsky into opposition to Stalin, relates in his autobiography that it was one of his students, Sylvia Ageloff, who unwittingly communicated Trotsky's whereabouts to his assassin.[23] Ageloff's sister served for a time as Trotsky's secretary in Mexico City, and when Ageloff visited there, Trotsky and his wife grew fond of her. After Ageloff had returned to New York, she was "casually" offered a ticket to Paris by a female friend who said that she was not going to be able to use it. Ageloff readily accepted. In Paris she met a dashing young journalist who said he was from Belgium— her first love. He was in fact Ramón Mercader, whose mother, a leading member of the Spanish Communist Party, was then living in Moscow with a general in the Narodnyi Komissariat Vnutrennikh Del (People's Commissariat of Internal Affairs), a predecessor of the KGB. In 1940, with Ageloff's guileless help, Mercader traveled to Mexico City, insinuated himself into Trotsky's household, and, when the opportunity arose, murdered him.

Back in New York, there now commenced yet another raging battle between Stalinists and Trotskyites. Questions of who and whom devolved into an eternity of commissions and conventions and contentions. As ever, the party-line Communists lied about everything; we now know that

Ramón Mercader was indeed a KGB agent and that in 1943 the KGB even planned a commando raid to free him from the Mexican prison where he was being detained.[24] Life-and-death issues in New York City, they were little noticed in the rest of the nation.

In 1948, Whittaker Chambers, who had been a contributor to the Communist publications the *Daily Worker* and *The New Masses* in the early 1930s and was later an editor at *Time*, would startle most of the nation with what seemed an astonishing assertion: in the mid-1930s he had been an undercover agent of the Soviet Union and a member of a Washington "cell" that included, most prominently, Alger Hiss. A great controversy arose. Was Chambers telling the truth?

Sidney Hook recounts that "everyone" in New York in the 1930s knew about Chambers's past: "I assumed—and I am confident that I was not the only one—that Chambers was engaged in underground work after he left *The New Masses*."[25] Only after Chambers had broken with the party did he realize that the penalty for this divorce could be death. As Hook recalls: "Chambers was on the verge of hysteria, . . . convinced that, because he had become a faceless, nameless, unknown creature of the underground, his elimination either by murder or kidnapping would remain undetected. His goal was to become a *public* character again, to emerge under his own name and thus prevent his disappearance into the shadows."[26]

Hook devised a complicated "'life insurance' policy" whereby Chambers would "draw up a detailed list of all the Soviet operatives he knew, all the 'sleepers' in Washington and elsewhere who had given him information," and send this to Earl Browder, then head of the CPUSA, with the further message that, if Chambers were murdered, the list would be made public. Hook adds, "When Chambers first publicly identified his fellow-conspirators in 1948, the names were quite familiar to me." They were the same names that Chambers had given to a mutual friend, Herbert Solow, in 1938. They were the same names that he had given to Adolph Berle, then an assistant secretary of state, in 1939. Many years later, in 1953, when Hook asked Berle about the incident and its aftermath, Berle talked about how confusing life was in Washington when he met Chambers, at the beginning of World War II with the world "falling to pieces" all around. "Nonetheless," Hook notes, "despite his initial incredulity at the bizarre tale, Berle steadfastly insisted that he had sent word of Chambers' story to the White House. Berle himself ended up convinced that it was true. Fortunately Berle kept his notes of his meeting with Chambers, which listed the names Chambers had identified as his confederates."[27]

It is not difficult to imagine how a memo from Berle could have been ignored. The anti-Communist hysteria of 1919–20 was remembered, especially by those associated with the administration of Franklin D. Roosevelt, as something of an embarrassment. No one would have wanted to be accused of similar credulity. And so the interval of 1918–39 concluded, and the Great War resumed. During that time the Soviet Union had put in place a fairly elaborate espionage apparatus, more or less reflexively. From the Soviet perspective, the United States was a somewhat marginal power, but even so, spies here might prove useful in time— as indeed they would, however briefly. For its part, the U.S. government was not much interested in such matters.

Looking back on this period, David Riesman wrote in 1952: "Twenty and even ten years ago, it was an important intellectual task . . . to point out to Americans of good will that the Soviet and Nazi systems were not simply transitory stages, nor a kind of throwback to the South American way—that they were, in fact, new forms of social organization, more omnivorous than even the most brutal of earlier dictatorships. At that time, there were many influential people who were willing to see the Nazis as a menace but insisted that the Bolsheviks were a hope."[28] It is a matter of the first importance that the people whom Riesman refers to were concentrated in New York City.

Among them was Lionel Trilling, a native of the city,

who spent most of his life at Columbia University and was one of the nation's foremost literary critics. In 1947 he published his only novel, *The Middle of the Journey*, which turns on the relations between Gifford Maxim, a former spy seeking to establish a higher profile in order to avoid being liquidated (in the usage of that period), and an upper-class couple, Arthur and Nancy Croom, who, although fictional representatives of a certain time and place, bear a remarkable resemblance to Alger and Priscilla Hiss. It happens that Trilling knew Chambers. He later wrote that Chambers's political career, including its underground phase, was "the openest of secrets while it lasted." But Trilling had never met either Alger or Priscilla Hiss, nor did he know anyone who had. Yet in a sense they *all* had. A few months after the novel was published, the Hiss case broke, and the previously obscure Chambers became "a historical figure."[29]

The novel, as the author remarked with a measure of understatement in his introduction to the 1975 edition, "was not well received." In fact it was attacked as a faintly disguised and politically incorrect account of real-life events. Trilling was even asked by one of Hiss's lawyers to testify against Chambers in court. Trilling refused, saying, "Whittaker Chambers is a man of honour," an assertion that provoked the lawyer into an "outburst of contemptuous rage." But Trilling stood by his assessment: "Whittaker Chambers had been engaged in espionage against his own country; when a change of heart and principle led to his defecting from his apparatus, he had eventually not only confessed his own treason but named the comrades who shared it, including one whom for a time he had cherished as a friend. I hold that when this has been said of him, it is still possible to say that he was a man of honour."[30]

It was the times that were out of joint. Trilling acknowledged that, a mere three decades afterward, the mentality of the Communist-oriented intelligentsia of the 1930s and 1940s strained comprehension, even among those who had observed it firsthand:

That mentality was presided over by an impassioned long-ing to believe. . . . What the fellow-traveling intellectuals were impelled to give their credence to was the ready fea-sibility of contriving a society in which reason and virtue would prevail. A proximate object of the will to believe was less abstract—a large segment of the progressive intellec-tual class was determined to credit the idea that in one country, Soviet Russia, a decisive step had been taken to-ward the establishment of just such a society. Among those people of whom this resolute belief was characteristic, any predication about the state of affairs in Russia com-manded assent so long as it was of a "positive" nature, so long, that is, as it countenanced the expectation that the Communist Party, having actually instituted the reign of reason and virtue in one nation, would go forward to do likewise throughout the world.[31]

Any characterization or evidence to the contrary was swiftly dismissed. Either the messengers were disparaged as being deficient in goodwill or the message itself was explained away. "Should it ever happen that reality did succeed in breaching the believer's defenses against it," Trilling wrote, "if ever it became unavoidable to acknowledge that the Com-munist Party, as it functioned in Russia, did things, or pro-duced conditions, which by ordinary judgment were to be deplored, . . . then it was plain that ordinary human judg-ment was not adequate to the deplored situation, whose moral justification must be revealed by some other agency, commonly 'the dialectic.'"[32]

But in time even these seemingly unassailable defenses were forced to give way. Trilling recounted:

But there came a moment when reality did indeed breach the defenses that had been erected against it, and not even the dialectic itself could contain the terrible assault it made upon faith. In 1939 the Soviet Union made its pact with Nazi Germany. There had previously been circum-stances—among them the Comintern's refusal to form a united front with the Social Democrats in Germany, thus allowing Hitler to come to power; the Moscow purge trials;

the mounting evidence that vast prison camps did exist in the Soviet Union—which had qualified the moral prestige of Stalinist Communism in one degree or another, yet never decisively. But now to that prestige a mortal blow seemed to have been given. After the Nazi-Soviet pact one might suppose that the Russia of Stalin could never again be the ground on which the hope of the future was based, that never again could it command the loyalty of men of good will.[33]

At the time of the Nazi-Soviet nonaggression pact, Richard Rovere, who later wrote the luminous "Letter from Washington" series in the *New Yorker,* was literary editor of *The New Masses* in New York. In his memoirs he recalls that, so great was his shock at the news, he cannot remember where he was during the next three or four days.[34] But as Trilling noted, even the Nazi-Soviet pact was not enough. War came; Hitler was the common enemy. The Soviets were allied with the West. And it was not until belief in the Soviet system had begun to fade in Moscow that something similar occurred in New York.

Now pay heed. New York City in the 1930s and early 1940s was the center of the country. It cast 7.3 percent of the votes in the 1944 presidential election. But it was not the capital. The capital was in Washington, D.C., a city that at this time was still provincial, with but little awareness of these matters. When the issue of Communists in government and Communists in general rose again, as it soon did, even Truman could easily dismiss it as reactionary hysteria. That he could do so was partly a consequence of the relative isolation of Communists in America.

There is another perspective, one perhaps best evoked by the anecdote told about Ernest Bevin, onetime head of the Transport and General Workers' Union in Britain and the British foreign secretary at the time of the Potsdam conference in 1945. When he returned from the conference, a fellow MP asked him what the Soviets were like. "Why," Bevin replied, "they're just like the bloody Communists!" By contrast, it is quite possible that Truman had never met a Communist until he sat down with Stalin at the same conference, and it is equally possible that Hoover had never knowingly met a Communist. This was a matter of regionalism in what was then a much more regionalist nation. The clandestine activities of the Communist Party of the United States of America were common knowledge within political and intellectual circles of Manhattan in the 1930s. They were a given. But they were almost completely unknown elsewhere, apart from a few midwestern industrial cities.

It may be wondered if Truman ever knew that he was chosen as the vice presidential candidate for FDR's 1944 reelection campaign by a cabal of Democrats whose leader was Edward J. Flynn of the Bronx. Flynn had encountered Communists at the polls in his borough. In 1944 the Liberal Party was founded to give antiorganization voters, Jewish for the most part, a "line" on which they could vote for Roosevelt. Previously the American Labor Party had served that purpose, but it was now under Communist control. These were serious matters to Democratic leaders. They judged that too many of these adversary organizations were too close to the incumbent vice president, Henry A. Wallace. Soon Wallace was out and Truman was in, thanks to Ed Flynn and his cohorts. These least sophisticated of politicians proved in some ways to be the most astute and prescient and, in the years ahead, crucial.

CHAPTER FOUR

The Experience of
World War II

The Great War resumed in 1939. The combatants were much the same; war itself, however, was changing dramatically, perhaps most significantly with the advent of aerial bombardment. The very idea had once seemed repellent. The First Hague Conference of 1899 had banned bombing from balloons, but the Germans went ahead even so, using dirigibles to develop the first strategic aerial bombing force. Soon airplanes and actual bombers followed, for which the all-important appurtenance was the bombsight.

In the 1920s an American inventor, Carl L. Norden, had developed a sighting device that promised precise aiming for high-altitude bombs. The Norden bombsight became the army's most important secret in the original understanding of the Espionage Act of 1917, which was primarily directed to military equipment, deployment, and installations. By November 1937, German spies had stolen the plans. The theft was the work of a large espionage operation directed from Hamburg by Colonel Nikolaus Ritter—the Ritter Ring, it was called. The Norden operation was carried out by Hermann Lang, a thirty-six-year-old native of Germany who was by then a naturalized U.S. citizen living in a German-American neighborhood in Queens, New York. He worked as an assembly inspector at the Norden plant on Lafayette Street in downtown Manhattan. (An equivalent facility today would be located in New Mexico and surrounded by an electrified fence. But we were learning.) Lang evidently considered himself a German patriot, and he copied the bombsight plans as an act of German patriotism.[1]

Soon, however, the Federal Bureau of Investigation was onto the operation. Another participant in the ring was Fritz Duquesne, an Afrikaner of Huguenot descent who had been born in Cape Province and had witnessed the British quashing of Afrikaner republics in the Boer War. By the 1930s, he too was a naturalized U.S. citizen, but he was willing to spy against the United States if, in so doing, he would be working toward the downfall of his "hated enemy," England.[2] On June 29, 1941, the FBI arrested twenty-three members of the Ritter Ring—nineteen in New York and four in New Jersey. On Walter Winchell's weekly radio program, FBI director J. Edgar Hoover called it "the greatest spy roundup in U.S. history."[3]

Espionage was becoming the stuff of entertainment. *The House on Ninety-Second Street,* a film released in 1945, was loosely based on the activities of the Ritter Ring. The FBI had by now acquired a firm place in the national imagery as the bane of foreign subversives, with German and later Japanese spies assuming the roles that gangsters had played in the 1920s and early 1930s. This was due partly to the director's law-and-order persona but also to the public's innate fascination with espionage, the subject of a great many 1930s spy novels and moving pictures. Much of this was merely entertainment; some part of it reflected national anxieties. But it also reflected a fact of consequence: the U.S. government was acquiring, principally but not exclusively through the FBI, an organized capacity to defend against foreign attack and, most important, was beginning to learn the art of infiltration where there was a domestic component to the foreign attack.

Note the pattern set in 1917. First, twentieth-century war requires or is seen to require measures directed against enemies both "foreign *and* domestic." Such enemies, real or imagined, will be perceived in both ethnic and ideological terms. Second, government responds to domestic threats with regulations designed to ensure the loyalty of those within the government bureaucracy and the security of government secrets, with similar regulations designed to protect against disloyal conduct on the part of citizens and, of course, foreign agents.

We do well to be wary of rules concerning organizational behavior, and even more so for such rules in political affairs. But, then, should we not also be mindful of the view of the framers of the Constitution—that they had discovered, in Hamilton's phrase, a new "science of politics" for bringing stability to the government that they had contrived?[4]

The record of 1917 and the years immediately following is instructive. President Wilson looked up the rules—in this case, the law of the sea—and decided that Germany was in gross and criminal violation. Whereupon the U.S. government declared war. New laws and regulations were dutifully enacted to ensure proper behavior in wartime. Events got out of hand. As fears of Communist conspiracies and German subversion mounted, it was the U.S. government's conduct that approached the illegal. A reasonable explanation for this is that at the time the government had no organized means of assessing these dangers accurately and responding to them appropriately.

It is notable that, in great contrast to the experience of World War I, there was little anti-German hysteria (not too strong a word) during World War II. This may partly be accounted for by the fact that the German presence in American civil life had already been suppressed during the earlier period, which saw what the *Harvard Encyclopedia of Ameri-*

can Ethnic Groups calls "the rapid dismantling of the asso-
ciational structure of German America," from the drasti-
cally reduced readership of German-language publications
to the dissolving of the National German-American Alliance
in April 1918, under Senate investigation.[5]

Even so, German Nazis made a considerable effort to establish an American base. They had already begun recruiting by 1924, but the first large-scale American organization,
the Friends of the New Germany, was not founded until July
1933.[6] A new immigrant, Fritz J. Kuhn, promptly joined. By
1936, Kuhn had become leader of the German-American
Bund (Amerika-Deutscher Volksbund), which was formed
at Buffalo, New York, and was thenceforth a not insignifi-
cant and more or less national political presence. In 1939,
on George Washington's birthday, Kuhn and his allies organized a mass rally in Madison Square Garden in New York.
The newsreel coverage was stunning: a full-fledged Nazi
rally, complete with uniforms and salutes, all intended to
rouse the masses in the struggle against "Rosenfeld's [that
is, Roosevelt's] Jew Republic."

Robin Edwin Herzstein estimates that the Bund probably consisted of some 6,500 activists at this time, with a combined pool of 50,000 to 100,000 sympathizers, family, and
friends.[7] In other words, about the same number of people
as the early Communist Party. There were other parallels.
Herzstein describes a similar immigrant core with similar
apocalyptic fantasies:

> When the Depression struck, many of these newly arrived
> Germans found themselves in dire straits. Unemployed or
> engaged in menial tasks like dishwashing, these disap-
> pointed people found solace in the Bund. They could leave
> their cramped cold-water flats, head for a local *Stube*, and
> sit around drinking beer. The conversation often turned to
> the Jews and to the misery of living in Roosevelt's America.
> Tens of thousands of such people attended Bund meetings
> and rallies. Better-educated leaders, like Fritz Kuhn, found
> them easy to manipulate.

Kuhn and his associate Gerhard Wilhelm Kunze made themselves the spokesmen of these alienated recent immigrants. Like Hitler, they hoped that the United States would fragment into an ethnic free-for-all. As one of the Bundists put it: "This will happen here. It is inevitable. When that day comes, and it is probably not far-off, we must be prepared to fight for the right kind of government. We must win the masses to our side." When *der Tag* (the Day) arrived, the Bund had to be ready to grab its share of the loot.[8]

There was even a similar reaching out to other ethnic groups: White Russians, Italians, Irish. The differences, however, were decisive. At the end of 1939 Kuhn was jailed for embezzlement, by 1941 Nazi Germany had declared war on the United States, and by 1945 the Third Reich was crushed. There was not time to generate the kind of influence or recruit the range of receptive audiences that Soviet Communism had.

To say again, the onset of World War II found the United States significantly better *organized* to deal with subversion, real or imagined. After war broke out in Europe in 1939, the government posted FBI agents in embassies in Latin America to compile information on Axis nationals and sympathizers. A worldwide regulatory regime was put in place that thereafter continally expanded, albeit with different players.[9] The FBI was, of course, active at home as well as abroad. Within three days of the bombing of Pearl Harbor, 1,291 Japanese, 857 Germans, and 147 Italians had been taken into custody.[10]

It is fair to say that by this time the federal government had bureaucratized its mode of dealing with subversion. State and local governments had no such experience or organizational framework, so such matters as mass evacuation of foreign elements became the concern of the federal government. Politics, not routine, set the order of the day (to use that expression correctly for a change). This was nicely encapsulated in a memorandum Hoover sent to Attorney

General Francis Biddle on February 3, 1942. He observed that, in California, "the necessity for mass evacuation is based primarily upon public and political pressure rather than on factual data. Public hysteria and in some instances, the comments of the press and radio announcers, have resulted in a tremendous amount of pressure being brought to bear on Governor [Culbert L.] Olson and Earl Warren, Attorney General of the State, and on the military authorities. . . . Local officials, press and citizens have started a widespread movement demanding complete evacuation of Japanese, citizen and alien alike."[11] Which was indeed the case. Soon congressional representatives from western states were joining in. Ten days after Hoover's memo to Biddle, Congressman Clarence Lea of California, the senior West Coast representative, wrote to Franklin D. Roosevelt on behalf of all members of Congress from California, Oregon, and Washington, recommending "the immediate evacuation of all persons of Japanese lineage and all others, aliens and citizens alike, whose presence shall be deemed dangerous or inimical to the defense of the United States from all strategic areas." The congressmen also recommended that "strategic areas" be defined as the states of California, Oregon, and Washington and the territory of Alaska.[12] These views prevailed.

On February 19, 1942, the matter was dealt with according to the regulatory mode. Roosevelt issued Executive Order 9066, "Authorizing the Secretary of War to Prescribe Military Areas." The order gave the secretary of war the power to exclude persons from designated areas in order to provide "protection against espionage and against sabotage to national-defense material."[13]

The executive order did not single out any specific group, ethnic or otherwise, but the result was that Japanese aliens, American citizens of Japanese descent, and Alaskan Aleuts were prohibited from living, working, or traveling on the West Coast. Between May 8, 1942, and March 20, 1946, a total of 120,313 people of Japanese descent who had been living on the West Coast were interned in relocation camps established elsewhere in the West. At the behest of the United States, sixteen Latin American countries interned at least 8,500 Axis nationals. Where governments were reluctant, the United States did the job for them: Peru, for instance, deported about one thousand Japanese, three hundred Germans, and thirty Italians to the United States in 1942.[14] Although the last American relocation camp was closed by March 1946, some Japanese detainees were still in custody as late as 1949.

Some argued that Germans and Italians should be dealt with in much the same way. But the members of these groups were far more numerous, and their political influence was far more formidable. Interning them all seemed inadvisable if not impossible. On May 15, 1942, Secretary of War Henry L. Stimson recommended to the president at a cabinet meeting that particular individuals should be excluded from militarily sensitive areas, but not entire classes of Germans or Italians.[15] Five months later, on October 12, Columbus Day, Attorney General Biddle announced that unnaturalized Italian immigrants would no longer be classified as enemy aliens.[16] German subjects in the United States technically remained enemy aliens, although by January 1943 most of the restrictions on them had been removed. Granted, first Imperial Japan and then Nazi Germany and Fascist Italy had attacked or declared war on the United States, and fascism, broadly defined, did have adherents in this country. Even so, eventually the U.S. government would regret these responses to the crises.

At the time, though, there was little protest at the internment of Japanese and others during World War II.[17] The Roosevelt administration never experienced any loss of reputation; Earl Warren went on to become chief justice of the United States. Much later—more than four decades later—Congress sought to make amends by means of the Civil Liberties Act of 1988, which states that the Japanese internment was "carried out without adequate security reasons and without any acts of espionage or sabotage documented" and was "motivated largely by racial prejudice, wartime hysteria, and a failure of political leadership."[18] The act provided redress for about eighty thousand survivors of internment, each of whom was eligible to receive twenty thousand dollars. More important, they also received an apology from Congress on behalf of the American people.

Extend the term "racial prejudice" to include ethnic and religious prejudice, and we can see a pattern of response to crisis that seems to have become fixed by World War II. In 1943, Lieutenant General John L. DeWitt, western defense commander, issued a report on the 1942 Japanese evacuation in which he reaches a bizarre conclusion: "In the war in which we are now engaged racial affinities are not severed by migration. The Japanese race is an enemy race and while many second and third generation Japanese born on United States soil, possessed of United States citizenship, have become 'Americanized,' the racial strains are undiluted. . . . There are indications that [West Coast Japanese] are organized and ready for concerted action at a favorable opportunity. The very fact that no sabotage has taken place to date is a disturbing and confirming indication that such action will be taken."[19] The last statement verges on the clinically paranoid. Interpreting the absence of overt threat as a device for allaying suspicion can be the mark of a seriously troubled mind. *Vide* Erving Goffman.

There were many such statements during World War II, and how could there not be? The Japanese had attacked the United States without warning. The losses seemed severe (more severe than they actually were). Germany and Italy promptly joined in the war against us. Europe had been conquered; Britain seemed all but lost; only Canada remained. In point of fact we kept our heads pretty well. The supreme Allied commander in Europe was a German American, with no notice taken. And for all the Japanese internees, there were also Japanese Americans like Daniel K. Inouye and

Spark M. Matsunaga, who emerged from the U.S. Army as decorated officers and went on to become U.S. senators.

World War II did see a reprise of the issue of press censorship when the *Chicago Tribune* revealed Roosevelt's plans for fighting a world war even before the United States had become involved. "FDR's War Plans!" shrieked the headline on December 4, 1941: "Goal Is 10 Million Armed Men." Robert R. McCormick, the *Tribune's* publisher, was an open foe of FDR's administration. Many thought that his paper's exposé was a demonstration of the press's impudence toward affairs of state. But in fact the incident may have been the first instance of the executive using the power of secrecy for his own purposes by "leaking" confidential information to the press.

In his biography of McCormick, Richard Norton Smith records the various sources that had provided the details about Roosevelt's "Victory Program," which the president had requested of the secretaries of war and navy five months earlier: "Citing 'a confidential report prepared by the joint Army and Navy high command by direction of President Roosevelt,' the *Tribune* revealed plans for total war on two oceans and three continents. An extensive air campaign against the German Reich, accompanied by offensive ground action in North Africa and the Near East, would theoretically culminate in a massive U.S.-led invasion of Fortress Europe no later than July 1, 1943." At a cabinet meeting two days after the story broke, Smith notes, Attorney General Biddle remarked that McCormick could perhaps be prosecuted under the Espionage Act of 1917. (He would not be the last attorney general to get this wrong.)[20]

The chief executive was surpassingly unperturbed. Smith speculates that Roosevelt might have seen McCormick's *Tribune* as having provided an opportunity. Michael Barone once suggested to the author that in this case Roosevelt's passivity, a matter that continues to perplex historians, was actually an example of government rationing secret information in order to affect third parties. By the 1960s, it would be routine for, say, the Johnson administration to give classified materials on the Vietnam War to friendly journalists and members of Congress, and almost certainly to friendly governments as well. But in this instance as in much else, it appears that FDR was the first to scout out the new territory. The essential "strategic" fact was that the secrets were created by executive regulation, and thereafter executives would feel free to use them as they might.

CHAPTER FIVE

The Bomb

W orld War II came to a close in August 1945, after the United States dropped two atomic bombs on Japan. The world now knew that the United States possessed the most fearsome secret in the history of warfare. In time, the United States would learn that the Soviet Union also possessed the secret, which had been spirited away by spies. The bomb changed international politics. It also changed the United States. Nothing has quite been the same since.

Prometheus-like, men had stolen fire from the gods. Maurice M. Shapiro, now chief scientist emeritus of the Laboratory for Cosmic Physics at the Naval Research Station in Washington, was one of the scientists who worked at the Atomic Research Laboratory at Los Alamos. He described the scene of the Trinity test, the first nuclear explosion, in the New Mexico desert on the morning of July 16, 1945: "At precisely 5:30 there was a blinding flash—brighter than many suns—and then a flaming fireball. Within seconds a churning multicolored column of gas and dust was rising. Then, within it, a narrower column of debris swirled upward, spreading out into an awesome mushroom-shaped apparition high in the atmosphere."[1]

But awe was almost immediately crowded out by "an oppressive sense of foreboding."[2] In his account of this moment, J. Robert Oppenheimer, then director of the Los Alamos laboratory, made an analogy often repeated since: "We waited until the blast had passed, walked out of the shelter and then it was extremely solemn. We knew the world would not be the same. A few people laughed, a few people cried. Most people were silent. I remembered the line from the Hindu scripture, the *Bhagavad-Gita:* Vishnu is trying to persuade the Prince that he should do his duty and to impress him he takes on his multi-armed form and says, 'Now I am become Death, the destroyer of worlds.' I suppose we all thought that, one way or another."[3]

The scientists at the site knew that if the test worked, not only would it end the war, as it did within the month, but it would forever change the nature of warfare. It was the culmination of four years of secret work, the fruit of the vast enterprise code-named the Manhattan Project. Before long we would learn that Communist sympathizers had stolen parts of the complex formula. *Our* punishment would now begin.

This was a complex fate. But then, so was that of Prometheus. For his audacity he was chained to a mountain where an eagle daily gnawed at his liver, which then healed itself every night. He was at length freed by Hercules. So, at length, would the United States be freed from the long torment of secrecy that followed, but only *after* a long ordeal and only to a degree.

The scientists present at the Trinity test had submitted to an unfamiliar and altogether uncongenial secrecy, for they knew what was at stake. (The physicists included some—Hans Bethe of Germany, Enrico Fermi of Italy, and James Chadwick of England, discoverer of the neutron and winner of the 1935 Nobel Prize for Physics—whose nationalities must have made them especially sensitive to what was in jeopardy.) Atomic fission itself was not a secret. German scientists knew of it; there are no secrets in science. Oppenheimer and his associates had "simply" figured out the techniques and found the resources to build the bomb before the Germans did. Later the Soviets did the same thing. But even in 1945, at that moment of profound concealment, scientific discourse was a remarkably open one, as Shapiro recorded: "While waiting for the rain to abate so that the test could begin, Dr. Bethe and I discussed his epochal discovery of the thermonuclear reactions that power the sun and stars. For me it was a memorable dialogue: we were about to witness the first massive fission explosion, yet we talked of controlled fusion—the steady burning of hydrogen in stars." Shapiro added, "We pointedly did not discuss the prospect of future H-bombs, also based on thermonuclear reactions."[4]

The H-bombs did come; it seemed that they had to come, once the A-bomb was no longer the American advantage. But even before then, in 1946, the United States did try to forestall a nuclear arms race. President Truman proposed to the United Nations a plan for international control of atomic energy. The Baruch Plan, as it came to be known (after Truman's representative Bernard M. Baruch), was blocked by the Soviet Union, whose leader Joseph Stalin was determined to have his own bomb.

And he soon had it. Thanks to successful espionage, the Russians tested their first atom bomb in August 1949, just four years after the first American test. Such alacrity on their part could mean only that they had somehow obtained at least part of our secret. And in fact the A-bomb that the Soviets detonated in August 1949 was a near-exact copy of "Fat Man," the American weapon that had destroyed Nagasaki in August 1945 (Figures 3 and 4).

Now the stakes were raised. When Truman and his advisors learned of the first Soviet test, they embarked on an intense, four-month, secret debate about whether to proceed with the hydrogen bomb project. A number of officials and atomic energy experts at the highest reaches of govern-

Figure 3. "Fat Man," the atomic bomb detonated over Nagasaki, Japan, on August 9, 1945. *Source:* National Archives and Records Administration, Washington, D.C.

Figure 4. Russian physicist Iulii Khariton with the first Soviet atomic bomb, detonated on August 29, 1949. Built according to designs stolen from the United States, the Soviet bomb was an almost exact copy of American weapon deployed four years earlier. Photograph by Victor Luk'yanov; printed courtesy of Dr. Alexey Semenov.

ment were quietly consulted, and then the president made his decision. In January 1950 Truman announced that the United States would continue researching and developing all forms of nuclear weapons, including H-bombs.

The arms race was on. Bethe described its first leg in a lecture, "My Road from Los Alamos," which he gave at the University of Maryland in December 1994. In the late 1940s, it was not clear whether a fusion weapon was technically possible. But in early 1951, a year after Truman's decision to accelerate the hydrogen bomb project, the mathematician Stanislaw Ulam and the physicist Edward Teller demonstrated that it was. Ulam and Teller's formulation was so "ingenious," so "convincing," Bethe recalled, "it was clear that not only the United States could make it but surely there were competent physicists in the Soviet Union who could do it as well": "And this being so, it was then clear that it had to be done, and in spite of my apprehension, I agreed to participate for a good half-year in developing the hydrogen bomb. We concluded it had to be done because the Soviets could, we believed, do it too." Then Bethe recounted, with the succinctness of the historical moment, what followed.

> First the U.S. tested a device which could not have been delivered in a war, which consisted of liquid deuterium. And it worked. It worked, in fact, impressively, giving a yield of some 10 megatons.
>
> This was followed in August 1953 by a Soviet test which [Andrei] Sakharov called the "layer cake," alternate layers of uranium and liquid deuterium to provide the nuclear fuel which is necessary for a fusion reaction. This would have been deliverable, its yield of energy of four-tenths of a megaton.
>
> In 1954 the United States made tests in the Pacific where they tested various variations, all with liquid deuterium, and developed some three or four different hydrogen bombs, each giving about 10 megatons.
>
> And finally in November 1955, there was an additional Soviet test. Sakharov had, in the meantime, hit upon the idea of Ulam and Teller, and produced a device just like

ours. They deliberately reduced the yield of it so they could deliver this bomb from a plane to the . . . test ground and the plane could get away. This could have been three megatons.

As Bethe's remarks make clear, the Soviet Union did not steal the Ulam-Teller method. Their own scientists discovered it, as scientists will do once certain principles are abroad. But the hydrogen bomb began, obviously, as a weapon, and because it was a weapon, details about it were kept, for the most obvious reasons, as secret as possible.

With, however, an all-important difference. There was no way to keep the whole world from knowing *about* the secret, for the simple reason that the bombs had to be tested. The weapons were new, there was much to be learned about them, and the only way to do so was to set them off. Thus began a series of tests by assorted nuclear powers that continues even to this day. But none has seized the world's imagination quite as much as did the underwater explosion in 1946 on Bikini, a small coral atoll in the Marshall Islands, an explosion designed to test the effect of the atom bomb on naval armament and equipment and on certain forms of animal life. The photographs were unforgettable. One caption read: "An awe-inspiring mushroom cloud rises above Bikini atoll in an underwater atomic bomb test. The mighty column of water dwarfs huge battleships." One ship captain, apprised of radioactive fallout, ordered the decks swabbed. Captain Cook might have done as much; no better remedy seemed at hand, such was the suddenness with which this new age had come upon us. The Bikini tests were followed in 1948 by tests of three weapons at Eniwetok atoll, two hundred miles west in what was termed the Pacific Proving Grounds.

The tension between great publicity and even greater secrecy finally led *Life* magazine to "tell all." In two lengthy articles, "The Atom" in May 1949 and "The Atomic Bomb" in February 1950, the fundamentals of the science and the particulars of the weapon were set forth in the language of laypeople. Americans were not yet used to all this secrecy—the kind of secrecy that we knew about, anyway. The editors of *Life* were clearly upset by the imbalance of what they called "necessary security and unnecessary secrecy." They were, even so, scrupulous. A headnote to the article "The Atomic Bomb" declares: "This article reveals no secrets. It is based on published, unclassified material that can be found by anyone, including the Russians, in public libraries." The article itself invokes a number of the nation's most respected journalists and commentators in support of the judgment that secrecy was getting out of hand.

> For the past five years the operations and results of the U.S. atomic weapons program have been almost completely unknown to the public. The critical facts about this greatest of all publicly owned enterprises have been withheld, partly because of essential security restriction. But a larger factor behind the present state of public ignorance is the extension of secrecy far beyond the limits of true security.
>
> This growing disparity between required security and officially imposed secrecy has recently come in for sharp criticism by many of the country's best-informed observers. Joseph and Stewart Alsop, writing about the world strategic situation and the H-bomb, say, "What the President has said [about the bomb] is not one third, or one tenth, of what it is his bounden duty to say." Hanson Baldwin, in the *New York Times,* writes, "Facts are the foundation of democracy—and facts we do not have."[5]

The Cold War had come. Americans were used to secrecy during wartime. The date of D day, for instance. But now a distinction was being made between a "hot war" like World War II and a "cold war" like the one then under way (the terms date from the 1940s), and secrecy was being presented as essential to both. This was wholly new. Profound aspects of the culture, even the nature of energy (the oldest of mysteries), were now to be known by a few but withheld from the rest. In a sense, it was the most primitive of arrangements in the most advanced of societies. The *Life* editors anguished: "So stifling are the effects of all-encompassing security that conscientious publications are unwilling to take the responsibility for presenting conclusions which they themselves could draw from the available, nonsecret literature. The government can and should take that responsibility—now, before it is too late."[6]

But it *was* too late—and for a complex of reasons, the most important being that the United States now had reason to fear for its security. Pearl Harbor had seemed devastating, but it represented an external threat, and that threat had passed. Now there appeared an *internal* threat in the form of American Communists serving as agents of the Soviet Union. What's more, the Soviet espionage attack, admittedly limited, had an unnerving capacity for penetrating key sites. Los Alamos, obviously. But also Arlington Hall, where Meredith Gardner and his fellow cryptographers (for the most part women, as it happens) were near to losing their minds decoding and deciphering the Venona cables, one arduous word at a time.

Looking over their shoulders was William W. Weisband, corporal, cipher clerk, spy. In 1945 he began work at Arlington Hall that made use of his fluency in Russian. Weisband was the first to tell the Soviet Union the critical information that its secret messages were being broken. In 1950 the U.S. Army discovered Weisband's treason, and, although he was suspended from his job, he was never prosecuted for espionage. Nothing was done, and no one outside the army and the FBI was informed. Bureaucracy has its uses.[7]

Here we come upon a large dilemma of our national life, one not readily if at all resolvable. We can but set forth the essentials and await some consensus—which may never come. The first essential concerns bureaucracy's tendency to amass official secrets, a tendency long ago noted by Max Weber. Although Weber's work was just being translated into English when the editors at *Life* produced their series on secrecy and the atom bomb, their critique could have been based on the Weberian model. *Wirtschaft and Gesellschaft*

(*Economy and Society*), published after Weber's death in 1920 but most likely written in part before World War I, includes a chapter entitled "Bureaucracy," where Weber delineates this tendency so clearly that the Commission on Protecting and Reducing Government Secrecy cited the following passage in its 1997 report.

> Every bureaucracy seeks to increase the superiority of the professionally informed by keeping their knowledge and intentions secret. Bureaucratic administration always tends to be an administration of "secret sessions": in so far as it can, it hides its knowledge and action from criticism. . . .
>
> The pure interest of the bureaucracy in power, however, is efficacious far beyond those areas where purely functional interests make for secrecy. The concept of the "official secret" is the specific invention of bureaucracy, and nothing is so fanatically defended by the bureaucracy as this attitude, which cannot be substantially justified beyond these specifically qualified areas. In facing a parliament, the bureaucracy, out of a sure power instinct, fights every attempt of the parliament to gain knowledge by means of its own experts or from interest groups. The so-called right of parliamentary investigation is one of the means by which parliament seeks such knowledge. Bureaucracy naturally welcomes a poorly informed and hence a powerless parliament—at least in so far as ignorance somehow agrees with the bureaucracy's interests.[8]

Clearly some aspect of this "sure power instinct" was behind the army's decision to keep Venona secret. It may be argued that the government ought to have been more open about these matters, ought to have made public what it knew about these spies: after all, we had rolled them up; their time was over. (As it was, the Soviet Union wasn't gaining much from its espionage efforts. In 1945 Bethe had estimated that the Soviets would be able to build their own bomb in five years; thanks to information provided by their agents, they did this in four. That was the edge that espionage gave them:

a year's worth, no more.) Yet who in the U.S. government could have made this information public? The president himself didn't know about it. And might not the public have panicked more than it did? Bethe, knowing that the Soviets would have the bomb in five years, began to believe that there would be atomic war in ten.[9] The ensuing arms race, along with war on the Korean peninsula, absorbed the energies of the executive. Too much was happening to expect something like a measured judgment. Instead, we began to accuse one another.

Trials arising from charges of espionage—perhaps most notably, the trials of Alger Hiss in 1949 and 1950—took place in quick succession. In Britain Klaus Fuchs confessed in January 1950 that he had been a Soviet agent at Los Alamos, setting in motion a chain of events that would expose the "Rosenberg ring." On February 9, 1950, in his infamous speech at Wheeling, West Virginia, Senator Joseph Mc-Carthy announced that he was in possession of a list of 205 Communists serving in the Department of State. In time, he was to accuse even General George C. Marshall of treason.

Also in 1950, Harry Gold became a suspect after Fuchs described meeting with a courier in Santa Fe, New Mexico, five years earlier. On May 22, Gold confessed after FBI agents found a map of Santa Fe in his closet. Gold had indeed been Fuch's courier, but it turned out that once, when KGB compartmentalization had been breached, Gold had received information from a second Los Alamos agent whom he described as a young soldier. On June 15, Gold identified a picture of David Greenglass as being that of the soldier, thus uncovering the second Los Alamos agent, code-named Calibre, mentioned in the Venona decryptions. Greenglass confessed immediately and implicated his sister, Ethel, and her husband, Julius Rosenberg. The FBI quickly identified Julius Rosenberg as the agent code-named Antenna, later changed to Liberal, in the Venona cables.

Beginning March 6, 1951, in a trial that was followed

the world over, the Rosenbergs, Greenglass (who pleaded guilty and testified against them), and a codefendant, Morton Sobell, were charged under the Espionage Act of 1917. Federal judge Irving R. Kaufman sentenced both Rosenbergs to death under section 2 of the Espionage Act, 50 *U.S. Code* 32 (now 18 *U.S. Code* 794), which prohibits transmitting or attempting to transmit to a foreign government information "relating to the national defense." Sobell and Greenglass were given prison sentences. And thus the Rosenbergs became the first American civilians executed for wartime spying. A month later, in May, two British intelligence officials, Donald Maclean and Guy Burgess, defected to Moscow. Would treason never end?

But for every accusation there was a denial. And the American government and the American public were being confronted with possibilities and charges that were at once baffling and terrifying. For all who believed Whittaker Chambers when he said that Hiss was indeed a Communist spy, there appeared to be a corresponding number convinced of Hiss's innocence. The same was true regarding the Rosenbergs. And for all who agreed that there were Communists in government, there were as many who saw the government as contriving fantastic accusations against innocent people.

In the more balanced history of this period that is emerging, the first fact is that a significant Communist constituency *was* in place in Washington, New York, and Los Angeles, but in the main those involved systematically denied their involvement. This was the mode of Communist operations the world over. In his memoirs the diplomat and historian George F. Kennan is quite clear-sighted about this: "The penetration of the American governmental services by members or agents (conscious or otherwise) of the American Communist Party in the late 1930s was not a figment of the imagination. . . . It really existed; and it assumed proportions which, while never overwhelming, were also not trivial."[10] Kennan must be read closely: "conscious or otherwise," he says. American Communism could be no more than a mindset, but it mattered. Communist spies tracking the bomb were tiny in number; Communist sympathizers were many more. In between were a considerable number of real-enough agents with not enough to do. There were just not that many *political* secrets. Never are; can't be.

The second fact is that many of those who came to prominence by denouncing Communist conspiracy and by accusing suspected Communists and "Comsymps" clearly knew little or nothing of such matters—and often just as clearly couldn't care less. Hence the dubious character of the accusers ironically served to lend credibility to the accused.

Add to this the political subtext of much of the debate, which only muddled matters further. Often those who were telling the truth about Soviet espionage were discredited or discounted as readily as those who knew little but who would accuse others of anything. The consequent ridicule could be devastating, and there was plenty of it; as one popular ditty of the time mocked, "Who's going to investigate the man who investigates the man who investigates me?" A fault line appeared in American society that contributed to more than one political crisis in the years that followed. Belief in the guilt or innocence of Alger Hiss became a defining issue in American intellectual life. Parts of the American government had conclusive evidence of his guilt, but they never told. The "anti-anti-Communists," to use Richard Gid Powers's term, were left to rant on about "scoundrel time" and witch-hunts and blacklists.[11] In an odd way, government stayed out of the most heated political argument of the time.

With the publication of the Venona documents, the evidence of Hiss's guilt became public (Figure 5). Hiss was indeed a Soviet agent and appears to have been regarded by Moscow as its most important. A Soviet cable of March 30, 1945, identified an agent code-named Ales as having attended the Yalta Conference of February 1945. He had then journeyed to Moscow, where, according to the cable, he and "his whole group"—that is, his colleagues back home—were "awarded Soviet decorations." This man could have been only Alger Hiss, deputy director of the State Department's Office of Special Political Affairs; the other three State Department officials in the delegation from Yalta to Moscow are beyond suspicion.[12] The party was met by Andrei Vyshinsky, the prosecutor in the Moscow trials of 1936–38. By no later than June 1950, the U.S. Army was persuaded that Ales *was* Hiss. But, as they say in combat, it maintained strict radio silence.

With or without the army signals intelligence, the Hiss case has been argued for half a century. More instructive has been the complete silence, maintained for the same half century, concerning Theodore Alvin Hall, a nineteen-year-old Harvard undergraduate who was recruited to work at Los Alamos. He arrived there in January 1944 and was assigned to work with Bruno Rossi on nuclear implosion. Entirely on his own, Hall passed on to the Soviets crucial information about implosion. A walk-in, as the tradecraft has it.* In May 1950, D. M. Ladd of the Federal Bureau of Investigation received a memorandum summarizing important investigation developments in the espionage field. One section was devoted to Hall and his classmate Saville Sax.

THEODORE ALVIN HALL and SAVILLE SAX
Recent information from [Venona] reflects that Theodore Hall, in November, 1944, was in New York City, where he was in contact with Saville Sax. Hall, at that time,

---

* John Lewis Gaddis observes that Klaus Fuchs was also a walk-in: "The Russians did not recruit Klaus Fuchs: he recruited them. The German émigré scientist, then in Britain, offered information about bomb development as early as the fall of 1941, and the Russians immediately accepted. This happened before anyone knew whether such a device could be made to work, and certainly prior to the 1944 Anglo-American agreement not to share atomic bomb information with 'third parties'; indeed there is reason to think that latter decision may have been influenced by preliminary indications that the Russians had already penetrated Manhattan Project security" (*The United States and the End of the Cold War: Implications, Reconsiderations, Provocations* [New York: Oxford University Press, 1992], p. 90).

MGB

From: WASHINGTON

To: MOSCOW

No: 1822

30 March 1945

Further to our telegram No. 283[a]. As a result of "[D⅟ A.'s]"[i] chat with "ALES"[ii] the following has been ascertained:

1.   ALES has been working with the NEIGHBORS[SOSEDI][iii] continuously since 1935.

2.   For some years past he has been the leader of a small group of the NEIGHBORS' probationers[STAZhERY], for the most part consisting of his relations.

3.   The group and ALES himself work on obtaining military information only. Materials on the "BANK"[iv] allegedly interest the NEIGHBORS very little and he does not produce them regularly.

4.   All the last few years ALES has been working with "POL'"[v] who also meets other members of the group occasionally.

5.   Recently ALES and his whole group were awarded Soviet decorations.

6.   After the YaLTA Conference, when he had gone on to MOSCOW, a Soviet personage in a very responsible position (ALES gave to understand that it was Comrade VYShINSKIJ) allegedly got in touch with ALES and at the behest of the Military NEIGHBORS passed on to him their gratitude and so on.

No. 431   VADIM[vi]

_____

Notes: [a] Not available.
Comments:
        [i]   A.: "A." seems the most likely garble here although "A." has
               not been confirmed elsewhere in the WASHINGTON traffic.
        [ii]   ALES: Probably Alger HISS.
        [iii] SOSEDI: Members of another Soviet Intelligence organization,
               here probably the GRU.
        [iv]   BANK: The U.S. State Department.
        [v]   POL': i.e. "PAUL," unidentified cover-name.
        [vi]   VADIM: Anatolij Borisovich GROMOV, MGB resident in WASHINGTON.

Figure 5. Decrypted Soviet cable that identified the agent code-named Ales—"probably Alger Hiss"—as having attended the Yalta Conference of February 1945. *Source:* National Security Agency, Washington, D.C.

was employed by MED* at Los Alamos. At the recommendation of Sax, Hall agreed to supply to Soviet Intelligence information concerning work being done at Los Alamos. Hall delivered to Beck (unidentified) certain information, and Sax contacted an official at the Soviet Consulate and delivered to him certain information. Based on the foregoing, an intensive investigation has been instituted.

Theodore Alvin Hall, who is identical with the Hall mentioned in the [Venona] information, presently is employed at the University of Chicago at the Institute of Nuclear Physics.

Sax also is residing in Chicago, where he is operating a mimeographing business.

Further investigation is being conducted to determine the current activities of these individuals and to identify Beck.†

Hall and Sax were both sons of first-generation Russian immigrants who brought their politics with them, especially in Sax's case. His family, Russian Jews from Vinnitsa, Ukraine, had emigrated to America in 1914 after pogroms struck their village. Sax's father had previously gotten into trouble for publicly criticizing the czar, and the family always remained devoted to the cause of the Russian revolution. Like Hall's father, Sax's father became prosperous in America, but unlike the Halls, the Saxes did not assimilate into American society.[13] The Halls were Jewish also and had no fondness for the old regime in Russia, but they did seem concerned about fitting into American society. (Hall and his brother, apparently concerned about anti-Semitism, changed their surname, Holtzberg, early on.) At Harvard, Hall was a member of the John Reed Society, a convinced Marxist as well as a brilliant physicist. With the war over, he decided quite on his own that the United States must never

* The MED was the Manhattan Engineer District, one of the atomic research centers constructed by the U.S. Army Corps of Engineers. In June 1942, the MED was put in charge of building research laboratories and manufacturing facilities across the country. In time the entire project was code-named the Manhattan Project.

† "Beck" was later identified as Sergei N. Kournakoff.

have a nuclear monopoly, and he proceeded to help the Soviet Union to break it.[14] Not a word of this was known outside government until the Venona decryptions were made public beginning in July 1995 (Figure 6).

A handful of journalists studying the documents promptly made the connection between a single reference to Hall and later ones to an agent code-named Mlad (Russian for "young" or "youngster"). In September 1995 Joseph Albright and Marcia Kunstel of the Cox newspapers met with Hall in Cambridge, England, where he had been teaching since 1962, and he signed an agreement with them to do a series of embargoed interviews. Michael Dobbs of the *Washington Post*, working separately, also spotted the connection; he flew to England, made his way to Cambridge, knocked on Hall's door, and asked him if he was the agent Mlad. Hall did not deny it; he merely replied that all of that had been a long time ago.[15]

Hall was more forthcoming with Albright and Kunstel. Their book, *Bombshell: The Secret Story of Ted Hall and America's Unknown Atomic Spy Conspiracy*, contains his account of what motivated him in 1944. Hall insists that he acted entirely on his own, uninfluenced by any party, person, or hope for personal gain. His political views had been shaped during the economic depression of the 1930s, he said, and he had seen how prosperity was restored not by Roosevelt's New Deal but by World War II. "What would happen when the war was over?" he wondered: "At nineteen I shared a common belief that the horrors of war would bring our various leaders to their senses and usher in a period of peace and harmony. But I had been thinking and reading about politics since an early age, and had seen that in a capitalist society economic depression could lead to fascism, aggression and war—as actually happened in Italy and Germany. So as I worked at Los Alamos and understood the destructive power of the atomic bomb, I asked myself what *might* happen if World War II was followed by a depression in the United States while it had an atomic monopoly."[16] Appar-

BRIDE

TOP SECRET

TO BE KEPT UNDER LOCK AND KEY :
NEVER TO BE REMOVED FROM THE OFFICE.

USSR

RUDAI-2A

Ref No: S/NBF/T193

Issued: 2/6/21/5/1952

Copy No: 205

1. LIST OF SCIENTISTS ENGAGED ON THE PROBLEM OF ATOMIC ENERGY.

2. UNSUCCESSFUL EFFORTS OF AN UNIDENTIFIED PERSON (POSSIBLY "STAR") TO CONTACT NICHOLA NAPOLI AND "HELMSMAN".

From: NEW YORK

To: MOSCOW

No: 1699   2 Dec 1944

Conclusion of telegram No. 940 [sic][i].

    Enumerates [the following][a] scientists who are working on the problem[ii] — Hans BETHE, Niels BOHR, Enrico FERMI, John NEWMAN, Bruno ROSSI, George KISTIAKOVSKI, Emilio SEGRE, G.I.TAYLOR, William PENNEY, Arthur COMPTON, Ernest LAWRENCE, Harold UREY, Hans STANARM, Edward TELLER, Percy BRIDGEMAN, Werner EISENBERG, STRASSENMAN
                    [7 groups unrecoverable]
our country addressed himself to NAPOLI[iii] and the latter, not wanting to listen to him, sent him to BECK [BEK][iv] as military commentator of the paper. On attempting to visit HELMSMAN [RULEVOJ][v] he was not admitted to him by the latter's secretary.

                              ANTON

Figure 6. The first Venona message indicating Soviet espionage, decrypted by Meredith Gardner. The message, which listed the scientists working at Los Alamos, was sent on December 2, 1944, and was decoded by Gardner on December 20, 1946. Eventually it was learned that the source for this information was Ted Hall, in his first act of espionage. *Source:* National Security Agency, Washington, D.C.

ently not liking the answers he was coming up with, Hall set about helping the Soviet Union break the monopoly. Afterward he was followed around a bit by the FBI before he finally decided to relocate to England. There he became a much-published physicist who traveled to and from the United States without concern.

It will require at least another generation to sort out the details of these incidents of subterfuge. But the facts now in hand surely attest that the U.S. government's pursuit of alleged sympathizers and spies in the post–World War II period did not amount to persecution, still less delusion. Not a few in fact were spies, and of these most were left untroubled. Never prosecuted, never named. Instead, the bureaucracies kept their secrets, especially the secrets that would not have held up in an American court.

Part of the reason for this reticence, as we have seen, was a reaction against the uproar over radical revolutionists in 1919–20, when there was a good deal of disorder and no small amount of government misconduct. Let us say now, in extenuation, that a world war, followed by what for a while seemed to be the onset of world revolution, required a fair amount of adjusting. A measure of balance did return, though, partly because of the isolationist bent that had appeared in national politics in reaction to Wilsonian activism but also because the legal profession had begun to brush up on the Bill of Rights.* Nothing like the Palmer Raids of

* On May 28, 1920, twelve of the nation's most respected lawyers and legal scholars (including Roscoe Pound, dean of Harvard Law School; Harvard law professors Felix Frankfurter and Zechariah Chafee, Jr.; and Francis Fisher Kane, former U.S. attorney for the Eastern District of Pennsylvania, who had resigned in protest over the Palmer Raids) issued a booklet entitled *Report upon the Illegal Practices of the United States Department of Justice.* The booklet, which has been called "the most authoritative denunciation of the anti-Red activities of the Justice Department yet made," documented that department's responsibility for a number of abuses of the Constitution—in particular, the Fourth, Fifth, and Eighth amendments (Robert K. Murray, *Red Scare: A Study in National Hysteria, 1919–1920* [Westport, Conn.: Greenwood Press, 1955], p. 25).

1919–20 would happen again in the United States; the trial of Sacco and Vanzetti, two anarchists, would take place in 1921, but it was a trial, not a raid. During the 1940s and 1950s, when the United States was going through much torment over Communism and Communist subversion, there were many displays of public alarm and political histrionics but few of the egregious excesses of the earlier period. No president since Wilson has sent a rival candidate to prison, whatever his party affiliation.

But another reason for the government's reticence was that secrecy had become the norm. As Weber had shown, a culture of bureaucracy will always tend to foster a culture of secrecy.

CHAPTER SIX

A Culture of Secrecy

T he Cold War settled in, a winter of many discontents. American society in peacetime began to experience wartime regulation. The awful dilemma was that in order to preserve an open society, the U.S. government took measures that in significant ways closed it down. The culture of secrecy that evolved was intended as a defense against two antagonists, by now familiar ones: the enemy abroad and the enemy within. Fallout shelters were built not only on the South Lawn of the White House but also in urban and suburban neighborhoods across the country, preparing the population for a Soviet attack with weapons that had by then become obsolete in nuclear arsenals. Cabinet officers routinely went through evacuation exercises, rushing to shelters miles from Washington. Schoolchildren learned to duck under desks. As for the enemy within, by 1950 or thereabouts the Communist Party was essentially neutralized. It still existed in outward appearance, but sometimes seemed to linger merely as a device maintained by the U.S. government to trap the unwary.

In each of these cases, the government overresponded,

but in none can it be blamed harshly. The Soviet Union was by now developing a nuclear and missile capacity very much on its own, if one allows for the contributions made by expatriate German scientists (a resource that both sides shared). And the Soviets continued an espionage offensive, although after Los Alamos there were no major successes—a fairly steady yield of random information, but nothing of coherent consequence.

Indeed, the terms of trade, if that image may be used here, had quite reversed since the 1940s. It was the Soviets who were now forced to deal with an enemy within. Marxism was a belief system that could evoke intense attachment, but all of a sudden it failed. Judgments vary, but probably the last member of the Politburo to have studied Marx and Lenin and adhered to their worldview was Mikhail A. Suslov, who became a member in 1952 and served almost continuously for thirty years.[1] Now came bureaucracy, disillusion, dissent, defection. Among the most conspicuous instances of the last-mentioned came in 1967, when Joseph Stalin's daughter, Svetlana, defected to the United States.

Thus the U.S. government, which at an earlier moment and to an as yet unknown extent had indeed been infiltrated by persons with pro-Soviet leanings or even actively treasonable intent, now stood unassailable. Not so the Soviet government. Disillusion grew from within. The promise of Marxism-Leninism had not been kept; the contrast with the Western world, and especially the United States, grew ever more painful. There was a good bit of internal exile; as time went on, there was more and more open defection.

The West probably undervalued the advantage of this situation, having had so little experience with such regimes. In 1975, for example, Arkady M. Shevchenko, then undersecretary-general for political and security council affairs of the United Nations, defected to the United States. Shevchenko was the highest-ranking Soviet in the U.N. system. (By unspoken agreement, a Soviet held the position of undersecretary for security council affairs, while an American held that of the undersecretary for general assembly affairs. The postwar settlement, that is, embodied in bureaucratic rank.) Shevchenko was able and effective; some said that he was on the shortlist to succeed an aging Andrei A. Gromyko. Then one day, with no hint, no notice, Shevchenko whispered to an American working in the Secretariat that he would like to defect. This was arranged, but in the tradecraft of the time, nobody was to know. Shevchenko was "kept in place," but as a source for what? For the cables that he could read. In time, Moscow sensed that something was wrong, evidently narrowing the suspects to Shevchenko, Oleg Troyanovsky (now ambassador to the United Nations), or Anatoly Dobrynin (the Soviet ambassador in Washington). By now no one was beyond suspicion.[2]

But before all this, the United States had to live through the aftermath of Soviet espionage, which had crested at Los Alamos. Several laws were enacted. The most important was the Atomic Energy Act of 1946, which introduced the principle that certain information was "born classified," meaning that no assessment was needed in order for that information to be deemed secret. In August 1945, for example, the government had released a history of the Manhattan Project, *A General Account of the Development of Methods of Using Atomic Energy for Military Purposes Under the Auspices of the United States Government, 1940–1945*, commonly known as the Smyth report (General Leslie R. Groves, head of the Manhattan Project, had asked Henry DeWolf Smyth, a physics professor at Princeton University, to write the account).[3] The Smyth report noted that most of the information on the development of the atomic bomb could be obtained from unclassified sources. But in the context of the Atomic Energy Act, this hardly seemed to matter. Automatic classification was by now a pattern of governance, and indeed it remains such. During the 1940s and 1950s, government regulation expanded as greatly as it had during the New Deal.

But during the 1930s, both supporters and opponents of Roosevelt's New Deal programs had grown concerned about the scope of the executive branch's assertion and had passed laws to counter it. In 1938, Roscoe Pound, chairman of the American Bar Association's Special Committee on Administrative Law and former dean of Harvard Law School, had denounced the trend of turning "the administration of justice over to administrative absolutism, . . . a Marxian idea."[4] In 1939, in response to such criticisms as well as to calls for greater openness in government as a means for assuring fairness in proceedings,[5] President Roosevelt had asked Attorney General Homer Cummings to organize a committee to study existing administrative procedures and recommend reforms.

The attorney general's Committee on Administrative Procedure, chaired by Dean Acheson, submitted a final report in 1941. After the war, this committee's efforts and hearings in the Senate Judiciary Committee resulted in the Administrative Procedure Act (APA) of 1946. The APA rests on a constellation of ideas: government agencies should be required to keep the public informed of their organization, procedures, and rules; the public should be able to participate in the rule-making process; uniform standards should apply to all formal rule-making and adjudicatory proceedings; and judicial review should be available in certain circumstances. Taken together with the Freedom of Information Act, an amendment to the APA that was enacted in 1966 and added to in 1974, 1986, and 1996, the APA was intended to foster more open government through various procedural requirements and thus to promote greater accountability in decision making.

As enacted, the APA recognized few exceptions to the standard of crafting a more open government, but the important one was set out in section 3 of the 1946 statute, which addressed "any function of the United States requiring secrecy in the public interest." Government manuals began to distinguish between agencies' ordinary operations, about which the public had a right to know, and agencies' confidential operations.[6] By its own terms, the APA's procedural requirements for both rule making and adjudication do not apply "to the extent that there is involved a military or foreign affairs function of the United States."

This very broad walling off of military and foreign affairs was consistent with the Supreme Court's decision ten years earlier in *United States v. Curtiss-Wright Export Corporation*, where the Court supported a sweeping range of executive discretion in the conduct of foreign affairs: "In this vast external realm, with its important, complicated, delicate and manifold problems, the President alone has the power to speak or listen as the representative of the nation. . . . The nature of transactions with foreign nations, moreover, requires caution and unity of design, and their success frequently depends on secrecy and dispatch. . . . He has his agents in the form of diplomatic, consular and other officials. Secrecy in respect of information gathered by them may be highly necessary, and the premature disclosure of it productive of harmful results."[7] Richard Frank has commented that the dichotomy between domestic politics and foreign affairs could not have been clearer: "Even in 1936, during the only era in which delegation of authority in the domestic area was being found unconstitutional, the Court was prepared, in most generous terms, to grant the Executive great latitude in foreign affairs."[8] Now, however, the definition of foreign affairs was becoming so inclusive that the distinction between foreign and domestic was dissolving.

The encounter with espionage, some of it involving employees and even military personnel of the U.S. government, led inevitably to the issue of loyalty. Wilson's executive order of April 7, 1917, had introduced the concept of loyalty as a condition of government service. Years of civil service reform had been designed to remove "party affiliation," as the term was, from considerations of government employment. In 1939, however, an amended Hatch Act prohibited federal employees from "membership in any political party or organization which advocates the overthrow of our constitutional form of government in the United States."[9]

The Hatch Act in turn was implemented through Civil Service Commission regulations devised in 1940; they were modified in 1942 to include the question "Do you advocate or have you ever advocated, or are you now or have you ever been, a member of any organization that advocates the overthrow of the Government of the United States by force or violence?" In 1942, President Roosevelt had also issued War Service Regulation 2, which denied a civil service examination or appointment to anyone whose loyalty was in "reasonable doubt." This was used by the Civil Service Commission to deny federal employment to a wide variety of individuals, ranging from members of the Communist Party to those associated with the German Bund and other allegedly fascist causes. Other wartime regulations gave the secretaries of war and the navy the authority to summarily remove employees considered risks to national security; after the war, this authority was extended to the Department of State and other departments. In 1944, the Civil Service Commission established a loyalty rating board to handle cases, referred by regional commission offices, involving "derogatory information" with regard to loyalty.[10]

Even so, during World War II the standards and procedures for conducting a loyalty program were not uniform; the development of such a program was left until after the war.[11] In March 1947 President Truman issued Executive Order 9835, establishing the Federal Employee Loyalty Program. The program set up uniform investigation procedures, authorized loyalty review boards across the government, and directed that federal employment be denied where "there is a reasonable doubt as to the loyalty of the person involved." Despite the wartime regulations, "personnel security" was still largely a new discipline. The Atomic Energy Act of 1946 had mandated a security program for its newly established Atomic Energy Commission and had directed the FBI to investigate employees' "character, associations, and loyalty," and in 1950 Congress had empowered certain agency heads to summarily suspend those deemed security risks. Nevertheless, most federal agencies still did not subject their employees to any formal security screening. Lieutenant General Leslie R. Groves, who had served in the army for thirty-two years and directed the Los Alamos project, put it succinctly when he testified in 1954 before the AEC board reviewing the suspension of J. Robert Oppenheimer's security clearance: "The Army as a whole didn't deal with matters of security until after the atomic bomb burst on the world because it was the first time that the Army really knew there was such a thing [as security]." A combination of the bomb's consequences and the growing fears about Communist and related threats to internal security led to a new "demi-jurisprudence" of security clearance procedures.[12]

The Truman order made loyalty a concern across the federal government. The approach generally proved popular, although a cross-section of legal scholars, including Zechariah Chafee, Jr., and Erwin Griswold, did criticize the lack of procedural safeguards and clear standards for assessing prospective and current government employees.[13]

In March 1948, the celebrated "Attorney General's List" was first promulgated. Seventy-one organizations and eleven schools viewed as "adjuncts of the Communist Party" were identified as "subversive," although in no case was the subversion defined. The list, published in the *Federal Register*, stated that "it is entirely possible that many persons belonging to such organizations may be loyal to the United States." But a striking aspect of the listing is the prominence of Japanese and German organizations, years after World War II. Similar diaspora groups—the American-Polish Labor Council, the Hungarian-American Council for Democracy, the Macedonian-American People's League—also appear. Some listings seem unlikely: Sakura Kai (the Patriotic Society, or the Cherry Association, for veterans of the Russo-Japanese War), the Dante Alighieri Society, even the Ku Klux Klan. But the list also included well-established Communist-front organizations (Figure 7).

It was a short step from proscribing organizations deemed subversive to querying government employees about their membership. The political pressure to establish a broader, more comprehensive security program—subsuming loyalty as one key criterion—had increased in 1950 with the passage of legislation "to protect the national security of the United States by permitting the summary suspension of employment of civilian officers and employees of various departments and agencies."[14] Moreover, during the 1952 presidential campaign, Eisenhower vowed to root out Communists and other security risks from the government and the defense industry, suggesting that their presence had been tolerated too easily by the Truman administration. In his first State of the Union address, Eisenhower promised a new system "for keeping out the disloyal and the dangerous." Executive Order 10450 followed within three months. It provided that the appointment of each federal employee would be subject to an investigation and that each agency head would be responsible for ensuring that the employment of each subordinate was "clearly consistent with the interests of the national security."[15] While abolishing the loyalty program of the Truman order, which had been criticized as both ineffective and inefficient,[16] the new order also made it clear that "the interests of the national security require that all persons privileged to be employed in the departments and agencies of the Government, shall be reliable, trustworthy, of good conduct and character, and of complete and unswerving loyalty to the United States."[17] Senator Joseph McCarthy praised the new order: "Altogether it represents a pretty darn good program. I like it."[18] The *New York Times* observed that the new program meant "a new investigation of many thousands of employees previously investi-

FEDERAL REGISTER

THE NATIONAL ARCHIVES OF THE UNITED STATES · 1934

VOLUME 13   NUMBER 56

Washington, Saturday, March 20, 1948

American League Against War and Fascism.
American Patriots, Inc.
American Peace Mobilization.
American Youth Congress.
Association of German Nationals (Reichsdeutsche Vereinigung).
Black Dragon Society.
Central Japanese Association (Beikoku Chuo Nipponjin Kai).
Central Japanese Association of Southern California.
The Central Organization of the German-American National Alliance (Deutsche-Amerikanische Einheitsfront).
Communist Party of U. S. A.
Congress of American Revolutionary Writers.
Dai Nippon Butoku Kai (Military Virtue Society of Japan or Military Art Society of Japan).
Dante Alighieri Society.
Federation of Italian War Veterans in the U. S. A., Inc. (Associazione Nazionale Combattenti Italiani, Federazione degli Stati Uniti d' America).
Friends of the New Germany (Freunde des Neuen Deutschlands).
German-American Bund (Amerikadeutscher Volksbund).
German-American Vocational League (Deutsche - Amerikanische Berufsgemeinschaft).
Heimusha Kai, also known as Nokubei Heieki Gimusha Kai, Zaibei Nihonjin, Heiyaku Gimusha Kai and Zaibei Heimusha Kai (Japanese Residing in America Military Conscripts Association).
Hinode Kai (Imperial Japanese Reservists).
Hinomaru Kai (Rising Sun Flag Society—a group of Japanese War Veterans).
Hokubei Zaigo Shoke Dan (North American Reserve Officers Association).
Japanese Association of America.
Japanese Overseas Central Society (Kaigai Dobo Chuo Kai).
Japanese Overseas Convention, Tokyo, Japan, 1940.
Japanese Protective Association (Recruiting Organization).
Jikyoku Iin Kai (Current Affairs Association).

Kibei Seinen Kai (Association of U. S. Citizens of Japanese Ancestry who have returned to America after studying in Japan).
Kyffhaeuser, also known as Kyffhaeuser League (Kyffhaeuser Bund), Kyffhaeuser Fellowship (Kyffhaeuser Kameradschaft).
Kyffhaeuser War Relief (Kyffhaeuser Kriegshilfswerk).
Lictor Society (Italian Black Shirts).
Mario Morganttini Circle.
Michigan Federation for Constitutional Liberties.
Nanka Teikoku Gunyudan (Imperial Military Friends Group or Southern California War Veterans).
National Committee for the Defense of Political Prisoners.
National Federation for Constitutional Liberties.
National Negro Congress.
Nichibei Kogyo Kaisha (The Great Fujii Theatre).
Northwest Japanese Association.
Protestant War Veterans of the U. S., Inc.
Sakura Kai (Patriotic Society, or Cherry Association—composed of veterans of Russo-Japanese War).
Shinto Temples.
Silver Shirt Legion of America.
Sokoku Kai (Fatherland Society).
Suiko Sha (Reserve Officers Association, Los Angeles).
Washington Book Shop Association.
Washington Committee for Democratic Action.
Workers Alliance.
Under Part III, section 3, of Executive Order No. 9835, the following additional organizations are designated.

American Polish Labor Council.
American Youth for Democracy.
Armenian Progressive League of America.
Civil Rights Congress and its affiliated organizations, including: Civil Rights Congress for Texas. Veterans Against Discrimination of Civil Rights Congress of New York.
Tom Paine School of Social Science, Philadelphia, Pa.
Tom Paine School of Westchester, New York.
Walt Whitman School of Social Science, Newark, N. J.

The Columbians.
Communist Party, U. S. A., formerly Communist Political Association, and its affiliates and committees, including: Citizens Committee of the Upper West Side (New York City). Committee to Aid the Fighting South. Dennis Defense Committee. Labor Research Association, Inc. Southern Negro Youth Congress. United May Day Committee. United Negro and Allied Veterans of America. Connecticut State Youth Conference. Council on African Affairs.
Hollywood Writers Mobilization for Defense.
Hungarian-American Council for Democracy.
International Workers Order, including People's Radio Foundation, Inc.
Joint Anti-Fascist Refugee Committee.
Ku Klux Klan.
Macedonian-American People's League.
National Committee to Win the Peace.
National Council of American-Soviet Friendship.
Nature Friends of America (since 1935).
New Committee for Publications.
Photo League (New York City).
Proletarian Party of America.
Revolutionary Workers League.
Socialist Workers Party, including American Committee for European Workers' Relief.
Veterans of the Abraham Lincoln Brigade.
Workers Party, including socialist Youth League.
Attention is also directed to certain organizations which are operated as schools. While the Attorney General is not of the view that any institution of learning, devoted to the advancement of knowledge, is subversive, it appears that these organizations are adjuncts of the Communist Party. They are as follows:
Abraham Lincoln School, Chicago, Ill.
George Washington Carver School, New York City.
Jefferson School of Social Science, New York City.
Ohio School of Social Sciences.
Philadelphia School of Social Science and Art.
Samuel Adams School, Boston, Mass.
School of Jewish Studies, New York City.
Seattle Labor School, Seattle, Wash.

Figure 7. A portion of the "Attorney General's List," a compilation of organizations and schools seen as "adjuncts of the Communist Party," published in the *Federal Register* 13 (March 20, 1948).

gated, as well as many more thousands who have had no security check."[19]

In the months to follow, concerns about personnel security heightened. In early November 1953, Attorney General Herbert Brownell alleged that President Truman had nominated a Soviet agent, Harry Dexter White, to serve as the executive director of the International Monetary Fund, despite knowing of White's involvement in Soviet espionage.* On December 3, President Eisenhower directed that a "blank wall be placed between Dr. [J. Robert] Oppenheimer and secret data," marking the beginning of the process that led to the AEC's suspension of Oppenheimer's security clearance later in December and its four-to-one decision on June 28, 1954, against restoring the clearance.

Thus the personnel security system that remains in place today, notwithstanding a fair amount of tinkering to ensure greater due-process protections, developed against the background of these deep concerns about loyalty and ideological associations. Edward Shils, writing in 1956, captured the moment: "The present system is centered around the assumption that spies are recruited from among those who feel an ideological kinship with the Soviet Union and from those who can be blackmailed or personally influenced or who by loose and careless talk disclose the secrets which have been entrusted to them."[20]

The concept of loyalty necessarily involved the notion of secrecy. Disloyal employees would reveal secrets; loyal employees would not. In such a setting apprehension rose,

---

* This squalid episode—White was five years dead, and Brownell was thinking Republican politics—is described in Richard Gid Powers's *Secrecy and Power: The Life of J. Edgar Hoover*. Former president Truman remarked, in an undated note written on stationery from the Waldorf-Astoria Hotel, where he stayed November 8–12, 1953, that his information on White had consisted of a report based on "statements made to the FBI by a crook and a louse, Mrs. Bentley and Whittaker Chambers" ("Post-Presidential File," box 619, Harry S. Truman Papers, Truman Library, Independence, Mo.).

as did the dimension of secrecy. More and more matters became classified. At about the same time that some were becoming concerned about public regulations involving mostly domestic activities, others were becoming worried about this newest form of regulation—classified secrets pertaining to foreign affairs.

This anxiety resulted in the first congressional inquiry. On January 18, 1955, Senators John C. Stennis and Hubert H. Humphrey introduced Senate Joint Resolution 21, an act to establish the Commission on Government Security.[21] In a floor statement, Humphrey put it bluntly: "Our present total Government mechanism for assuring security does not inspire confidence." He stated the reason for the proposed measure: "Not since 1917, when the Espionage Act was under consideration by the Congress, has there been full-dress consideration by the Congress of the problems of protecting national secrets, and national defense generally, against subversive penetration." After discussing particular problems in the administration of the personnel security system, Humphrey observed: "As a practical matter, our present security system is a phenomenon of only the past decade. We have enacted espionage laws and tightened existing laws; we have required investigation and clearance of millions of our citizens; we have classified information and locked it in safes behind locked doors, in locked and guarded buildings, within fenced and heavily guarded reservations. But each of these actions has been taken sporadically and independently and not as part of a rational overall master plan for security." Humphrey posed these questions: "What are we trying to protect, and against what? What can we effectively protect? What specific measures will give us the degree of protection we want or need? What price are we willing to pay for security?"[22]

Having cited the duplication and contradiction among the "complex of Government security statutes, regulations, and procedures," Humphrey then noted how limited congressional involvement had been.

To the extent Congress has legislated at all in this area, it has been primarily concerned with the problems of espionage and unauthorized disclosure of national defense secrets. The basic statute is the Espionage Act of 1917. We have amended this statute a number of times to tighten it in the light of current needs, but we have never really studied it to make sure that a statute written in 1917 to reflect the political, military, and technological problems of that era is adequate in the era of hydrogen bombs, radar, and guided missiles, and the world's most infamous conspiracy, the international Communist conspiracy, which surely is not comparable in its ramifications, its subtleties, and its treachery, to some of the old tyrannies of years gone by.[23]

We encounter here (yes, even in the Congress) the bureaucratic desire for uniformity and predictability—"each of these actions has been taken sporadically and independently and not as part of a rational overall master plan"— but also and equally a concern for civil liberties, a fear of too much government with too few restraints. Loyd Wright, former president of the American Bar Association, was named chairman of the commission, with Senator Stennis as vice chairman. The spirit of the enterprise may be seen from President Eisenhower's appointments, which included the likes of Franklin D. Murphy, then chancellor of the University of Kansas, and James P. McGranery, who had served as attorney general under President Truman.

The commission set about reviewing and studying all phases of the government's security and loyalty programs, which it called a "vast, intricate, confusing and costly complex of temporary, inadequate, uncoordinated programs and measures designed to protect secrets and installations vital to the defense of the Nation against agents of Soviet imperialism." There had been a reason for the welter of programs that had sprung up between 1947 and 1955: "the ceaseless campaign of the Soviet Union and international communism to infiltrate our Government, industry, and other vital areas and to subvert our citizenry for purposes of espionage and sabotage." But now a stricter, more orderly approach was called for. The *Report of the Commission on Government Security*, published in June 1957, called for a "sound Government program" to establish the following: "procedures for security investigation, evaluation, and, where necessary, adjudication of Government employees, and also appropriate security requirements, with respect to persons privately employed or occupied on work requiring access to national defense secrets or work affording significant opportunity for injury to national security"; "vigorous enforcement of effective and realistic security laws and regulations"; and "careful, consistent, and efficient administration of this policy in a manner which will protect the national security and preserve basic American rights."[24]

The commission report—all 807 pages of it—was encyclopedic and fair-minded. It revealed a clear concern that the idea of loyalty not mutate into a caste system dividing the born-again from the untouchable. The commission distinguished between "the loyalty problem" and the problem of suitability and security, recognizing that "all loyalty cases are security cases, but the converse is not true." Someone who talks too freely when in his cups or someone whose personal life makes them vulnerable to blackmail may be a security risk but may also be a loyal American. The commission recommended that "as far as possible such cases be considered on a basis of suitability to safeguard the individual from an unjust stigma of disloyalty."[25]

In the end, however, the commission had only two legislative proposals: first, to penalize unlawful disclosures of classified information by persons outside as well as within the government (in the past, only disclosures by government employees had been punishable); second, to make admissible in court evidence of subversion that federal agencies had obtained by wiretapping.[26]

Little came of the commission's work. The proposal to outlaw disclosures of classified information by anyone, federal employee or no, was quickly perceived as prior restraint on the press: censorship. Responses from journalists and editorial boards were at once swift and predictable. Four days after the commission had issued its report, James Reston wrote an article for the *New York Times*, "Security Versus Freedom: An Analysis of the Controversy Stirred by Recommendation to Curb Information." Reston's article is notable for its specificity.

> The history of recent years is full of illustrations of the dangers of such broad legislative proposals.
>
> Franklin D. Roosevelt's deal with Joseph Stalin at Yalta to bring the Ukraine and Bylo-Russia into the United Nations was classified "top secret." Elaborate efforts were made to conceal the arrangement. The late Bert Andrews, Washington correspondent of the *New York Herald-Tribune*, found out about it.
>
> He "willfully," even gleefully, reported it, knowing full well that it was classified "top secret." Under the proposals of the Commission on Government Security, if law at the time, he would have been subject to a fine of $10,000 and five years in jail. . . .
>
> This newspaper also published the original plans of the United States, Britain, France and the Soviet Union on the formation of the United Nations. Again, they were marked "top secret" and the Federal Bureau of Investigation was called in to make an official investigation of disclosure.
>
> In this case, though the Government maintained that publication would block formation of the United Nations, the main result was a long debate on the Big Five veto power and the assumption that the five major powers could agree on a post-war settlement. This, in turn, helped clarify the issue and contributed to some modifications of the Charter, but under the legislation now proposed by the Commission on Government Security, it would have been a clear case for criminal action.[27]

(In this last-mentioned case, we would note that the potential felon would have been Reston himself, who had a friend in the Chinese delegation.)

Reston's assumption that journalists would act responsibly in such matters had a certain innocence. So did Wright's opposing assumption that, by making secret information public, the instigator was in effect a traitor: "The purveyor of information vital to national security, purloined by devious means, gives aid to our enemies as effectively as the foreign agent."[28]

Now then. Even at that time, the most frequent purveyors of "information vital to national security" obtained it, not by "devious means," but through routine channels. Officials often provided classified information to journalists, sometimes to enhance their own prestige, sometimes to gain advantage in an internal dispute, sometimes to let the public know something that the purveyor thought the public had a right to know. The matter has never been quantified, but it is reasonable to think that most "leaking" was coming from the higher reaches of the system. (We have Kennedy's testament that the Ship of State is the only ship that leaks from the top.) As Max Frankel of the *New York Times* has observed, presidents soon came to realize that "even harmless secrets were coins of power to be hoarded."[29]

It was beyond the range of a commission report to speculate on the allure of secrecy, but this must never be discounted. The official with a secret *feels* powerful. And is. In 1960, three years after the *Report of the Commission on Government Security* was published, the Committee on Government Operations of the House of Representatives declared: "Secrecy—the first refuge of incompetents—must be at a bare minimum in a democratic society, for a fully informed public is the basis of self-government. Those elected or appointed to positions of executive authority must recognize that government, in a democracy, cannot be wiser than the people."[30] Which is very likely true, but not of necessity widely believed by those in authority, howsoever brief.

The Commission on Government Security was not as bold or explicit in stating the problem, but it did attempt, in its most instructive proposal, to provide a solution. As a remedy for "one of the principal deficiencies of past loyalty and security programs"—the "shortage of trained, qualified personnel to administer them"—the commission recommended an independent central security office in the executive branch. The first duty of its director would be "to select eminently qualified personnel, including hearing examiners to conduct loyalty hearings under the Federal civilian employee program and security hearings under the industrial, atomic energy, port and civil air transport programs."[31] This strategy fit well with public administration doctrine of this time. It could well have been proposed by one of the several Hoover commissions of the postwar period. Like the Civil Service Commission, the new federal agency would operate according to uniform rules administered by trained, qualified, well-managed personnel.

But this, too, ran athwart the changed political culture of Washington. It was turning out that secrets were an asset not to be centralized and shared.

Organizations with the morale, incentives, and structure enabling them to hold information closely were increasingly disinclined to cooperate with organizations that were not. This is perhaps too generous. A less charitable view is that secrets had become assets; organizations hoarded them, revealing them sparingly and only in return for some consideration. Such as these wanted no part of some central security office busying itself with their internal affairs. This, of course, is conjecture, but it is certainly true that no central security office emerged.[32]

Instead, the dispersal of secrecy centers within the government continued. The Federal Bureau of Investigation began operations, as against investigations, overseas. This was a logical extension of its internal task of keeping abreast of domestic espionage and, from an organizational perspective, provided an opportunity of considerable import.

A dramatic instance of this extension can be seen in the interesting relationship that the FBI developed with a naturalized American named Morris Childs, born Moishe

Chilovsky in the Ukraine in 1902 of Jewish parents. His father, who had been engaged in anticzarist activities and had been exiled to Siberia, fled to the United States in 1910, and his family came the following year. Morris Childs later became a charter member of the Communist Party of the United States of America. Following the expulsion of Jay Lovestone (born Jacob Liebstein in 1898 in Lithuania), Childs became a party official under Browder; in 1929 he was sent to Moscow for further training. In 1934, he became a member of the American Central Committee, and in 1945 he succeeded Budenz as managing editor of the *Daily Worker*. In 1947, Childs returned to Moscow, where he learned of the repression there and specifically of Stalin's persecution of Jews. Thoroughly disillusioned, he was "turned" by the FBI in the early 1950s. In 1957, Childs became deputy head of the CPUSA and the primary contact with Soviet, Chinese, and other parties abroad, traveling regularly to Moscow and Peking. He led the U.S. delegation to the Twenty-First Party Congress in Moscow in 1959. Reportedly a source of considerable information about Kremlin politics and especially of Sino-Soviet tensions, Childs's role as an American agent was kept entirely within the FBI until President Gerald R. Ford was informed in 1974. In 1987, he was awarded the National Security Medal in a ceremony held *in camera* at FBI headquarters.

Meanwhile, the Eisenhower administration began an inquiry of its own. In August 1956 Secretary of Defense Charles E. Wilson established the five-member Committee on Classified Information, chaired by Charles A. Coolidge, a former assistant secretary of defense. (The other four members were retired high-ranking military officers.) In his letter establishing the committee, Secretary Wilson stated that he was "seriously concerned over the unauthorized disclosure of classified military information"; he called on the committee to examine the adequacy of all laws and regulations on classification and the safeguarding of classified information, as well as the procedures utilized at the Defense Department in this area and the department's ability to "fix responsibility" for unauthorized disclosure of classified information.

Three months after it was set up, on November 8, 1956, the Coolidge committee issued a report containing twenty-eight recommendations—ten covering overclassification, eleven relating to unauthorized disclosures of information, and the remaining seven relating to department policies vis-à-vis Congress, industry, and the press. The first recommendation—based on a finding that Defense Department officials had a tendency to "play it safe" and classify too much—called for "a determined attack" on overclassification, "spearheaded by the responsible heads within the Department of Defense, from the Secretary of Defense down." Another called on senior officials to "throw back over-classified matter received from subordinates." The committee also urged the department to make clear that the classification system "is not to be used to protect information not affecting the national security, and specifically prohibits its use for administrative matters." What the committee did not propose was any disciplinary action when classification procedures were abused. And in July 1957, when Secretary Wilson issued a new directive consolidating the department's rules for classification, it did not impose any procedures to address the matters that he had caused to be so strikingly set forth.

In addition to the several commissions organized to examine the security classification system, in 1955 the House of Representatives created the Special Government Information Subcommittee of the Government Operations Committee. The subcommittee was created because some representatives were concerned about the growth of postwar secrecy, especially the Eisenhower administration's establishment in November 1954 of the Office of Strategic Information, in the Commerce Department. The new agency was responsible for formulating policies about production and distribution of "unclassified scientific, technical, industrial, and economic information, the indiscriminate release of which may be inimical to the defense interests of the United States."[33]

In 1953, Representative John Moss, a freshman Democrat on the House Post Office and Civil Service Committee, had raised the issue of public access to government information. He had sought information from the Eisenhower administration's Civil Service Commission to verify its claim that 2,800 federal employees had been fired for "security reasons"; he wanted to know whether these reasons were based on allegations of disloyalty or espionage or on other matters that could also be grounds for discharge—like a misstatement on a job application. The commission refused to release the information, and Moss found that he had no means to compel its release. Two years later, he urged the creation—and subsequently was made chairman—of the Special Government Information Subcommittee, tasked with monitoring executive secrecy.

The Moss subcommittee undertook a lengthy inquiry (spanning the duration of both the Coolidge committee and the Wright commission) of the classification system's administration and operation and, more generally, the availability of information from agencies and departments. Among its chief concerns was the lack of any action against overclassification of information: "In a conflict between the right to know and the need to protect true military secrets from a potential enemy, there can be no valid argument against secrecy. The right to know has suffered, however, in the confusion over the demarcation between secrecy for true security reasons and secrecy for 'policy' reasons. The proper imposition of secrecy in some situations is a matter of judgment. Although an official faces disciplinary action for the failure to classify information which should be secret, no instance has been found of an official being disciplined for classifying material which should have been made public. The tendency to 'play it safe' and use the secrecy stamp has, therefore, been virtually inevitable."[34] But aside from effecting some attention to declassification of historical documents, the subcommittee's recommendations—including those intended to provide disincentives for overclassification and to establish a security classification system based in statute—were "largely ignored" by the executive branch.[35]

The Moss subcommittee did, however, remain at the forefront of legislative efforts to enhance public access to government information. Beginning in the mid-1950s, it focused more attention on how the security classification system related to the rights of both Congress and the public to obtain information from the executive branch. This would lead in 1966, after eleven long years, to enactment of the Freedom of Information Act (FOIA), which established any person's statutory right of access to all federal records except those falling into one of nine listed categories.

In 1958, Moss succeeded in narrowing the use of the 1789 "housekeeping" statute, an oft-litigated provision that had allowed government agencies to withhold information. In 1962, he helped persuade President Kennedy to narrow the use of "executive privilege" in denying the release of records. And in 1965 Moss, with Representative Donald Rumsfeld, introduced legislation to establish a presumption that, with only narrow exceptions, executive-branch documents should be available to the public and that judicial review should be available as a check on agency decisions to withhold information. By 1966, bipartisan support for the effort had grown, and it appeared that the issue of public access to information might even come up in the fall congressional elections. The legislation passed the Senate first, then the House. On July 4, 1966, President Johnson signed the FOIA into law. It went into effect exactly one year later, in order to give the executive branch time to prepare for its implementation.

Notable as that achievement was and remains, it did not much change the practices of the bureaucracy. In 1972, the

House Foreign Operations and Government Information Subcommittee, now chaired by Representative William Moorhead of Pennsylvania, concluded that "the efficient operation of the Freedom of Information Act has been hindered by five years of foot dragging by the Federal bureaucracy." Agency procedures were deficient and employees untrained, large fees were charged in order to deter requests, responses were long in coming, and the exemption categories were being applied too broadly. Again Congress responded. With Moorhead's leadership, the FOIA was amended substantially in 1974 (the amendment became law after Congress voted overwhelmingly to override a presidential veto) to close some of the loopholes and strengthen several provisions.

Notwithstanding the accomplishments of Representatives Moss and Moorhead and their colleagues, an inevitable conflict remains between the right of access prescribed in the FOIA and the authority of the executive branch to preserve certain secrets. The very first exception to the general FOIA principle of public access applies to matters that are "specifically authorized under criteria established by an Executive order to be kept secret in the interest of national defense or foreign policy" or to matters that are "in fact properly classified pursuant to such Executive order."[36] This exception is not surprising; as noted, such matters had been treated differently in the original Administrative Procedure Act. The difference now is the availability of procedures, including use of the courts, to review bureaucrats' decisions to deny the release of information requested under the FOIA.[37]

From the onset of the atomic age there had been a tension between the defense establishment (generally defined) and the scientific community over the nature of secrecy in science. From the time of the Smyth report and the arguments of Bethe and others as to the inevitability of a Soviet H-bomb, the level of irritation between the two camps was not inconsiderable. The scientists had said that the United

States could not hide nature from Russians. Now an argument arose about the disutility of trying to hide nature from Americans. As noted earlier, the Wright commission was on to this, stressing "the dangers to national security that arise out of overclassification of information which retards scientific and technological progress, and thus tends to deprive the country of the lead time that results from the free exchange of ideas and information."[38]

This aspect of the Wright commission's report was echoed in resounding fashion thirteen years later. In July 1970, a special task force on secrecy, convened by the Defense Science Board and led by Frederick Seitz of Rockefeller University, issued its final report on how to address problems with the system for classifying scientific and technical information.[39] The task force, whose members included Edward Teller and Jack P. Ruina of the Massachusetts Institute of Technology, deemed it unlikely that any classified scientific and technical information would remain secure for as long as five years; more likely, the information would become known to others in as little as one year by means of "independent discovery" or clandestine disclosure.[40] The report also cited the costs of classification, urging that its effect in inhibiting the flow of information should be considered, and balanced against the benefits, when classification decisions were made. If greater care was taken to classify fewer documents and for shorter periods, the task force concluded, the amount of scientific and technical information that was classified could be reduced by as much as 90 percent.

In its most telling passage, the Seitz task force wrote that "more might be gained than lost" if the United States were to adopt "unilaterally, if necessary—a policy of complete openness in all areas of information." Recognizing, however, that this proposal was not practical in light of prevailing views on classification, it recommended instead a "rigid schedule" for automatic declassification, with a general period of one to five years, subject to exemptions for specified categories.[41] That nothing came of this recommendation speaks to the culture of secrecy that was settling on Washington. This task force was not a band of outsiders; its members included Teller and Ruina, men who had designed and built the weapons under scrutiny. In matters of constructing weaponry their judgment was unquestioned, but by some bizarre dissociation, their judgment could not be trusted where secrecy was concerned.

Nor did time mellow these attitudes. To the contrary: "The security classification of information became in the 1980s an arbitrary, capricious, and frivolous process, almost devoid of objective criteria." Thus was the conclusion of Glenn T. Seaborg, co-discoverer of plutonium and chairman of the Atomic Energy Commission from 1961 to 1971. During this time he kept a journal, much of it consisting of a diary written at home each evening, the rest containing correspondence, announcements, minutes, and the like. Seaborg was careful about classified matters; nothing was included that could not be made public. While he was at the AEC, the portions of his journal relating to the Kennedy and Johnson administrations were microfilmed and placed in the appropriate presidential libraries. Before he left the AEC, Seaborg had the entire journal cleared virtually without deletion.

Then lunacy descended. Or, rather, the Atomic Energy Commission became the Department of Energy and bureaucracy got going. Seaborg writes of all this in an article, "Secrecy Runs Amok," published in *Science* in 1994. It seems that in 1983 the chief historian of the department asked to borrow one of two sets of the journal, some twenty-six volumes in all, for work on a history of the commission. By the time Seaborg got his journal back, passage after passage had been redacted, much of it explicitly public information (like the published code names of nuclear weapons tests), some of it purely personal (like his account of going trick-or-treating with his children on Halloween).[42]

The twenty-six volumes of the journal, "in expurgated form," as Seaborg puts it, are now available in manuscript archives of the Library of Congress. But where does one go for sanity? Seaborg notes that, "with the beginning of the Reagan administration, the government had begun to take a new, much more severe and rigid position with regard to secrecy."[43] The balance between the right of the public to know and the right of the nation to protect itself was simply lost as (often apologetic) investigators pored over the papers of one of the great Americans of our time.

Again to the theme that organizations in conflict— make that "competition"—become like one another. By the 1990s the Central Intelligence Agency had created a history staff at the Center for the Study of Intelligence. (History staffs were by then standard appurtenances of Washington agencies.) The center engaged a young scholar, Nick Cullather, to write a history of the agency's early involvement in Guatemala. In 1994, the CIA published a redacted version of Cullather's *Operation PBSUCCESS: The United States and Guatemala, 1952–1954*. One of the redacted portions: a passage quoted from President Eisenhower's memoirs.[44]

CHAPTER SEVEN

The Routinization of Secrecy

As the Cold War gathered, the United States, in no wise the aggressor, had to organize itself to deal with aggression from a different kind of adversary. The Soviet Union's very name reflected the new phenomenon: a federation of soviets, towns or village councils made up of workers and peasants. The hamlet as nation-state as international movement. The red flag knew no boundaries: it represented mankind, and the Supreme Soviet in Moscow spoke for mankind. This was not German or Japanese nationalism. It was something wholly new, and now the United States organized itself in a wholly new fashion.

The Cold War is probably best understood as the third in a succession of civil wars in Western civilization. The first began in 1914, the second in 1939. The third began in Central Europe, as had the two earlier conflicts, with the Soviets pressing to expand their dominion in the wreckage of previous regimes. In 1949 Communists triumphed in a civil war in China; suddenly, the conflict became global.

In all this the United States, as the preeminent world

power, began to recognize that it would be managing disputes, and very likely engaged in warfare, around the world and indefinitely. As a consequence, a large peacetime military establishment began to take shape. Foreign policy began to anticipate, rather than merely react to, conflicts. Seeing that the United States would inevitably be drawn in if the Soviets were to invade West Germany, we chose to become engaged in advance, helping to formulate the North Atlantic Treaty in 1949; for the first time in our history, we entered a peacetime alliance committing us to war if others were attacked. In 1955 the Soviets organized the Warsaw Pact, and the symmetry was complete. Central Powers versus Allied Powers, Axis Powers versus Allied Powers, Warsaw Pact versus North Atlantic Treaty Organization.

The extraordinary fact of the final stage of this hundred years' war is that warfare never broke out between the major contesting powers. Proxy conflicts of all sorts did occur. U.S. forces did see action. Still, this time, global confrontation did not result in global war. The reason, of course, was the atomic bomb and the strategic thinking that began with the onset of the atomic age. American strategic doctrine, with its emphasis on "second-strike" capability—on developing a nuclear-weapons force able to withstand nuclear attack and deliver a retaliatory attack—was surely key in ultimately achieving nuclear stability. But during the Cold War this outcome was by no means clear. As ideological conflict between the two powers raged, so did efforts to gain tactical advantage through espionage or subversion. Both parties organized alliances, built conventional forces and strategic forces, cultivated dissent among adversaries, hoarded information, and built up intelligence forces of unprecedented size and global reach.

As we have seen, part of the U.S. response to what seemed a new world order was to rationalize, modernize, and routinize its intelligence operations. The National Security Act of 1947 created the National Security Council to advise the president about all domestic, foreign, and military policies relating to national security and the Department of Defense, bringing American armed forces under unified command. It also created the Central Intelligence Agency to provide "national intelligence"—"timely, objective, independent of political considerations, and based upon all sources available to the intelligence community"—to the president and agency heads.[1] Thus the CIA essentially began its life as a committee. It was to make sense of the cable traffic, publish the *National Intelligence Daily* for the president and a few others, keep an eye out for the unexpected. Truman had originally understood that the agency would work "for the benefit and convenience of the President of the United States . . . [so that] instead of the President having to look through a bunch of papers two feet high, the information was coordinated so that the President could arrive at the facts."[2]

In short order, however, the CIA became a worldwide organization involved with espionage, insurgency, and counterinsurgency—operations of every sort. By the late 1950s, it had grown to about the size of the State Department, with some twenty thousand employees. After setting up in temporary buildings on Navy Hill, across the road from the State Department, it acquired its magnificent headquarters on the banks of the Potomac, at Langley, Virginia. (Senate lore has it that Senator Richard B. Russell of Georgia slipped the building into a defense appropriations bill in the guise of an aircraft carrier.) And with the vast expansion in bureaucratization came a remarkable routinization of secrecy. Until 1997, the intelligence budget was secret; even now that the total budget is public information, its details remain classified. Covert operations, often paramilitary, became a signature activity. A half century after the CIA was founded, a newly confirmed director told the press, and, by indirection, agency employees, that the mission of the CIA was "to pursue the hardest targets that threaten American interests around the world": "At the end of the day, this is an espionage organization. . . . Otherwise I don't know why we are here."[3]

As we shall see, there were several reasons for the CIA's having embraced concealment as a modus vivendi. But the routinization of secrecy worked against the very purpose it was designed to serve: to see clearly the nature of the Soviet threat, and to respond accordingly.

In his magisterial summa *Bureaucracy: What Government Agencies Do and Why They Do It,* James Q. Wilson states: "An organization is like a fish in a coral reef. To survive, it needs to find a supportive ecological niche." If an organization's niche is not specified by law, as it was with the Social Security Administration or the Internal Revenue Service, its founding executives can sometimes achieve that autonomy by other means. Wilson uses the CIA as the prime example of how this transformation can be brought about: "First, [the founding executives must] seek out tasks that are not being performed by others. . . . The first directors of the Central Intelligence Agency faced plenty of rivals—the military services as well as the State Department had active intelligence services. This fact . . . led it to define a new role for itself in the area of covert operations."[4]

The agency lost little time in defining this role. Its reach, it determined at the outset, would be global. In *Operation PBSUCCESS,* Nicholas Cullather records that CIA agents arrived in Guatemala in March 1947, just months after the agency was created; they were to keep an eye on Peronists and Communists and, in time, start a civil war.[5] This operation became the model for the Cuban operation that culminated in the Bay of Pigs. In the meantime, the Eisenhower administration used covert actions to build a government in South Vietnam and support a separatist movement in Sumatra.[6] The activities in Iran are now well known (though the full story will never be known, as the agency destroyed the files in 1960s). There were others, less dramatic but no less adventurous.

But of course the CIA was chiefly concerned with carving out its sphere of influence with regard to the Soviet

Union. And in the drive to pursue an active agenda, it often disregarded voices that seemed to argue for a quieter approach. In July 1947, three months after CIA agents had arrived in Guatemala, the magazine *Foreign Affairs* published "The Sources of Soviet Conduct," by a writer identified only as "X." Although the piece was attacked and even grossly misread by those with interventionist leanings, it was surely the most prescient position paper in the history of modern American diplomacy. Its author, George F. Kennan, who at that time was head of the State Department's policy planning staff, argued the case for containment as a largely passive policy. There was no urgency, he asserted, for the simple reason that Soviet doctrine itself decreed there was none. Marxism-Leninism had famously declared that capitalism contains the seeds of its own destruction, that its inescapable result was a revolutionary transfer of power to the working class. A final phase would lead to war and revolution, but all in good time. In tracing intentions from ideology, Kennan perceived that the Soviet leadership may have been less aggressively expansionist than many assumed: "We have seen that the Kremlin is under no ideological compulsion to accomplish its purposes in a hurry. Like the Church, it is dealing in ideological concepts which are of long-term validity, and it can afford to be patient. . . . The very teachings of Lenin himself require great caution and flexibility in the pursuit of Communist purposes."[7]

Moreover, the faith was dying at home. Kennan saw that Soviet Communism contained its own seeds of destruction: the hardships of Soviet rule, especially with regard to human freedoms, and the hardships of the troubled Soviet economy. The Russian people, he observed, "are disillusioned, skeptical and no longer as accessible as they once were to the magical attraction which Soviet power still radiates to its followers abroad. The avidity with which people seized upon the slight respite accorded to the Church for tactical reasons during the war was eloquent testimony to the fact that their capacity for faith and devotion found little expression in the purposes of the régime."[8]

As for the Russian economy, some parts of it had developed—notably, the metallurgical and machine industries (which would be crucial in producing nuclear weapons). But for the rest, it was a backward economy devastated by war and hobbled by an increasingly outdated infrastructure (a primitive railroad system, an inadequate highway network, a rudimentary air transport industry). Kennan clearly foresaw the consequences: "The future of Soviet power may not be by any means as secure as Russian capacity for self-delusion would make it appear to the men in the Kremlin." He recalled Thomas Mann's analogy in the great novel *Buddenbrooks:* human institutions, like stars, often appear to shine most brilliantly when their inner decay is in reality farthest advanced. "And who can say with assurance that the strong light still cast by the Kremlin on the dissatisfied peoples of the western world is not the powerful afterglow of a constellation which is in actuality on the wane? This cannot be proved. And it cannot be disproved. But the possibility remains (and in the opinion of this writer it is a strong one) that Soviet power, like the capitalist world of its conception, bears within it the seeds of its own decay, and that the sprouting of these seeds is well advanced."[9]

Kennan, of course, wrote at a time when the United States was pursuing a postwar policy of accommodation with the Soviet Union.[10] But he was warning of obstacles ahead. We were in for a time of trouble, but we needed to keep it in perspective; it was trouble that we could handle.

All this seemed to change in August 1949, with the intelligence reports that the Soviet Union had "probably" achieved a successful nuclear explosion.[11] Truman directed the State Department and Defense Department to conduct a joint study of nuclear weapons policy, including the advisability of proceeding with not just developing but stockpiling nuclear weapons. The resulting text, called NSC-68, was principally associated with Paul H. Nitze, who replaced Kennan as head of the State Department's policy planning staff. It proposed that the nation move to the more aggressive footing that we now associate with the Cold War: the Soviets were to be rolled back, not merely contained.

In his biography of Allen Dulles, Eisenhower's first director of Central Intelligence, Peter Grose suggests that the assessment in NSC-68 was all but unbalanced: "Democrats and Republicans both believed that the Free World confronted a global adversary that would yield to nothing less than an overwhelming counterforce. This conviction had been enshrined in NSC-68, . . . which perceived the world through a Manichaean prism."[12] Looking back in 1997, Nitze recalled that the drafters of NSC-68 relied on threat assessments from the intelligence community, and that parts of the assessments turned out to be "significantly inflated." He gave the example of a CIA report that put the number of combat-capable Soviet divisions at 175, when in fact only a third of these divisions were at full strength, another third were at half strength, and the rest were only skeletal.[13]

This misinformation regarding Soviet military strength also colored the debate about Soviet intentions. Among those involved with NSC-68, neither Kennan nor Charles E. "Chip" Bohlen were swayed.* They argued that the leaders of the Soviet Union were first of all concerned with maintaining their own power, then with keeping control of Soviet satellites; global expansion of socialism came last. They raised their objections, and Nitze explains that NSC-68 was modified to some extent, though never to Kennan and Bohlen's satisfaction.[14]

Withal, NSC-68 echoed Kennan's basic assessment: "The greatest vulnerability of the Kremlin lies in the basic nature of its relations with the Soviet people. That relationship is characterized by universal suspicion, fear and denuncia-

---

* At the time, Bohlen was a specialist in Russian affairs, while Kennan was a special assistant to the secretary of state. Both would go on to become ambassador to Russia: Kennan in 1952, Bohlen from 1953 to 1957.

tion. It is a relationship in which the Kremlin relies, not only for its power but its very survival, on intricately devised mechanisms of coercion. The Soviet monolith is held together by the iron curtain around it and the iron bars within it, not by any force of natural cohesion."[15]

The policy of containment that NSC-68 described was one of seeking, "by all means short of war," to block further expansion of Soviet power, expose Soviet pretensions, induce retractions of the Kremlin's control and influence, and "so foster the seeds of destruction within the Soviet system that the Kremlin is brought at least to the point of modifying its behavior to conform to generally accepted international standards."[16]

The history of American foreign policy in the second half of the twentieth century could be written in terms of how this message was lost.[17] One component, surely, is that during this time so much became secret. Kennan's views were published in *Foreign Affairs*. But in the years that followed, typically as one administration succeeded another, most documents, studies, and other informed assessments were classified. NSC-68 itself was classified until 1975. Policy planners moved about in a fog of secrecy so thick that they did not entirely recognize when they had changed directions. Thus, by the time of the Nixon administration, the movement from containment to détente was based on an assumption of the Soviet regime's permanence and power. American government had lost touch with the concept that the Soviet Union was bound to self-destruct in time.* (As Nixon himself commented in his book *The Real War* (1980), "During all of my presidency we were engaged in a 'war' with the Soviet Union," predicting that the struggle with the Soviets "will continue to dominate world events for the rest of this century.")[18]

A few did recognize that the haze of secrecy was growing denser, especially at the CIA, and they warned of its dan-

* The author so attests. In 1976, he was fired from Ford's cabinet for thinking otherwise.

gers. One such moment came during the McCarthy period, after the senator's committee had begun targeting the agency. On July 9, 1953, McCarthy's staff summoned William P. Bundy, a CIA employee and son-in-law of Dean Acheson, to testify that very morning about his four-hundred-dollar contribution to Alger Hiss's legal defense fund. (Before joining the agency, Bundy had informed his new superiors of his contribution; Hoover had come upon the information and almost certainly passed it on to McCarthy.) On the spot, Director Dulles decided that his officers were not to testify before Congress. Irate, McCarthy took to the Senate floor. But the next day, Dulles made his way to Capitol Hill. Remaining pleasant but firm, he asked Vice President Nixon to call McCarthy off, which Nixon did, at a small dinner gathering with committee members.[19]

The fallout for the CIA was a good bit of public criticism. Walter Lippmann wrote, speaking of Dulles's stand, "Secrecy is not a criterion for immunity." The agency had to submit to congressional accountability just like every other executive agency: "The argument that the CIA is something apart, that it is so secret that it differs in kind from the State Department or, for that matter, . . . the Department of Agriculture, is untenable." Hanson W. Baldwin of the *New York Times* went further, warning of "a philosophy of secrecy and power, of the ends justifying the means, of disagreeable methods for agreeable ends."[20] These critics were not outsiders, radicals denouncing the government in New York's Union Square or in Chicago's Haymarket Square. They were personal friends, Dulles and Lippmann having been at the Paris Peace Conference together in 1919. They were journalists of reputation and experience, setting high standards for public affairs. Secrecy seemed out of place to them. *Fin de ligne*.

But even had the government been inclined to heed warnings like these, the routinization of concealment would have prevented assessments from receiving a fair hearing. Not long after the Bundy episode, former president Herbert

Hoover announced that, as part of the work of the Second Commission on Organization of the Executive Branch of the Government, he had named General Mark W. Clark to a task force to look into the "restructure and administration" of the CIA.[21] President Eisenhower evidently became concerned that Clark's inquiry might get too close to sensitive matters, so he asked Lieutenant General James H. Doolittle, who had led the bombing raid on Tokyo in April 1942, to head a panel of consultants to review the agency's covert activities. In a letter of July 26, 1954, Eisenhower told Doolittle that the Clark task force, in keeping with the Hoover commission's mandate, was to concern itself with means "to accomplish the policy of Congress to promote economy, efficiency, and improved services." Because that work was to get under way shortly, the president suggested that the two generals confer in order to avoid "unnecessary duplication." Then Eisenhower gave explicit instructions. "The distinction between the work of your Study Group and of the Hoover Task Force is this: 'You will deal with the covert activities of the CIA, . . . and your report will be submitted to me.' . . . . Reports of the Hoover Commission are made to the Congress."[22] Doolittle's report was to be secret.

The sixty-page report, marked Top Secret, was delivered to the president on September 30, 1954—two months' work, but a great divide. Doolittle was confident about his assessment of CIA tactics. "Infiltration by human agents" wasn't working: "The information we have obtained by this method of acquisition has been negligible and the cost in effort, dollars and human lives prohibitive." It was time to explore "every possible scientific and technical avenue of approach to this scientific problem."* There was a tendency at CIA "to

---

* The first U-2 test flight took place one year later, on August 1, 1955. The first operational flight, targeting Moscow and Leningrad, took place in early July 1956. Francis Gary Powers's U-2 was shot down on May 1, 1960. This would seem an average life for a technical secret. Satellites came next, whereupon both sides knew that both sides knew what was going on in the Fulda Gap, or wherever. This was the great intelligence feat that brought stability to the Cold War.

over-classify documentary data originating in the Agency, a condition which operates in derogation of the security classification system as a whole." Translation: secrets are hoarded. "The Armed Services should be allowed to engage in espionage and counterespionage operations." Translation: the military was still here; there must not be a civilian monopoly on intelligence. Doolittle's most significant recommendation, however, is found in the first few pages of his report: containment would not do; the United States was at war. "We must develop effective espionage and counterespionage services and must learn to subvert, sabotage and destroy our enemies by more clever, more sophisticated and more effective methods than those used against us," he urged. "It may become necessary that the American people be made acquainted with, understand and support this fundamentally repugnant philosophy."[23]

The American people would not be "made acquainted" with this outlook. Only the president and a few others read the report. Nothing of substance was leaked. On October 14, 1954, Baldwin did file a long story in the *New York Times*, "Doolittle Heads Inquiry into CIA," noting that General Clark was also leading a similar inquiry. But not much of substance was reported—certainly not a profound shift away from containment as national policy.

The Clark report—actually two reports, one public, one classified—was finished the following May 1955 and transmitted to Congress in June by the Hoover commission. It was a credible exercise in the never-ending quest for efficiency in American government. Although it found Director Dulles in possession of many admirable qualities, the report concluded that he had taken on too many duties and responsibilities. The CIA as a whole was spread too thin. The task force recommended that the agency focus on collecting intelligence on Communist China and Russia and her satellites, not allowing itself to get distracted by operations elsewhere around the globe. "The task force is deeply concerned over the lack of adequate Intelligence data from behind the

Iron Curtain. . . . The glamor and excitement of some angles of our Intelligence effort must not be permitted to over-shadow other vital phases of the work or to cause neglect of primary functions."²⁴ Thus the judgment of the Clark report was in line with that of the Doolittle report: covert action was getting in the way of intelligence.

The Clark report seems not to have been well received at the agency. In a memorandum of July 19, Frank O. Wis-ner, then the CIA's deputy director of plans—which is to say, covert action—took a more than defensive tone. The "Clark Committee," he charged, had "solicited advice from Senator McCarthy, and the more or less public solicitation of any and all adverse information concerning cia and its personnel." Wisner wasn't in the mood for this, and he responded much as J. Edgar Hoover would have done. He concluded his three-page Secret memorandum by lumping the investiga-tions of General Clark together with those of Senator Mc-Carthy and portraying the CIA as an embattled organization: "The personnel of this Agency are entitled to feel very reas-sured and, in fact, proud to belong to an organization which has so successfully withstood the acid test of these *unprece-dented* investigations. I consider that we are entitled to hold our heads high and to indulge ourselves in a modest amount of self-congratulation. Certainly there is no longer any rea-son for the personnel of this Agency to feel that the Agency is under the gun or required to offer apologies. . . . I believe that we should let it be understood that the 'open season' on CIA is closed and that it is no longer a fashionable or prof-itable pursuit to sling mud at our people."²⁵

Wisner and his colleagues did have some reason to be indignant. Here they were, devoting their careers to the struggle against Communism, routinely risking their lives in the endeavor (some, like William Buckley in Beirut years later, were tortured to death), while the likes of Senator Mc-Carthy had the audacity to question their loyalty. But this surely was not General Clark's purpose, and his task force was onto something. Secrecy was beginning to cause problems. The agency was seen to be deceptive. In early 1967 it was revealed that the agency had secretly funded the Congress for Cultural Freedom, whose journal, *Encounter*, was first edited in London by Irving Kristol and Stephen Spender. The journal was assertively anti-Communist, but more liberal than conservative. Kristol was wholly unapologetic. Correct opinion in New York was not reassured. The CIA? Indeed, the U.S. government? By far the most important of the task force's critiques concerned "the quality and quantity of the Agency's intelligence on the Soviet Union." Was there insufficient room in the CIA's ecological niche, as Wilson calls it, for *intelligence?* In two years' time, the U.S. government was to adopt the view of Soviet capabilities and prospects that argued the task force's case in stunning terms.

For all the distraction of covert action and military engagement on the periphery of Eurasia and in parts of what was coming to be known as the Third World, the central, all-consuming task of statecraft during the Cold War was to establish an effective system of deterrence by which the Soviet Union would be dissuaded from nuclear war. The big "secret" of the American government during the early and middle years of the Cold War was that Soviet economic and military power was advancing at a rate that made deterrence problematic at best. In 1957, a Top Secret report, "Deterrence and Survival in the Nuclear Age," warned of the Soviets' "spectacular progress" in achieving substantial parity in the essentials of military strength, forecasting a crossover, as the term was: a time when the USSR would achieve military superiority over the United States. Soviet growth was so phenomenal that a crossover could also be anticipated for Soviet economic superiority.

The document, known as the Gaither report, for H. Rowen Gaither, Jr., then head of the Ford Foundation, was a product of the Security Resources Panel of the president's Science Advisory Committee. (PSAC as it would be known, had been created by President Eisenhower to provide science advice independent of Pentagon counsels.)* The National Security Council had requested the report, and the job was done in six months. It was forwarded to the president just weeks after the October 4, 1957, launching of Sputnik. The conclusions were stark to the point of startling:

> The Gross National Product (GNP) of the USSR is now more than one-third that of the United States and is increasing half again as fast. Even if the Russian rate of growth should decline, because of increasing difficulties in management and shortage of raw materials, and should drop by 1980 to half its present rate, its GNP would be more than half of ours as of that date. This growing Russian economic strength is concentrated on the armed forces and on investment in heavy industry, which this year account for the equivalent of roughly $40 billion and $17 billion, respectively, in 1955 dollars. Adding these two figures, we get an allocation of $57 billion per annum, which is roughly equal to the combined figure for these two items in our country's current effort. If the USSR continues to expand its military expenditures throughout the next decade, as it has during the 1950s, and ours remains constant, its annual military expenditures may be double ours. . . .
>
> This extraordinary concentration of the Soviet economy on military power and heavy industry, which is permitted, or perhaps forced, by their peculiar political structure, makes available economic resources sufficient to finance both the rapid expansion of their impressive military capability and their politico-economic offensive by which, through diplomacy, propaganda and subversion, they seek to extend the Soviet orbit.

The charts that followed were uncompromising. The first showed the Soviets reaching toward U.S. production levels in coal and steel and already producing twice the number of machine tools. This while the United States frittered away resources on consumer goods like automobiles, wash-

* This, at all events, was the understanding of committee members in later years. The author was a member from 1971 to 1973.

ing machines, and refrigerators. The second showed that the military effort of the USSR was about to surpass that of the United States.

The assertion that the Soviet GNP was growing "half again as fast" as that of the United States was traumatic. In 1956, nominal growth in the United States was 5.5 percent, which would give the Soviets a nominal rate of 8.25 percent. The former rate was in line with the forecasts prepared by the Council of Economic Advisers, which had been estimating long-run real growth of 3.5 percent, with inflation at about 2 percent. And so the "crossover" date would be 1998. By the end of the century, the Soviet Union would have a larger economy than the United States would and presumably vastly greater military strength as well.[26]

The intelligence community accepted and "improved" the assessment of the Gaither commission. In May 1958, Director Dulles spoke to the annual meeting of the Chamber of Commerce of the United States. His talk was entitled "Dimensions of the International Peril Facing Us," and he described these as formidable: "Whereas Soviet gross national product was about 33 percent that of the U.S. in 1950, by 1956 it had increased to about 40 percent, and by 1962 it may be about 50 percent of our own. This means that the Soviet economy has been growing, and is expected to continue to grow through 1962, at a rate roughly twice that of the economy of the United States. Annual growth overall has been running between 6 and 7 percent, annual growth of industry between 10 and 12 percent." Dulles then provided more statistics showing that Soviet consumption as a proportion of GNP was significantly lower than U.S. consumption, whereas Soviet investment was significantly higher. Furthermore, investment funds in the USSR were plowed back into expansion of electric power, the metallurgical base, and producer goods. Defense expenditures, as a proportion of GNP in the USSR, were significantly higher than in the United States, "in fact about double." Soviet industrial production was rapidly expanding, increasing 11 percent in 1957–58; in comparison, industrial production had declined 11 percent in the United States. The output of coal in the Soviet Union was about 70 percent of that in the United States. In steel production, reported Dulles, "In the first quarter of 1958, the Sino-Soviet Bloc has for the first time surpassed the United States. . . .The three months figures show that the USSR alone turned out over 75 percent of the steel tonnage of the U.S."[27]

At a 6 percent growth rate for the USSR, the crossover date would be 1992. At 7 percent, 1983. As best this now receding history can be reconstructed, the Department of State was almost alone in questioning such fantasy. In 1962, Walt Rostow, then head of the policy planning staff, privately demurred that he was not one of those "6 percent forever" people.[28]*

The Gaither report remained Top Secret until 1973. But, of course, it had leaked well before then. On November 5, 1957, two days before it was forwarded to the president, the *New York Times* reported that a secret study of the entire scope of national defense was about to be sent to the NSC;

* Also in 1962, G. Warren Nutter, an economist of the Chicago school, published *The Growth of Industrial Production in the Soviet Union* (Princeton: Princeton University Press, National Bureau of Economic Research, 1962). As was often the case with those of the Chicago school at this time, Nutter was wholly at odds with the general disposition of the academic profession. He judged that Soviet growth rates did not equal those of the czarist period, preceding the 1917 revolution, and did not at all match growth rates in contemporary West Germany and Japan. He dismissed Soviet statistics as propaganda. Withal, he was no less alarmed by the state of affairs. As Paul Craig Roberts would later write: "Nutter's studies of the Soviet system also foretold that serious economic problems would not constrain the Communist leadership from building a military machine that was openly aggressive and a formidable threat to the rest of the world" ("Warren Nutter: An Economist for All Times," in *Ideas, Their Origins, and Their Consequences: Lectures to Commemorate the Life and Work of G. Warren Nutter* [Washington, D.C.: American Enterprise Institute for Public Policy Research, 1988], p. 159). From 1969 to 1973 Nutter served as assistant secretary of defense in the Nixon administration but felt not the least sympathy for the administration's détente approach to the Soviet Union. It would, he felt, only embolden the Soviet military.

then, on December 23, the *Washington Post* published a detailed article.[29] The term "missile gap" now appeared. The report had been explicit in this matter: "By 1959, the USSR may be able to launch an attack with ICBMs carrying megaton warheads, against which SAC [Strategic Air Command] will be almost completely vulnerable under present programs. By 1961–1962, at our present pace, or considerably earlier if we accelerate, the United States could have a reliable early-warning capability against a missile attack, and SAC forces should be on a 7- to 22-minute operational 'alert.' The next two years seem to us critical. If we fail to act at once, the risk, in our opinion, will be unacceptable."[30]

It is not clear whether the Gaither panel had access to the U-2 photographs then available, which evidently showed no sign of a massive ICBM buildup. In any event, President Eisenhower did know about the photographs and was disinclined to see a crisis. Probably Senator John F. Kennedy did not know about them, and so the "missile gap" entered the rhetoric of the 1960 presidential election. Journalist Joseph Alsop knew all manner of leading figures within the intelligence community. In August 1958 he had written: "At the Pentagon they shudder when they speak of the 'gap,' which means the years 1960, 1961, 1962, and 1963. They shudder because in these years, the American government will flaccidly permit the Kremlin to gain an almost unchallenged superiority in the nuclear striking power that was once our specialty."[31]

In 1976, the Congressional Joint Committee on Defense Production published the Gaither report. In an introduction to the volume, Senator William Proxmire wrote, "Few documents have had as great an influence on American strategic thinking in the modern era."[32] The missile gap turned out not to exist, but nearly four decades later the United States is still contemplating modes of missile defense.[33] *Civil* defense has pretty much disappeared from policy debates, but in weapons negotiations and appropriations, the aftermath of the scare echoes on.

The question must be asked: what was gained by secrecy? What would have been lost had the report been made public, as Senator Lyndon B. Johnson requested at the time? For fifty years, as Bryan Hehir has observed, the United States confronted a direct, unambiguous issue: "how to deter a conscious, rational choice to use nuclear weapons against American territory."[34] Given the nature of the issue—a rational choice—a case surely can be made that our deliberations ought to have been more public. Save for the Smyth report of 1946, this case was never made. The bomb created a mystique of secrecy that resisted a disposition to openness.

To be sure, vigorous public debate about nuclear strategy did occur, principally at universities and various think tanks. But within government, decision making proceeded on the basis of tightly held (unless deliberately leaked) classified information and analysis. Of the roughly one hundred people associated with the Gaither report, few were economists. None of the principals had any specialized knowledge about the Soviet system, certainly not enough to add "investment in heavy industry" to outlays on the armed forces to produce an index of Soviet geopolitical strength defined as nuclear strike power. These passages from the report now seem absurd. What seems merely painful is the image of physicists measuring the overall strength of an economy in terms of coal and steel production, thirteen years after one of the first computers began operating at Harvard University.

Now, it would be an exaggeration to say that government secrecy alone caused this muddled state of affairs. The disposition put in place in the Eisenhower years—to see the Soviets as a modern industrial economy growing ever stronger—resulted partly from accepting Soviet data at face value. In July 1990, one year before the collapse of the Soviet regime, Nicholas Eberstadt of the American Enterprise Institute testified before the Senate Committee on Foreign Relations, and he was careful to acknowledge that, for estimates on Soviet economic output, the "most comprehensive and authoritative" were those produced by the U.S. government, principally under the auspices of the Central Intelligence Agency. "In fact," he added, "I believe it may be safe to say that the U.S. Government's effort to describe the Soviet economy may be the largest single project in the social science research ever undertaken." But the project had shortcomings, contradictions that were evident "even in a fairly cursory assessment of the published research." Eberstadt pointed first to the problems attendant upon using the notoriously inflated statistics provided by the Soviet Union. "The limitations of these official statistics are well known," he said. But "very often the U.S. analysis took these figures at face value, with only minor adjustments." The consequences of such credulousness were seen in the latest CIA *Handbook of Economic Statistics*, which suggested that the per-capita output of milk was higher in the USSR than in the United States, "making the Soviet Union not only a nuclear power, but a dairy superpower." What's more, "these estimates suggest Soviet meat output in the late 1980s to be about the same as in the United States in 1960, during the Eisenhower years." Such estimates, of course, were totally out of step with impressions of Western tourists and Soviet citizens alike. "Now, it is widely believed that the Soviet Government routinely hides many of its efforts from outside view," Eberstadt granted. "But where, one wonders, are the hidden stockpiles and reserves of Soviet meat?"[35]*

Using Soviet data was one problem; another was that the tendency to overestimate Soviet strength was pandemic. At the same hearing of the Senate Committee on Foreign Re-

* Poorly stocked grocery stores and the long queues outside them were just part of the story. By the 1960s, it was commonplace for journalists and other visitors to return from Moscow with tales about Soviet hotels, particularly the Stalinist behemoth known as the Ukraine. *Always* get a room on a lower floor, the advice was, as the elevators *never* worked. A former defense official in the Kennedy administration proposed the ironic theory that such scenes were part of a demonic device by which Soviet officials concealed the vibrant, progressive society in which everyday Russians actually lived.

lations that Eberstadt spoke at, Michael J. Boskin, then chairman of the Council of Economic Advisers, estimated that the economy of the Soviet Union was "about one-third" that of the United States.[36] At this time, the official *Handbook of Economic Statistics* put the ratio at 52 percent.[37] The disposition to overstate, which had begun with the Gaither-era projections, was still much in evidence. The U.S. GDP for 1990 was $4.8 trillion. The intelligence community put Soviet GDP at $2.5 trillion. The president's chief economist made it more like $1.6 trillion. The difference, $900 billion, would buy a lot of missiles.

But the CIA, which had made its estimates of Soviet GDP public as early as 1959, did have company. Many economists failed to grasp the stagnation that had settled on the Soviet economy after a brief post–World War II spurt in industries beloved of Heroes of Soviet Labor. Dale W. Jorgenson writes that "this has to be one of the great failures of economics— right up there with the inability of economists (along with everyone else) to find a remedy for the Great Depression of the 1930s."[38] Henry S. Rowen of Stanford University, whose distinguished government service included his chairmanship of the National Intelligence Council (1981–83), has echoed this sentiment; Sovietologists both within the intelligence community and in academia, trained to rely on the same general assumptions and data, had engaged in a form of "group think" that resulted in a monumental failure of analysis. In 1985, Rowen circulated a paper to senior officials in the Reagan administration, outlining his conclusion that actual Soviet economic growth was close to zero; in 1986, he expressed his views directly to the president and vice president.[39] Even so, the analytic system failed, and the United States paid a price.

Moreover, the system had failed from the beginning. In 1997, the CIA's Center for the Study of Intelligence convened a conference to coincide with the release of intelligence estimates prepared between 1946 and 1950. In addressing the conference, Kennan noted that intelligence assessments of

Soviet military intentions began suffering from "a certain deterioration" beginning in late 1948: "There were evidences of the assumptions, and the tendency to overrate allegedly blindly aggressive military commitments on the Soviet side, commitments quite divorced from the political restraints and awareness of the basic weaknesses in the civilian and economic backgrounds that inevitably modified Soviet diplomacy."[40] To repeat Stansfield Turner's query of 1991, "Why were so many of us so insensitive to the inevitable?"[41]

The answer has to be, at least in part, that too much of the information was secret. The intelligence community's valuations were not sufficiently open to the critique of the likes of Eberstadt or the Swedish economist Anders Åslund, who for a long time described the Soviet Union as "a reasonably well developed Third World country, calling to mind Argentina, Mexico, or Portugal."[42] In 1997, the European Comparison Project, looking at Soviet per capita GDP for 1990, estimated it to be only 32 percent of U.S. per capita GDP. Åslund calculates this at 30 percent lower than the U.S. intelligence estimate. And thus the crossover somehow never came about. This, of course, is just what Kennan had been saying, but that message had been lost.

There was an element of organizational aggrandizement in all this routinization of secrecy. By the 1990s, the budget of the intelligence community was five times that of the State Department. By the late 1990s, the military budget of the United States would about equal those of Russia, China, Japan, France, Germany, and the United Kingdom combined (the countries with the six next largest defense budgets).[43] In an address to the National Press Club in 1997, President Gerald R. Ford looked back on his early days in the House of Representatives, where for twelve years he was a member of the Defense Appropriations Committee. Every year, before the committee began hearings in preparation for putting together a defense bill, the members were briefed by the CIA. The director and his analysts "were very prestigious, they were acknowledged to be the wisest, brightest people we had in the government," Ford recalled. "They had charts on the wall, they had figures. And their conclusion was that in ten years, the United States would be behind the Soviet Union in military capability, in economic growth, in the strength of our economy. It was a scary presentation." But as it turned out, they were wrong by 180 degrees. "These were the best people we had, the CIA so-called experts," Ford mused. "How they could be so in error, I don't understand, but they were. Thank goodness they were wrong."[44]

Better to have overspent than otherwise, one might argue. But what was the good of getting the Soviet trajectory so very wrong? A good deal was put at risk in all this, and we ought to learn something from it.

Risks still persist, among them the relations between Russia and the former members of the Soviet Union as well as among nationality groups within Russia. But recent history suggests that lessons still need to be learned. The differences among these groups of the former Soviet Union are so profound that the Strategic Arms Reduction Treaty (START), the most important weapons-reduction agreement of the nuclear age, might not have gone forward at all. Yet START was negotiated without the least awareness that the Soviet Union might break up by the time the negotiations were completed.

NSC-68 had alerted us to the fact that "the Soviet system might prove to be fatally weak": "the well-known ills of colonialism" were compounded by the Kremlin's demands that its satellites not only accept its authority but believe in and proclaim its ideological primacy and infallibility. "These excessive requirements can be made good only through extreme coercion," the authors observed. "The result is that if a satellite feels able to effect its independence of the Kremlin, as Tito was able to do, it is likely to break away."[45]

But such sagacity got lost. In the 1980s, George P. Shultz, a masterful secretary of state, began to sense that the new Soviet leader, Mikhail Gorbachev, was interested in great reductions in nuclear weapons. (We would at least get START I.) The cultural exchanges seemed to be getting off the ground. The word from Moscow was positive. Not so from Langley. As Schultz later recounted, "In Washington, and especially from the CIA and its lead Soviet expert, Bob Gates, I heard that the Soviets wouldn't change and couldn't change, that Gorbachev was simply putting a new face on the same old Soviet approach to the world and to their own people. 'The Soviet Union is a despotism that works,' Gates said."[46] Soviet despotism would stop working in about four years; by then, Gates would be director of the CIA. Somehow it came to be that that is how a career officer rose to the top.

When the START treaty—with four different countries—came to the Senate Committee on Foreign Relations, the negotiators conceded that the thought of a Soviet break had never occurred to them. At a committee hearing on the treaty in 1992, I asked one of the negotiators, Ambassador Ronald F. Lehman, then director of the U.S. Arms Control and Disarmament Agency: "When did you, as negotiators, first contemplate the possibility that you would be signing a treaty with four countries and not one?"

Lehman replied, "Well, if you mean informal speculation, it probably began about two years ago [June 1990]. In terms of would this actually have come to pass, I think at the time of the Moscow coup [August 1991] people began to realize that some of the themes we were hearing around the Soviet Union might begin moving very quickly."

"Two years ago you began to think it might be possible; one year ago it became very real?" I asked.

"I think it became quite obvious that we had to step up to the issue with the dissolution of the Soviet Union in December of last year," said Lehman.

In other words, the negotiators had to begin dealing with the proposition of the dissolution of the Soviet Union in December of 1991, when the Soviet Union was already dissolving. I then asked Ambassador Linton F. Brooks whether anyone had suggested that by 1992 they would be negotiating with four governments, not one. He replied, "Senator, I certainly do not remember that . . . . I think very few of us on our end of the street predicted the collapse."[47]

Now, it was not the negotiators' job to follow the internal dynamics of the Soviet regime. Their concern was with throw weights. But they were entitled to intelligence, some whiff of caution, and they got none.[48] An age that began with state papers of unequaled clarity and prescience ended in a bureaucratic mode that never devised an effective mode of self-correction.

CHAPTER EIGHT

A Culture of Openness

T he Cold War ended; secrecy as a mode of governance continued as if nothing had changed. On the premise that data is the plural of anecdote, a small incident: early in 1993, the Senate Committee on Foreign Relations asked to be briefed on the conflict that had broken out in Bosnia and adjacent countries. A sizable contingent of generals arrived, accompanied by civilians. In the manner of President Ford's briefings decades earlier, the man from the agency began. But first the question: is everybody here cleared? One asked oneself: cleared for what? Premature Chetnik sympathies? Latent Titoist tendencies? We *had* no secrets about the Balkans. But this was now government routine.

The routine is best represented by the annual report of the Information Security Oversight Office (ISOO) of the National Archives and Records Administration. Every year since 1979, ISOO has counted the number of secrets created by various agencies of government. The report for 1996, a model of clarity and concision, provides a two-page listing of agency acronyms and abbreviations. Seventy-six in all, including exotica like MCC, for the Marine Mammal Commission. But in 1996, after years of expanding secrecy, there now appeared some evidence of shrinkage. As noted, the number of government officials who could classify a document had indeed been reduced; presumably this would have reduced the number of classifications, but the number of classifications *increased* by nearly two-thirds (see Chapter 1). The report was the first under the regime of Executive Order 12958, "Classified National Security Information," which was signed by President Clinton April 17, 1995, and which was, as the report states, "a radical departure from the secrecy policies of the past."[1] Original classifications were to be cut back, documents were to be released. But on the first count, results were surely mixed.

Credit to Clinton and his aides, notably John D. Podesta, sometime professor at the Georgetown University Law Center. They had acted on the slowly cumulating perception in Washington that secrecy could be the ruin of presidents and could put at risk the constitutional order itself. This was clear enough in the Iran-Contra affair but most dramatic, if not always perceived as such, in the resignation of Richard M. Nixon, which began with an effort to protect inane government secrecy.

In a well-worn story, Robert S. McNamara, toward the end of his tenure as secretary of defense, ordered a study of American intervention in Vietnam. In 1971, the documents known as the Pentagon Papers made their way to the *New York Times* and the *Washington Post*, both of which decided to publish. Nixon, grievously ill advised, decided to go to court to prevent publication. On the anniversary of the event in 1996, Max Frankel of the *Times* wrote: "Twenty-five years ago today, reporters, editors and owners of *The Times* stood accused in Federal court of treasonous defiance of the United States. We had begun to publish a 10-part series about the Pentagon Papers, a 7,000-page study of how four Administrations became entrapped in Vietnam—progressively more committed and more frustrated than they dared at every stage to admit to the public. Although the documents were historical and lacking any operational value, they were stamped 'Top Secret' and therefore withheld, like trillions of other Government papers, from public, press, Congress and even Executive officials not duly 'cleared' into the priesthood of 'national security.'"[2] The problem, as the writings of Henry Cabot Lodge, Sr., could have told Nixon, is that no law prohibited publishing documents like these. Such a law had been proposed by a previous president—Wilson—but Congress, having considered it, had decided against it. By roll call vote. Somehow this memory, if it had ever taken hold (recall Biddle and the *Chicago Tribune*), had evanesced.

Harold Edgar and Benno C. Schmidt, Jr., have exhausted the subject in their analysis of the earlier espionage laws, published in 1973 against the backdrop of the Pentagon Papers litigation. The courts found that there was literally "no law" to prevent publication. The problem could be traced to the time of creation, 1917, when Wilson failed in his efforts to achieve a sweeping ban on publication of defense information. The U.S. espionage laws, as Edgar and Schmidt had showed, are "in many respects incomprehensible," with the result being that "we have lived since World War I in a state of benign indeterminacy about the rules of law governing defense secrets."[3]

Most of the executive orders on national security information issued in succession since 1951 do not even refer to espionage law. And, as in the case of the Commission on Government Security's proposal in 1957, Congress has not been willing to make unauthorized disclosure of classified information an action subject to criminal sanctions without consideration of the *intent* of the communicator. This being so difficult to prove, such cases have been all but impossible to prosecute. As a former assistant general counsel of the CIA concluded (in an unpublished paper cited by Edgar and

Schmidt): "An individual who simply reveals to the public at large classified data is for all practical purposes immune from prosecution since his defense, of course, would be that he thought the American public had a right to know and the Government would not be able to prove intent to aid a foreign government or to harm the United States. The fact that any reasonable man would know that revelation to the general public ipso facto reveals to foreign governments is immaterial. Even if the one making the exposure is a government employee well versed in the rules governing classified information, there can be no presumption of intent which would bring him within the terms of present espionage laws."[4]

President Nixon's attempt to suppress the Pentagon Papers was doomed from the start. And indeed what followed was all so hapless. It was no secret that the United States was involved in a war in Vietnam. If we could publish our correspondence with Britain in 1861, we were surely in a position to reveal much less consequential matters with assorted lesser powers in 1971. And just as surely was Justice Hugo L. Black correct when he wrote, in the Pentagon Papers case, "The guarding of military and diplomatic secrets at the expense of informed representative government provides no real security for our Republic."[5]

How sensitive was the material in the Pentagon Papers? Erwin N. Griswold, who had been President Nixon's solicitor general at the time of the crisis and accordingly had argued the government's case before the Supreme Court, summed it up well nearly two decades later: "I have never seen any trace of a threat to the national security from the publication. Indeed, I have never seen it even suggested that there was such an actual threat. . . . I doubt if there is more than a handful of persons who have ever undertaken to examine the Pentagon Papers in any detail—either with respect to national security or with respect to the policies of the country relating to Vietnam." Like vast numbers of other classified materials, the Pentagon Papers were kept secret not so much to prevent harm to national security but to prevent "governmental embarrassment of one sort or another." Griswold concluded: "There may be some basis for short-term classification while plans are being made, or negotiations are going on, but apart from details of weapons systems, there is very rarely any real risk to current national security from the publication of facts relating to transactions in the past, even the fairly recent past. This is the lesson of the Pentagon Papers experience."[6]

This is an apt critique of the culture of secrecy. It is a belief system, a way of life. It can be, as it was during the Cold War, all consuming. Judgment blurs. And so, three days after the *New York Times* began printing the Pentagon Papers on June 13, 1971, the Nixon administration obtained a temporary restraining order against further publication; a mere fifteen days later, the Supreme Court rejected the president's attempt at prior restraint, and the newspaper resumed its publication of the Papers. One month later, Nixon created "the Plumbers," a White House unit with a mission to prevent leaks of classified material.

Leonard Garment writes that Nixon's political demise began with Daniel Ellsberg's massive dump of the Pentagon Papers: "Nixon let his anger undermine his political judgment."[7] William Safire concurs: "The Pentagon Papers case led [Nixon] into an overreaction that led to his most fundamental mistakes." The breach of *secrecy,* however inconsequential, caused him "to lose all sense of balance, to defend his privacy at the expense of everyone else's right to privacy, and to create the climate that led to Watergate."[8] The Plumbers commenced domestic covert operations, which continued into the 1972 presidential campaign. In 1974, Nixon would become the first president in American history to resign.

What would become known as the Iran-Contra affair began as a matter of agency routine. But one determining difference separated this from earlier covert operations abroad: the House of Representatives and the Senate had each now established a select committee on intelligence. These had come about in the aftermath of the Church and Pike committees, which, in studying the intelligence community, had found that agencies too often abused the civil rights of American citizens and pursued activities in violation of law. In May 1976, one month after the Church committee issued its report, the Senate created the Select Committee on Intelligence, the measure passing by a vote of seventy-two to twenty-two. The following year, the House established a comparable committee. The resolution creating the Senate committee (S. Res. 400, Ninety-Fourth Congress) stated that the heads of intelligence agencies should keep the committee "fully and currently informed" of their agencies' operations, including "any significant anticipated activities."*

Three years later in Nicaragua, in July 1979, the regime of Anastasio Somoza fell to a general uprising, after which the Marxist-led Sandinista National Liberation Front took power. The following November in Iran, the U.S. embassy in Tehran was seized by Islamic extremists, and fifty-two Americans were taken hostage. The events marked the onset of a new era, the fading of another. Islamic hostility to the West, part of what Samuel P. Huntington would describe as the "clash of civilizations," was emerging. Marxism as a political force was waning. Nicaragua would appear to have been the site of the last classically Marxist revolutionary regime to seize power anywhere. When an idea dies in Madrid, it can take two generations for word to reach Managua. (Word never did reach Langley. A reasonable American response to the new Communist government in Managua would have been a statement of condolence. We

* The author was a member from February 1977 to January 1985, the last four years as vice chairman, with Senator Barry Goldwater of Arizona as chairman.

regretted the misfortune that had visited the people of Nicaragua: in the event of earthquakes, they could be assured of American aid; when the first crop failure came, however, they would need to look to Havana. In the meantime, no, repeat no, Soviet aircraft or missiles.)

A visit to Nicaragua in December 1983 induced this thought. Managua had been leveled by an earthquake. The cathedral was a ruin. The one new building, nine or ten stories high in the best international style, was the Ministry of the Interior. One fine morning, I set out to pay a visit to Commandant Tomas Borge, who was at work in his suite on the top floor. On the sidewalk outside, television cameras greeted the arriving guest. But before the elevators had been reached, the power had gone off, and there followed something of a climb. In the commandant's suite an hour of dialectic ensued, after which lunch was suggested. The commandant turned to theretofore silent aides; in unison, they proposed that the barrio Sandino, a farmers' market with a restaurant, would be just the place. A bus happened to be waiting. At the restaurant, a table happened to be set. The visitor declined the tureen of goulash that was promptly served, along with the obligatory Pepsi Cola (soft drink of the people), asking instead for rice and beans. While waiting for the requested dish, the guests were treated to a quarter hour of street theater, in which a succession of workers and peasants came to express assorted disaffections in the best polemic mode. The week previous, the new orthopedic hospital, or whatever, had been opened in barrio Guavera, and the commandant had not shown the elementary courtesy of being on hand for the ceremony. Another delegation reported that the new irrigation system in Las Palmas, or wherever, was not yet working at full capacity. Still another group complained that the new highway to León was at least five weeks behind schedule. The commandant assertively acknowledged his failings but firmly resolved to change his ways and those of the regime. The people were correct: mistakes had been made; there would be no more of this. He asked forgiveness. That concluded, a somewhat hesitant aide came up to report that no beans were to be had.

This and other reports ought to have been enough to indicate to the American government the likely longevity of this regime, if left on its own. But counterrevolution was now agency routine, and the new Reagan administration was all for it. (The Carter administration had at first rather welcomed the revolution and sent food aid, much as Wilson had done with Russia in 1917.) And so to the jungles again, this time with neighboring Honduras providing a cooperative military regime. The idea was addled. The new Sandinista regime was already beginning to show its colors, but the United States seemed to be recruiting opposition from supporters of a previous, no less vile regime. The airport apron at Tegucigalpa, capital of Honduras, was littered with abandoned Nicaraguan air force transport planes in which assorted Somozan officials had fled, now presumably to organize a counterrevolution.

For the moment the United States needed a rationale for intervention. On March 3, 1986, President Reagan would allow that we might have to make our final stand at Harlingen, Texas. A prospect of some portent—the missing evidence for which was soon enough produced. The Sandinistas were providing arms to a Marxist guerrilla faction in El Salvador. The long march north had commenced.

In the end, nothing of the kind was ever proved. Heroic surveillance measures were put in place; outside the occasional pickup truck or small boat, nothing showed up. While in the capital, San Salvador, in 1983, I asked to see the rector and vice rector of the Central American University (both were Basque Jesuits subsequently murdered by the regime). I put the question to them directly: "Were the Sandinistas shipping arms to the Salvadoran insurgents?" "No," replied the rector. "But they had been?" "True." "Then why no longer?" "Because you are doing it now."* And, indeed, American equipment costing millions of dollars was being flown down, along with American military advisors. We had even built a small gem of a central intelligence agency, complete with fountains in the lobby. In the way of that world, the arms were being shared.

President Reagan saw a global issue at stake. In January 1984, he approved a CIA plan to mine harbors on the west coast of Nicaragua. That the mines were thereafter laid was no secret, but it was assumed the Contras had done it. On April 6, however, David Rogers of the *Wall Street Journal* reported that, in a covert operation, the CIA had mined the harbors. A constitutional crisis now commenced.

As noted, the statute creating the Senate Select Committee on Intelligence stated that the committee would be informed of any "significant anticipated events," meaning covert actions. The committee had not been informed. On April 9, Chairman Goldwater sent a furious letter to Director of Central Intelligence William J. Casey: "[How can I] most easily tell you my feelings about the discovery of the President having approved mining some of the harbors of Central America[?] . . . I am pissed off!" The letter, which went on at some length, contained two sentences contributed by the vice chairman: "This is an act violating international law. It is an act of war."[9]

The letter made it to the *Washington Post*, and tumult followed. The administration lied. First it lied about Goldwater: getting on, don't you know—memory problems. Then Robert C. McFarlane, national security advisor, lied to cadets at the U. S. Naval Academy—something never to be done. On April 15, the author resigned from the committee. Two weeks later, in an honorable act, Casey apologized to the

---

* Six years later, in November 1989, not only the rector, Ignacio Ellacuria, and the vice rector, Ignacio Martin-Baro, but also four other Jesuits, their cook, and her fifteen-year-old daughter were shot and brutally dismembered by government agents.

vice chairman and to the committee. It seemed a crisis had been avoided.

A legitimate question arose. In the statute providing that the committees were to be told in advance of "significant anticipated activities," what was meant by "significant?" We suggested that the term be defined as anything personally approved by the president. This understanding was dutifully drawn up and signed by all parties, the president included.

In the meantime, Congress, at the behest of Edward P. Boland, chairman of the House Select Committee on Intelligence and close associate of House Speaker Thomas P. "Tip" O'Neill, Jr., imposed a ban on further aid to the Contras. The administration set about secretly raising funds abroad; in the end they would sell arms to the ostensibly untouchable Iranians. The Casey Accord, as our agreement had come to be known, was ignored; the committees, again, were told nothing. Instead, it happened that the nation found out about the arms deals from a magazine published in Beirut.

There was a chilling, systemic quality to the event. Despite the statute, despite the accord, the executive kept quiet about its activities, which were certainly "significant." Nor should the executive have been concerned that the committees were politically unfriendly, for there were no politics, at least not on the Senate side. Goldwater was a Reagan loyalist, thought of the president as a protégé. His letter to Casey asked how was he going to defend the president's foreign policy if he wasn't told what it was. Goldwater and I had worked together to get the intelligence community pretty much whatever it felt it had to have, especially by way of satellites.

We escaped, you could say. The administration did not. Secrecy almost ruined yet another presidency. Off it went to buy arms abroad, with the National Security Council now opting for covert action of its own, all hidden by secrecy.

Whatever the intelligence community might have done, it was done by professionals. And the president was kept out of it. Now lieutenant colonels and the like were putting the presidency of the United States at risk. It was only luck that when it all finally came out, as it did in the subsequent joint congressional investigation, there seemed no point in destroying a popular president in his final years in office. No one wanted to replay the denouement of an all-too-recent Watergate. And yet, secrecy had got us into difficulties unlike any we had ever known.

Had it not been possible for those involved with Iran-Contra to act under a vast umbrella of secrets, they would have been told to stop. Recall that most of what they were doing was kept from the rest of the government. (It is still not clear what the CIA knew, outside the director himself.) During the congressional investigation Senator Paul S. Sarbanes of Maryland used the term "junta," something never known to American government. Hardly hyperbole. The behavior of the CIA and especially its director in the Nicaraguan mining episode was nothing less than the outset of a challenge to American constitutional government, the "first acts of deception that gradually mutated into a policy of deceit," as I told Theodore Draper for his history of the event, *A Very Thin Line;* the Iran-Contra affair two years later was the culmination of this insidious policy. I also told Draper that I didn't believe the American republic had ever seen so massive a hemorrhaging of trust and integrity. The very processes of government were put in harm's way by a conspiracy of faithless or witless men—sometimes both.[10]

In an earlier essay on the tormented congressional hearings, Draper began: "If ever the constitutional democracy of the United States is overthrown, we now have a better idea of how this is likely to be done. That may be the most important contribution of the recent Iran-Contra congressional hearings."[11] In his book *Firewall: The Iran-Contra Conspiracy and Cover-Up*, Lawrence E. Walsh, the independent counsel in the Iran-Contra investigation, concluded:

"What set Iran-Contra apart from previous political scandals was the fact that a cover-up engineered in the White House of one president and completed by his successor prevented the rule of law from being applied to the perpetrators of criminal activity of constitutional dimension."[12] Walsh uses the term "national security crime."[13]

In all this we need to be clear that those involved never set out to be criminals; they were trapped in a system. In his study, *The National Security Constitution: Sharing Power After the Iran-Contra Affair,* Harold Hongju Koh agrees that we saw "a nearly successful assault upon the constitutional structures and norms that underlie our postwar national security system." But it was not a case "of bad people violating good laws . . . or of good people violating bad laws . . . but of seriously misguided people violating seriously ineffective national security laws."[14] In Koh's judgment, the American government has not found a stable mode of national security decision making, and the likes of the Iran-Contra crisis—the parallel, in his view, being not Watergate but Vietnam—"waits to afflict us anew."[15] Surely this is true, and just as surely is it an element in this ongoing crisis, for only secrecy enables a constitutionally weak executive to bypass the legislature in making decisions that the legislature will not support when things go wrong.

A more serious development was that operations displaced intelligence and in fact became, in James Q. Wilson's phrase, "the culture-defining task of the CIA."[16] Many operations endeavors were more trouble than they were worth. Trouble not least at home, for Americans were never able to resign themselves to such CIA projects as how-to manuals on political assassinations. Nor were the national nerves appreciably improved by "The Routinization of Crisis Government," as Donald L. Robinson described it in 1974,[17] which had taken its toll in Vietnam. The intelligence community— the whole of it, not merely the CIA—surely failed to impress on the White House (Congress, again, was left out) that the Red Chinese and the Soviet Union were not engaged in a great sweep down the perimeter of Asia and up the Bay of Bengal to Calcutta, through which, as Trotsky had decreed, the road to Paris ran. While we were in the jungles hoping to stop this, the Soviets and the Chinese were all but going to war with one another. In 1978 Robert Novak had a long interview with Deng Xiaoping in which the Chinese leader declared his desire "to join the Americans in confronting the Soviet Union." Taiwan could rest easy; he "had no objection to U.S. troops in South Korea."[18] And later, not four years after the fall of South Vietnam to what had been represented as an international Communist alliance, the People's Republic of China invaded the North. It is not clear that U.S. foreign policy agencies quite follow this even now.

The Cold War has bequeathed to us a vast secrecy system that shows no sign of receding. It has become our characteristic mode of governance in the executive branch. Intelligence agencies have proliferated and budgets grown even as the military has subsided. As old missions fade, the various agencies seek new ones. In 1967, Anthony Downs described this process whereby a government bureau, as it ages, becomes willing to modify its original formal goals in order to survive: a bureau's more senior officials "would rather alter the bureau's formal goals than admit that their jobs should be abolished because the original goals have been attained or are no longer important."[19] Exactly thirty years later, in September 1997, some wondered whether a similar process was taking place at the Central Intelligence Agency. The occasion was the fiftieth anniversary of the agency's founding, and the event was celebrated at Langley with a ceremony, complete with a display of "lipstick pistols" and other devices of spycraft. The *Washington Post* reported, matter-of-factly: "These artifacts were standard fare during the Cold War, an era from which critics say the CIA has yet to fully emerge. CIA analysts failed to forecast the Soviet Union's collapse, and some on Capitol Hill have questioned whether the agency, which has an estimated 16,000 employees, has adequately redefined its mission for a new era."[20]

President Clinton spoke on the occasion, setting forth the agency's future mission as outlined in an earlier directive. He repeated his top priorities for focusing intelligence resources "in the areas most critical to our national security": "First, supporting our troops and operations, whether turning back aggression, helping secure peace or providing humanitarian assistance. Second, providing political, economic, and military intelligence on countries hostile to the United States so we can help to stop crises and conflicts before they start. And, third, protecting American citizens from new trans-national threats such as drug traffickers, terrorists, organized criminals, and weapons of mass destruction."[21] The first task is ambiguous at best. The military supports the military and uses military intelligence. The second task is quite in order. That is the mission the agency acquired during the Cold War. The third task, as regards "trans-national threats" like drug traffickers and weapons dealers, is an invitation to marginalization or worse. There are already several dozen federal agencies engaged with drugs and crime (none of them with notable success). To nudge its way in, the CIA would have to begin competing with the Bureau of Alcohol, Tobacco and Firearms. As Downs had forecast.

At the time Clinton spoke, the CIA had had five chiefs in ten years, not to mention several aborted nominations. By contrast, the Federal Bureau of Investigation had had one director for its first forty-eight years: J. Edgar Hoover, who died in office. In an organizational mode not perhaps sufficiently appreciated, he had spent much of that time trying to keep his agency away from tasks that it couldn't perform. Tasks at which no organization could expect much success. Hoover "was strong enough to resist for many years FBI involvement in organized crime and civil rights cases,"* as

---

* As an aide to Governor Averell Harriman of New York in the 1950s, I became interested in the subject of organized crime after it was discovered that an extraordinary assembly of mob leaders from around the country

James Q. Wilson notes, "but when the time came, in his eyes, to change, he was also strong enough to make the organization change with him."[22]

It may be too much to suppose that other organizations will learn on their own. There was only one Hoover. Now is the time for law. Eighty years from the onset of secrecy as an instrument of national policy, now is the time for a measure

---

had convened in the hamlet of Apalachin in southern New York State. I also worked peripherally with Robert F. Kennedy, who was pursuing the subject as a Senate staffer. In July 1961, I published an article, "The Private Government of Crime," in *Reporter* magazine, arguing that what could reasonably be termed "organized crime" had its roots in Prohibition, that it was serious, and that no government bureau had found a way of dealing with it because doing so would have offered insufficient organizational rewards. Almost in passing, I noted that the FBI, which had "not hesitated to take on the toughest problems of national security," had "successfully stayed away from organized crime." It would have given Hoover nothing but institutional trouble.

By now I had joined the Kennedy administration as an aide to Arthur J. Goldberg, then secretary of labor. In a matter of weeks after the article appeared, the Department of Labor building was literally raided by G-men. In unison they hit our floor, went door to door, told everyone save the hapless author but including the secretary himself that a dangerous person had infiltrated their ranks, clearly implying that the secretary should go. I can't demonstrate this but offer the judgment that at any other department at this time in Washington, the person in question would have gone. Hoover had files on everyone, or so it was said.

The Department of Labor was different only insofar as Arthur J. Goldberg was different. On August 2, just after my article appeared, C. D. "Deke" DeLoach of the FBI had informed the secretary that "it would appear to be impossible to deal with Moynihan on a liaison basis in view of his obvious biased opinion regarding the FBI." The secretary called me in, told me that I had a problem, and sent me to explain my point of view to the director. The next day, DeLoach agreed to see me but made plain he could barely stand the sight. In my FBI file is a three-page, single-spaced memorandum of the meeting, sent to the director through John Mohr. It concludes: "Moynihan is an egghead that talks in circles and constantly contradicts himself. He shifts about constantly in his chair and will not look you in the eye. He would be the first so-called 'liberal' that would scream if the FBI overstepped its jurisdiction. He is obviously a phony intellectual that one minute will back down and the next minute strike while our back is turned. I think we made numerous points in our interview with him, however, this man is so much up on 'cloud nine' it is doubtful that his ego will allow logical interpretation of remarks made by other people." The director appended a handwritten notation, "I am not going to see this skunk." I was put on the "Not to Contact" list.

of definition and restraint. In 1997, the Commission on Protecting and Reducing Government Secrecy proposed a statute for achieving just these ends, noting the wisdom of John F. Kennedy's remark, "The time to repair the roof is when the sun is shining."

The Secrecy Commission noted that after the U.S. Army had adopted the three-level classification model used by the British—For Official Use Only, Confidential, and Secret (later Confidential, Secret, and Top Secret)—just what any of the various terms meant was never defined. With the beginning of the Cold War, presidents took to issuing executive orders about classification: Eisenhower, E.O. 10501; Kennedy, E.O. 10964; Nixon, E.O. 11652; Carter, E.O. 12065; Reagan, E.O. 12356; and Clinton, E.O. 12958. The one criterion conspicuously missing from all but President Carter's was a balancing test of the public's right to know and the government's need to protect national security. The Secrecy Commission proposed a simple enough framework for a statute that would do just that. First, information shall be classified only if its protection is demonstrably in the interests of national security, with the goal of keeping classification to an absolute minimum. Standards shall be established to determine whether information should be or remain classified, and these standards shall weigh the benefit from public disclosure against the need for its initial or continued protection; where doubt exists, information shall not be classified. Next, as a parallel program to the classification system, a declassification system shall be established. Information shall remain classified for no longer than ten years, unless it is specifically reclassified because of current risks; all information shall be declassified after thirty years, unless it is shown that doing so will harm an individual or ongoing government activities. Finally, a National Declassification Center shall be established to coordinate, implement, and oversee these declassification policies and practices. The commission report was unanimously endorsed by its members; the congressional members, one each of both parties from both bodies, have introduced legislation to establish this new framework.

The proposed National Declassification Center may seem a matter of concern mainly to scholars, but it is more of a national interest even than that. Secrecy has come at a price. As we have seen, the nation paid heavily in the McCarthy moment, when, as Shils wrote, "the phantasies of apocalyptic visionaries attained the level of a reasonable interpretation of events." Not for another forty years would government tell what it actually knew about the Communist conspiracy: there had indeed been one, but it had never been massive; it had first been contained, then suppressed. A democracy does not leave its citizens uninformed in these matters. As Paul McMasters comments, "The Government's obsession with secrecy creates a citizen's obsession with conspiracy."[23]

By coincidence, in 1997, forty-seven years after Senator Joseph McCarthy's famous speech in Wheeling, West Virginia, a new conspiracy was uncovered in the same city. James Rogers, a member of a right-wing extremist group, the Mountaineer Militia, was convicted of trying to help terrorists blow up an FBI fingerprint-records complex in nearby Clarksburg. Rogers had photographed blueprints that detailed the FBI complex and given the photographs to Floyd Looker, founder of the Mountaineer Militia. Looker then sold the pictures to an FBI agent posing as an explosives expert who worked for Middle East terrorists. Looker is reported to have told the agent, "That installation is a threat to national security. I don't care who knocks it out."[24]

Rogers was convicted under the Antiterrorism and Effective Death Penalty Act of 1996. The law is not a pretty thing. Among its provisions is one mandating that prisoners sentenced to death have but six months to file habeas corpus petitions after all state appeals are exhausted and, with few exceptions, allowing for consideration of only one habeas corpus petition. It also requires federal judges to defer to the findings of state courts unless their rulings are "unreasonable." In sum, it holds that in these cases constitutional protections do not exist unless they have been unreasonably violated—an idea that would have confounded the framers. No such law, nothing approaching such a law, was ever enacted during the Cold War. We are reminded of Richard Gid Powers's observation that the McCarthy experience had persuaded some people that the general public was too unsophisticated, too easily inflamed, to be informed of the real underlying issues of the Cold War; in similar fashion, the American government, almost as a matter of policy, left its citizens to think what they chose about international threats for fear that they might find out the truth or react unpredictably. Now, with the Cold War behind us, Congress got serious. There was to be no bombing of FBI records plants. Measures of a severity hardly contemplated and certainly never enacted during earlier crises now became statute with a minimum of objection. The Antiterrorism and Effective Death Penalty Act of 1996 passed the U.S. Senate by a vote of ninety-one to eight.

As Richard Hofstadter and others have recorded, conspiracy theories have been part of the American experience for two centuries, but they appear to have grown in dimension and public acceptance in recent decades. The most notorious conspiracy theories, of course, play upon the unwillingness of the vast majority of the American public to accept that President Kennedy was assassinated in 1963 by Lee Harvey Oswald. In 1964 the United States President's Commission on the Assassination of President John F. Kennedy, commonly called the Warren commission, released its report concluding that Oswald had acted alone. In 1964, a poll found that 36 percent of respondents accepted this finding, whereas 50 percent believed others had been involved in a conspiracy to kill the president. In 1978 only 18 percent responded that they believed the assassination had been the act of one man; fully 75 percent believed there had been a broader plot. The numbers have remained relatively steady since; a 1993 poll also found that three quarters of those surveyed believed (consistent with the film *JFK*, released that year) that there had been a conspiracy: the CIA had murdered the president in order to prolong the war in Vietnam.[25]

More painful yet was the 1997 request by the family of Martin Luther King, Jr., that the federal government establish a commission to offer amnesty to anyone with new information on the assassination of Dr. King. His son Dexter has alleged that Dr. King was killed "by Army intelligence, the Federal Bureau of Investigation and the Central Intelligence Agency, with the probable knowledge of President Lyndon Johnson."[26] This view is evidently shared by Dr. King's widow.

To go from assassination conspiracies to coverups of unidentified flying objects and extraterrestrial life is to trivialize the matter, but apparently the leap doesn't seem that great to the 80 percent of Americans who, according to a CNN-*Time* poll of June 15, 1997, believe that their government is hiding knowledge of the existence of extraterrestrial life forms.

Lest these be thought merely cases of mass dementia or the personal torment of survivors, keep in mind that for some decades into the Cold War (and since?), many of the men and women who ran the American government had a lively conviction that the government was spying on *them*.*

---

* In 1977, having been elected to the U.S. Senate, I took the precaution of asking for my own FBI file. In short order I had a three-inch stack of folders, 561 pages in all, including a Confidential report of an investigation conducted by the air force in 1952. Part of the report contained enclosures indicating "possible communist tendencies on the part of PATRICK J. MOINYHAN, DAY Civilian." The setting is London, where I had arrived as a Fulbright scholar in 1951. Wanting to stay a bit longer in Europe, and half expecting to be called back into the navy, I had taken a job at an air force installation on the outskirts of London. All of which, and more, are duly noted: "MOINYHAN, an American citizen, was employed in Air Installations sometime in the fall of 1951. His employment was due to the efforts of DANA M. HICKS, Major, A0912552, former Air Installations Officer. . . . Prior to his present employment MOINYHAN was doing research and study in the UK under a Fulbright scholarship. 'His thesis was something to do with labor.' HICKS had alleged that during his research, MOINYHAN had access to US Em-

Evan Thomas, writing of the early years of the CIA, speculates that such a conviction may have been behind Kennedy's swift reappointment of Allen Dulles as director of the CIA and J. Edgar Hoover as director of the FBI. Both men were "legends," explained the newly elected president; they were better left undisturbed. "His deference may have been encouraged by the knowledge that the CIA and FBI had thick files on the president-elect's past, including his brief affair with a German spy during World War II," observes Thomas. "The family patriarch, Joseph Kennedy, had urged his son to play it safe by reappointing Hoover and Dulles."[27]

We are not going to put an end to secrecy, nor should we. It is at times legitimate and necessary. But a culture of secrecy, a culture of the sort that we associate with Dulles and Hoover, need not remain the norm in American government as regards national security. It is possible to conceive that a competing culture of openness might develop, and that it could assert and demonstrate greater efficiency. The central fact is that we live today in an Information Age. Open sources give us the vast majority of what we need to know in order to make intelligent decisions. Decisions made by people at ease with disagreement and ambiguity and tenta-

bassy records. Some time after his employment at Air Installations, MOINYHAN was observed by informant to be reading the 'Daily Worker.' Informant reported that fact to HICKS who stated 'It's been looked into and it's all right.' HICKS also stated that MOINYHAN was permitted to 'go to the Unity Theatre.' U-OI-1 informed the writer that the Unity Theatre was run by communists and presented anti-American and Anti-Conservative (British Political Party) reviews. HICKS did not qualify any of his statements concerning SUBJECT. ROSENFELD [a colleague] remarked that all Communists should be lined up and shot. MOINYHAN quickly defended communism and told ROSENFELD that he was as bad as the communists to advocate such treatment. The discussion became heated. . . . MOINYHAN maintained his defense of communism . . . [and seemed] sincere in his defense of communism and they gained the impression that MOINYHAN was either a communist or a communist sympathizer."

In retrospect I suppose I ought not to have brought a copy of the *Daily Worker* to work, but I was young. On the other hand, the Unity Theater *was* good vaudeville, albeit of a pinkish cast.

tiveness. Decisions made by those who understand how to exploit the wealth and diversity of publicly available information, who no longer simply assume that clandestine collection—that is, "stealing secrets"—equals greater intelligence. *Analysis*, far more than secrecy, is the key to security.

There is no way to make certain that this new model of decision making will happen, yet the competitive spirit *can* be put to work here. In seeking victories where others had failed, policy-makers may begin to see that their devotion to secrecy has not served them well. An example, on a subject that still troubles U.S. foreign relations, is the Bay of Pigs invasion of Cuba in April 1961. Planned and carried out in secret, the object was to arouse a popular revolt against the regime of Fidel Castro, which had become unmistakably Communist in its orientation. No such uprising occurred, and the events set in motion arguably led to the Cuban missile crisis of 1962, the closest the United States and the Soviet Union came to a nuclear exchange during the Cold War.

It need never have happened. The Bay of Pigs debacle could have been avoided if foreign policy experts in the United States had but paid attention to published research already available to them. In the spring of 1960, Lloyd A. Free of the Institute for International Social Research at Princeton had carried out an extensive public opinion survey in Cuba. The polling techniques now common to American politics were then being developed by scholars such as Free and his associate Hadley Cantril. Free had asked one thousand Cubans to rank their well-being at that moment in time, five years previously, and five years hence. The Cubans reported that they were hugely optimistic about the future; many dreaded the return of Castro's predecessor, the dictator Fulgencio Batista. Free's report ended on an unambiguous note: Cubans "are unlikely to shift their present overwhelming allegiance to Fidel Castro."[28] His colleague Cantril later recalled: "This study on Cuba showed unequivocally not only that the great majority of Cubans supported Castro, but that any hope of stimulating action against him or exploiting a powerful opposition in connection with the United States invasion of 1961 was completely chimerical, no matter what Cuban exiles said or felt about the situation, and that the fiasco and its aftermath, in which the United States became involved, was predictable."[29] Free's report, published July 18, 1960, was readily available in Washington. (Indeed, the Cuban embassy sent for ten copies.) It is difficult not to think that the information in the public opinion survey might have had more influence had it been secret. In a culture of secrecy, that which is not secret is easily disregarded or dismissed.*

Now open sources compete with covert ones. The Cuban missile crisis provides the example of the shift in intelligence sources. As is well known, a key event of the crisis turned on the photographs taken by American U-2 planes, which showed unequivocally that the Soviets had landed and were beginning to assemble missiles in Cuba. These overflights were an important American secret for many years. After the spy planes came the spy satellites and the National Reconnaissance Organization, whose very name was a secret until 1992. But in the late 1990s, governments' monopoly on spying from space came to an end. An American firm, EarthWatch, in partnership with a Japanese firm, Hitachi, and others, built the spacecraft *Earlybird 1*, which was launched from Svobodny Cosmodrome, a military base in eastern Russia. The Russian booster was formerly a military missile known as *Start 1*, for the control talks that restricted

* In October 1961, six months after the Bay of Pigs, Lyman B. Kirkpatrick, inspector general of the CIA, prepared a detailed "Survey of the Cuban Operation," twenty copies in all. It was as blunt as such documents ever get: the Bay of Pigs was as painful a failure as the United States had yet experienced in the Cold War (and would lead step by step to the Cuban missile crisis). The survey, made public in 1997, stated that the CIA "failed to collect adequate information on the strengths of the Castro regime and the extent of the opposition to it; and it failed to evaluate the available information correctly." However, there is no mention of Free's survey, which was known to the agency and might have spared the United States, Cuba, the world, the trauma of the moment and the ultimate peril that followed. Open sources simply had no standing.

them. Fifteen minutes after launch, a ground station in Norway reported that the satellite was doing a fine job of taking pictures of the earth, distinguishing features as small as cars and trucks. EarthWatch sells these digital images over the Internet (www.digitalglobe.com), and at quite reasonable prices—$300 to $725 an image. Other such satellites will follow, and other pictures of high-definition, golf-ball-on-the-green precision cannot be long in coming to a Web site near you. Surely times have changed.

They have assuredly changed in Moscow. On December 26, 1997, the Moscow *Rossijskaya Gazeta,* an official journal of the Council of Ministers, published a 14,500-word "Russian Federation National Security Blueprint," with the subtitle "Russia Within the World Community." It is a singular document. It can be described as liberal in the traditional understanding of the term. As translated by the Foreign Broadcast Information Service and broadcast on the Internet, the "National Security Blueprint" acknowledges, for example, that the Russian Orthodox church and the churches of other confessions play "a most important role in the preservation of traditional spiritual values." In a section entitled "Russia's National Interest," the document declares: "The system of Russia's national interests is determined by the aggregate of the basic interests of the individual, society, and the state." (The basic interests of the individual consist in "the real safeguarding of constitutional rights and freedoms and personal security, in improved quality of life and living standards, and in physical, spiritual, and intellectual development." The interests of society include "the consolidation of democracy, the attainment and maintenance of social accord, the enhancement of the population's creative activeness, and the spiritual renaissance of Russia." The interests of the state lie in "the protection of the constitutional system, the sovereignty and territorial integrity of Russia, the establishment of political, economic, and social stability, . . . and the development of international cooperation on the basis of partnership.")[30] The document is open about ethnicity and the "centrifugal tendencies of Russian Federal components" to an extent few regimes would contemplate. Or risk: "The ethnic egotism, ethnocentrism, and chauvinism that are displayed in the activities of a number of ethnic social formations help to increase national separatism and create favorable conditions for the emergence of conflicts."[31] And the document is all but brutally candid about the deterioration of Russian conventional forces, "manifested in the extremely acute nature of social problems in the Russian Federation Armed Forces and other troops and military formations and organs, the critically low level of operational and combat training, . . . the intolerable decline in the level of . . . weapons and military equipment, and in general the reduction of the state's potential for safeguarding the Russian Federation's security."[32]

And so to the only remaining source of Russian power—nuclear weapons. Here the policy paper is not alarmist: "The threat of large-scale aggression against Russia is virtually absent in the foreseeable future." The blueprint refers repeatedly to international law. But, then, NATO is expanding. Wars along the federation's borders keep breaking out. So "until the nonuse of force becomes the norm in international relations, the Russian Federation's national interests require the existence of a military might sufficient for its defense." But the blueprint's description of how this will be achieved by the hollow Russian military is sobering: "The most important task for the Russian Federation Armed Forces is to ensure nuclear deterrence in the interests of preventing both nuclear and conventional large-scale or regional wars. . . . In order to perform this task the Russian Federation must have nuclear forces with the potential to guarantee the infliction of the required damage on any aggressor state or coalition of states."[33]

Thus, for a moment in the 1980s, it appeared that the nuclear era might slowly recede, that a weaponless world was at least conceivable. No longer, or at least not soon. President Boris Yeltsin of the Russian Federation had issued the "National Security Blueprint" less than two weeks after the Duma had declined to take up the START II treaty, the embodiment of a "building down" strategy. The treaty (which may yet be ratified by Moscow) had come about after long decades in which NATO developed a military doctrine of graduated, or flexible, response to a Soviet threat: weapons systems would escalate, but a full-scale nuclear exchange was to be the very last resort. The Soviet planners had begun to think in much the same terms (yet again to the theme of organizations in conflict). Then came the 1980s, when both the Soviet Union and the United States could contemplate serious cutbacks in strategic nuclear weapons. Then came the collapse of the Soviet system. Now the Russian core has reverted to a doctrine of inflexible response. One false step and it's nuclear war.

The "what-ifs" are intriguing. What if the United States had recognized Soviet weakness earlier on and accordingly kept its own budget in order, so that upon the breakup of the Soviet Union a momentous economic aid program could have been commenced?

What if we had better calculated the forces of ethnicity so that we could have avoided going directly from the "end" of the Cold War to a new Balkan War, leaving little attention and far fewer resources for the shattered Soviet empire?

There it rests, with the one remaining large and positive possibility. Openness. East and West paid hideous costs for keeping matters of state closed to the people whom the states embodied. The Russian policy paper, it should be noted, calls for "an appropriate statutory legal base" for dealing with "security tasks." Whether that should ever happen in the Russian federation is for others to say. It *can* happen here. In order for a culture of openness to develop within government, the present culture of secrecy must be restrained by statute. Let law determine behavior, as it did in the case of the Administrative Procedure Act. A statute defining and limiting secrecy will not put an end to overclassification and needless classification, but it will help.

After all, a huge proportion of the government's effort at

classifying is futile anyway. Let Kennan have the last word. In a letter of March 1997 he writes: "It is my conviction, based on some 70 years of experience, first as a government official and then in the past 45 years as an historian, that the need by our government for *secret* intelligence about affairs elsewhere in the world has been vastly over-rated. I would say that something upwards of 95% of what we need to know about foreign countries could be very well obtained by the careful and competent study of perfectly legitimate sources of information open and available to us in the rich library and archival holdings of this country." As for the remaining 5 percent, we could easily, and nonsecretively, find most of that in similar sources abroad. Kennan concludes: "There may still be areas, very small areas really, in which there is a real need to penetrate someone else's curtain of secrecy. All right. But then please, without the erection of false pretenses and elaborate efforts to deceive—and without, to the extent possible—the attempt to maintain 'spies' on the adversary's territory. We easily become ourselves, the sufferers from these methods of deception. For they inculcate in their authors, as well as their intended victims, unlimited cynicism, causing them to lose all realistic understanding of the interrelationship, in what they are doing, of ends and means."[34]

A case can be made, not different from that of Seitz and his fellow scientists a generation ago, that secrecy is for losers. For people who don't know how important information really is. The Soviet Union realized this too late. Openness is now a singular, and singularly American, advantage. We put it in peril by poking along in the mode of an age now past. It is time to dismantle government secrecy, this most pervasive of Cold War–era regulations. It is time to begin building the supports for the era of openness that is already upon us.

Notes

Introduction

1. Theodore Draper, "Getting Irangate Straight," *New York Review of Books,* October 8, 1987, p. 47; see also Draper, *A Very Thin Line* (New York: Touchstone, 1991).

2. Daniel Patrick Moynihan, letter to Richard Gid Powers, July 22, 1997.

3. Daniel Patrick Moynihan, "The United States in Opposition," *Commentary,* March 1975, p. 42.

4. DPM to RGP, July 22, 1997.

5. Daniel Patrick Moynihan, "Letter from Peking," January 26, 1975, intended for publication in the *New Yorker* but not printed due to Moynihan's appointment to the United Nations.

6. Daniel Patrick Moynihan, "Will Russia Blow Up?" *Newsweek,* November 19, 1979, p. 144.

7. Ibid.

8. Ibid.

9. Daniel Patrick Moynihan, commencement address at New York University, May 24, 1984.

10. DPM to RGP, July 22, 1997.

11. Ibid.

12. Max M. Kampelman, letter to DPM, December 3, 1991.

13. Conference on the future of intelligence, Washington, D.C., sponsored by the Richard M. Nixon Library, Yorba Linda, Calif., March 12, 1992.

14. Henry A. Kissinger, letter to DPM, April 2, 1992.

15. Daniel Patrick Moynihan, "Secrecy as Government Regulation," the Marver H. Bernstein Lecture, Georgetown University, Washington, D.C., March 3, 1997, p. 11.

16. Daniel Patrick Moynihan, "How America Blew It," *Newsweek*, December 10, 1990, p. 14.

17. Ibid.

18. Ibid.

19. The other commissioners were John M. Deutch, the former director of Central Intelligence; Martin C. Faga, the former director of the National Reconnaissance Office and assistant secretary of the Air Force for Space; Alison B. Fortier, former staff director of the National Security Council; Richard K. Fox, Jr., former ambassador and career foreign service officer; Representative Lee H. Hamilton of Indiana; Senator Jesse Helms of North Carolina; journalist Ellen Hume; Samuel P. Huntington, professor at Harvard University and former coordinator of security planning for the National Security Council; John D. Podesta, White House deputy chief of staff for the Clinton administration; and Maurice Sonnenberg, of Clinton's Foreign Intelligence Advisory Board. Eric R. Biel of the Senate Finance Committee staff served as director of the commission's staff of sixteen, which had several members on loan from the Departments of State and Defense, the Central Intelligence Agency, and the National Security Agency.

20. Commission on Protecting and Reducing Government Secrecy, *Secrecy: Report of the Commission on Protecting and Reducing Government Secrecy* (Washington, D.C.: Government Printing Office, 1997), p. xxi.

21. Ibid., p. xiii.

22. Edward A. Shils, *The Torment of Secrecy: The Background and Consequences of American Security Policies* (1956; reprint, Chicago: Ivan R. Dee, 1996).

23. Herbert J. Gans, "Best-Sellers by Sociologists: An Exploratory Study," *Contemporary Sociology* 26, no. 2 (March 1997): 134.

24. Daniel Patrick Moynihan, introduction to Shils, *Torment of Secrecy,* pp. x–xi.

25. Commission on Protecting and Reducing Government Secrecy, *Secrecy,* p. xxi.

26. Moynihan, introduction to Shils, *Torment of Secrecy,* p. xxi. The economist was Anders Åslund.

27. Commission on Protecting and Reducing Government Secrecy, *Secrecy,* p. xxi.

28. For a detailed discussion of the Venona project, see Robert Louis Benson and Michael Warner, *Venona: Soviet Espionage and the American Response* (Washington, D.C.: National Security Agency, Central Intelligence Agency, 1996).

29. Moynihan, introduction to Shils, *Torment of Secrecy*, p. xvi.

30. See, for example, Richard Hofstadter, *The Paranoid Style in American Politics and Other Essays* (1964; reprint, Chicago: University of Chicago Press, 1979); David Brion Davis, *The Fear of Conspiracy: Images of Un-American Subversion from the Revolution to the Present* (Ithaca: Cornell University Press, 1971).

31. For an overview of the events of these years and J. Edgar Hoover's activities, see Richard Gid Powers, *Not Without Honor: The History of American Anticommunism* (New York: Free Press, 1995), chap. 2, and *Secrecy and Power: The Life of J. Edgar Hoover* (New York: Free Press, 1987), chaps. 3–4.

32. For classic examples of early Red Web conspiracy theories, see Blair Coan, *The Red Web, 1921–1924* (1925; reprint, Boston: Western Islands, 1969); Richard Whitney, *Reds in America* (1924; reprint, Belmont, Mass.: Western Islands, 1970).

33. R. G. Brown et al., *Report upon the Illegal Practices of the United States Department of Justice* (1920; reprint, New York: Arno, 1969), generally referred to as the "Lawyers' Report."

34. The definitive account of the Brown Scare of the late 1930s and early 1940s is Leo P. Ribuffo, *The Old Christian Right: The Protestant Far Right from the Great Depression to the Cold War* (Philadelphia: Temple University Press, 1983).

35. Elizabeth Dilling, *The Red Network* (Kenilworth, Ill.: published by author, 1934), and *The Roosevelt Red Record and Its Background* (Chicago: published by author, 1936); J. B. Matthews, *Odyssey of a Fellow Traveler* (New York: Mt. Vernon, 1938); Eugene Lyons, *The Red Decade: The Stalinist Penetration of America* (Indianapolis: Bobbs-Merrill, 1941); Daniel Aaron, *Writers on the Left* (New York: Avon, 1961); William L. O'Neill, *A Better World: The Great Schism, Stalinism, and the American Intellectuals* (New York: Simon and Schuster, 1982).

36. John Roy Carlson [Avedis Derounian], *Undercover: My Four Years in the Nazi Underground in America* (New York: Dutton, 1943).

37. For a survey and refutation of Pearl Harbor conspiracy theories, see Gordon Prange, *Pearl Harbor: The Verdict of History* (New York: McGraw-Hill, 1986). For the 1944 sedition trial, see Ribuffo, *Old Christian Right;* Lawrence Dennis and Maximilian St. George, *A Trial on Trial: The Great Sedition Trial of 1944* (New York: National Civil Rights Committee, 1945).

38. The standard account of McCarthy and his career is David M. Oshinsky, *A Conspiracy So Immense: The World of Joe McCarthy* (New

York: Free Press, 1983). McCarthy published his notorious speech on Marshall in *America's Retreat from Victory: The Story of George Catlett Marshall* (1951; reprint, New York: Devin-Adair, 1962).

39. For an account of this episode, see Powers, *Not Without Honor,* chap. 10. For the notorious biography of Eisenhower, see Robert Welch, *The Politician* (1963; reprint, Belmont, Mass.: Western Islands, 1964).

40. Stanley Mosk and Howard H. Jewel, "The Birch Phenomenon Analyzed," *New York Times Magazine,* August 20, 1961, p. 12.

41. See Powers, *Not Without Honor,* chap. 10.

42. For Goldwater's own bitter account of these episodes, see Barry M. Goldwater with Jack Casserly, *Goldwater* (New York: Doubleday, 1988), pp. 143–44, 171, 176, 205.

43. See Powers, *Not Without Honor,* pp. 333–39; Peter Schrag, *Test of Loyalty: Daniel Ellsberg and the Rituals of Secret Government* (New York: Touchstone, 1964); Sanford J. Ungar, *The Papers and the Papers: An Account of the Legal and Political Battle over the Pentagon Papers* (1972; reprint, New York: Columbia University Press, 1989).

44. Neil Sheehan, introduction to Sheehan et al., eds., *The Pentagon Papers* (New York: Bantam, 1971), p. xii.

45. Ibid., pp. xiii, xv.

46. Gravel is quoted in Ungar, *The Papers and the Papers,* p. 37.

47. Mark Felt, *The FBI Pyramid: From the Inside* (New York: Putnam's, 1979), pp. 88, 93, 98. For an account of the raid at Media, Pennsylvania, see Powers, *Secrecy and Power,* pp. 464–66. See also Cathy Perkus, ed., *COINTELPRO: The FBI's Secret War on Political Freedom* (New York: Monad, 1975).

48. For detailed accounts of the Senate and House investigations of the intelligence agencies, see Loch K. Johnson, *A Season of Inquiry: The Senate Intelligence Investigation* (Lexington: University Press of Kentucky, 1985); Kathryn S. Olmsted, *Challenging the Secret Government* (Chapel Hill: University of North Carolina Press, 1996); Senate Select Committee to Study Governmental Operations with Respect to Intelligence Activities, *Final Report,* 64th Cong., 2d sess., H. Rept. 94–755.

49. Senate Select Committee to Study Governmental Operations, *Final Report,* book 3, p. 376.

50. Ibid., book 3, p. 3.

51. House Select Committee on Intelligence, testimony of retired special agent Arthur Murtagh, *Hearings Before the Committee on Intelligence,* 94th Cong., 1st sess., November 18, 1975, part 3, p. 1048.

52. Olmsted, *Challenging the Secret Government.*

53. Quoted in ibid., pp. 66, 79.

54. William Appleman Williams, *Tragedy of American Diplomacy* (Cleveland: World, 1959); Denna Fleming, *The Cold War and Its Origins* (New York: Doubleday, 1961); Gabriel Kolko, *Politics of War: The World and United States Foreign Policy, 1943–1945* (New York: Random House, 1968); Lloyd C. Gardner, *Architects of Illusion: Men and Ideas in American Foreign Policy, 1941–1949* (Chicago: Quadrangle, 1970); Gar Alperovitz, *Atomic Diplomacy: Hiroshima and Potsdam, the Use of the Atomic Bomb, and the American Confrontation with Soviet Power* (New York: Simon and Schuster, 1965). The quotation is from Gardner, *Architects of Illusion,* p. 317.

55. David Horowitz, *Free World Colossus: A Critique of American Foreign Policy in the Cold War,* rev. ed. (New York: Hill and Wang, 1971), pp. 4–6.

56. Robert James Maddox, *The New Left and the Origins of the Cold War* (Princeton: Princeton University Press, 1973), p. 19.

57. Gerald Posner, *Case Closed: Lee Harvey Oswald and the Assassination of JFK* (New York: Random House, 1993), p. 241.

58. Natalie Robins, *Alien Ink: The FBI's War on Freedom of Expression* (New York: William Morrow, 1992); Buckley's comment appears as a blurb on the back of the jacket.

59. Herbert Mitgang, *Dangerous Dossiers: Exposing the Secret War Against America's Greatest Authors* (New York: Donald I. Fine, 1988), p. 314.

60. Bud Schultz and Ruth Schultz, *It Did Happen Here: Recollections of Political Repression in America* (Berkeley: University of California Press, 1989), p. 413; Griffin Fariello, *Red Scare: Memories of the American Inquisition* (New York: Norton, 1995); Athan G. Theoharis and John Stuart Cox, *The Boss: J. Edgar Hoover and the Great American Inquisition* (Philadelphia: Temple University Press, 1988); and Ellen Schrecker, *The Age of McCarthyism* (New York: Bedford, 1984).

61. Edward Pessen, *Losing Our Souls: The American Experience in the Cold War* (Chicago: Ivan R. Dee, 1993), p. 11.

62. Bruce Cummings, foreword to I. F. Stone, *The Hidden History of the Korean War, 1950–1951* (1952; reprint, Boston: Little, Brown, 1988), pp. xi–xii.

63. Jim Garrison, *On the Trail of the Assassins* (New York: Warner, 1988), p. 324.

64. Anthony Summers, *Official and Confidential: The Secret Life of J. Edgar Hoover* (New York: Putnam's, 1993); Athan Theoharis, *J. Edgar Hoover, Sex, and Crime* (Chicago: Ivan R. Dee, 1995).

65. Seymour Hersh, *The Dark Side of Camelot* (Boston: Little, Brown, 1997); Gore Vidal, "Coached by Camelot," *New Yorker,* December 1, 1997, pp. 85–92.

66. Allen Weinstein, *Perjury: The Hiss-Chambers Case* (New York: Knopf, 1968), p. xvii.

67. Ibid., pp. 548–49.

68. Ibid., p. 565.

69. O'Neill, *A Better World*, p. 367.

70. Ronald Radosh and Joyce Milton, *The Rosenberg File*, 2d ed. (New Haven: Yale University Press, 1997), pp. 471–72.

71. Ibid., pp. 450–51.

72. Ibid., pp. 453, ix.

73. Ibid., pp. xxv, xxix–xxx.

74. Ibid., p. xxi.

75. Harvey Klehr, John Earl Haynes, and Fridrikh Igorevich Firsov, *The Secret World of American Communism* (New Haven: Yale University Press, 1995), pp. 18–19.

76. John Lewis Gaddis, *We Now Know* (New York: Oxford University Press, 1997), pp. 292–93.

77. Ibid., pp. 294, 25.

78. Ibid., pp. 74–75.

79. Ibid., p. 49.

80. Ibid., p. 14.

81. Ibid., pp. 293–94.

Chapter 1: Secrecy as Regulation

1. Foreign Relations Authorization Act for Fiscal Years 1994 and 1995, 50 *U.S. Code* 401.

2. Robert Lewis Benson, *Introductory History of Venona and Guide to the Translations* (Fort George G. Meade, Md.: Center for Cryptologic History, National Security Agency, 1995), pp. 3, 6.

3. J. Edgar Hoover, letter to George E. Allen, May 29, 1946, file "FBI–Atomic Bomb," in subject file "President's Secretary's File," Harry S. Truman Papers, Truman Library, Independence, Mo.

4. D. M. Ladd, memorandum to J. Edgar Hoover, May 28, 1946, Library of Congress.

5. H. B. Fletcher, memorandum to D. M. Ladd, October 18, 1949, archives of the Federal Bureau of Investigation.

6. Allen Weinstein, *Perjury: The Hiss-Chambers Case* (New York: Random House, 1978; reprint, New York: Random House, 1997).

7. Office of Management and Budget, *Historical Tables: Budget of the United States Government, Fiscal Year 1998* (February 1997); calculations are based on constant 1998 dollars.

8. Information Security Oversight Office, *1996 Report to the President* (Washington, D.C.: Information Security Oversight Office, 1996), p. ii.

9. Ibid.

10. James Risen and Ronald J. Ostrow, "East Germany's Spy Files at Center of FBI-CIA Clash," *Los Angeles Times*, October 25, 1995.

11. Tim Weiner, "For First Time, U.S. Discloses Spying Budget," *New York Times*, October 16, 1997.

12. Evan Thomas, "A Singular Opportunity: Gaining Access to CIA's Records," *Studies in Intelligence* 39 (1996): 19.

13. Sherman Kent, "Studies in Intelligence," September 1955, in *Studies in Intelligence, Index 1955–1992*.

14. R. Jeffrey Smith, "The Dissenter," *Washington Post Magazine*, December 7, 1997, pp. 18–20.

15. Stansfield Turner, "Intelligence for a New World Order," *Foreign Affairs* 70 (Fall 1991): 162.

Chapter 2: The Experience of World War I

1. John A. Rohr, *To Run a Constitution: The Legitimacy of the Administrative State* (Lawrence: University Press of Kansas, 1986), p. 156.

2. Floyd M. Riddick and Alan S. Frumin, *Riddick's Senate Procedure: Precedents and Practices*, 101st Cong., 2d sess., 1992, S. Doc. 101–28, p. 275.

3. James Parton, *Life of Andrew Jackson* (New York: Mason Brothers, 1860), 3:607.

4. William Z. Slany, "Draft History of the Foreign Relations Series," p. 4.

5. Wilson, "An Address to a Joint Session of Congress," January 8, 1918, in *The Papers of Woodrow Wilson*, edited by Arthur S. Link (Princeton: Princeton University Press, 1984–92), 45:536.

6. Ibid., p. 537.

7. *World Book Encyclopedia*, 1994 ed., s.v. "Alien and Sedition Acts," by Jerald A. Combs.

8. William H. Seward, letter to Charles Francis Adams, 1861, in *Annual Message of the President*, 37th Cong., 2d sess., S. Doc. 21, serial 1117, 1:108.

9. David M. Halbfinger, "Political Role of Immigrants Is Still Lagging," *New York Times*, December 1, 1997.

10. Sir William Schwenck Gilbert, *Iolanthe*, libretto by W. S. Gilbert, edited by William-Alan Landes (Studio City, Calif.: Players Press, 1997).

11. Nathan Glazer, "From Socialism to Sociology," in *Authors of Their Own Lives: Intellectual Autobiographies*, edited by Bennett M. Berger (Berkeley: University of California Press, 1990), p. 191.

12. Melvyn Dubofsky, *We Shall Be All: A History of the Industrial Workers of the World* (Chicago: Quadrangle Books, 1969), p. 271.

13. Ibid., p. 146, quoting Lewis S. Gannet.

14. Robert Lansing to Wilson, November 20, 1915, *Papers of Woodrow Wilson* 35:230.

15. Wilson, "An Address in Philadelphia to Newly Naturalized Citizens," May 10, 1915, *Papers of Woodrow Wilson* 33:147–50.

16. Wilson, "Annual Message on the State of the Union," December 7, 1915, *Papers of Woodrow Wilson* 35:306–7.

17. *An Act Requiring an Oath of Allegiance and to Support the Constitution of the United States, to Be Administered to Certain Persons in the Civil Service of the United States*, 12 Stat. 326 (August 6, 1861).

18. U.S. Department of Justice, *Annual Report of the Attorney General, 1916* (Washington, D.C.: Government Printing Office, 1916), pp. 12–20.

19. Robert Lansing, memorandum, March 20, 1917, *Papers of Woodrow Wilson* 41:442.

20. Wilson, "Address to a Joint Session of Congress," April 2, 1917, in *Papers of Woodrow Wilson* 41:524.

21. McIlhenny and others to Woodrow Wilson, April 5, 1917, in *Papers of Woodrow Wilson* 41:546.

22. S. 2, chap. 2, sec. 2(c).

23. H.R. 291, sec. 4.

24. Harold Edgar and Benno C. Schmidt, Jr., "The Espionage Statutes and Publication of Defense Information," *Columbia Law Review* 73, no. 5 (May 1973): 950–51.

25. *The Encyclopedia of the United States Congress* (New York: Simon and Schuster, 1995), 2:774.

26. *Congressional Record* 55, pt. 1:789 (April 18, 1917).

27. Ibid., pt. 2:2263 (May 14, 1917).

28. Ibid., pt. 2:2119 (May 11, 1917).

29. Ibid., pt. 1:787–88 (April 18, 1917).

30. Ibid., pt. 3:2262 (May 14, 1917).

31. Ibid., pt. 3:3144 (May 31, 1917).

32. Sedition Act of 1918, 40 Stat. 553.

33. Edgar and Schmidt, "Espionage Statutes," p. 1023.

34. 42 U.S. Code 2274.

35. Wilson, speech of September 5, 1919, *Papers of Woodrow Wilson* 63:46–47.

36. Madison to Jefferson, May 13, 1798, *The Republic of Letters: The Correspondence Between Thomas Jefferson and James Madison, 1776–1826,* edited by James Morton Smith (New York: W. W. Norton, 1995), 2:1048.

37. Jules Witcover, *Sabotage at Black Tom: Imperial Germany's Secret War in America, 1914–1917* (Chapel Hill, N.C.: Algonquin, 1989), p. 42; Captain Henry Landau, *The Enemy Within: The Inside Story of German Sabotage in America* (New York: G. P. Putnam's Sons, 1937), pp. 7–8.

38. Marc Mappen, "Jerseyana," *New York Times,* July 14, 1991.

39. "Ram Chandra in Toils with Four Hindoo Plotters," *San Francisco Chronicle,* April 8, 1917.

40. Joan M. Jensen, "The 'Hindu Conspiracy': A Reassessment," *Pacific Historical Review* 48 (February 1979): 65.

41. Ibid.

42. John L. Heaton, *Cobb of "The World"* (New York: Dutton, 1924), p. 270.

43. Wilson, "Address to a Joint Session of Congress," April 2, 1917, in *Papers of Woodrow Wilson* 41:523.

44. Samuel Eliot Morison, Henry Steele Commager, and William E. Leuchtenburg, *The Growth of the American Republic,* 6th ed. (New York: Oxford University Press, 1969), 2:383.

45. Ibid.

46. Ibid., 2:386.

47. *Theodore Roosevelt Cyclopedia,* edited by Albert Bushnell Hart and Herbert Ronald Ferleger (New York: Roosevelt Memorial Association, 1941).

48. *Encyclopedia of the United States Congress* 2:774.

49. Morison, Commager, and Leuchtenburg, *American Republic* 2:384.

50. Louis W. Koenig, *Bryan: A Political Biography of William Jennings Bryan* (New York: G. P. Putnam's Sons, 1971), pp. 502–3.

51. Arthur S. Link, *Wilson: The Struggle for Neutrality, 1914–1915* (Princeton: Princeton University Press, 1960), p. 420.

52. "Josephus Daniels Dies at Age of Eighty-Five," *New York Times,* January 16, 1948.

53. "Baker to Be New Secretary of War," *New York Times,* March 7, 1916.

54. *Schenck v. United States,* 249 U.S. 47 (1919).

55. *Debs v. United States,* 249 U.S. 211 (1919).

Chapter 3: The Encounter with Communism

1. Wilson's executive order of April 7, 1917, is quoted in Paul P. Van Riper, *History of the United States Civil Service* (Evanston, Ill.: Row, Peterson, 1958), p. 266; for the actions of the Civil Service Commission after the war, see pp. 265–67.

2. *World Book Encyclopedia*, 1994 ed., s.v. "Anarchism," by James D. Forman.

3. "General Orders No. 64, General Headquarters, American Expeditionary Force," November 22, 1917, in Harold C. Relyea, *The Evolution of Government Information Security Classification Policy: A Brief Overview (1775–1973)*, Congressional Research Service, September 11, 1973, p. 22.

4. Robert Lansing, memorandum, March 20, 1917, *The Papers of Woodrow Wilson*, edited by Arthur S. Link (Princeton: Princeton University Press, 1984–92), 41:438.

5. Ibid., p. 440.

6. Robert A. Rosenstone, *Romantic Revolutionary: A Biography of John Reed* (Cambridge: Harvard University Press, 1990), p. 330.

7. Harvey Klehr, John Earl Haynes, and Fridrikh Igorevich Firsov, *The Secret World of American Communism* (New Haven: Yale University Press, 1995), p. 22.

8. Theodore Draper, *The Roots of American Communism* (Chicago: Ivan R. Dee, 1957), p. 189. Draper also reproduces a breakdown of the total membership of the CPUSA, estimated at 26,680 members: English, 1,900 (including 800 from the Michigan organization, which soon dropped out); Estonian, 280; German, 850; Hungarian, 1,000; Jewish, 1,000; Lettish, or Latvian, 1,200; Lithuanian, 4,400; Polish, 1,750; Russian, 7,000; South Slavic, 2,200; Ukrainian, 4,000; and members from nonfederation countries, 1,100 (ibid.).

9. Klehr, Haynes, and Firsov estimate that fewer than 4,000 members of both the Communist Party of America (about 24,000 members) and the Communist Labor Party (about 10,000 members) spoke English (*Secret World*, p. 5).

10. Draper, *Roots of American Communism*, p. 191.

11. Ibid.

12. Ibid., p. 323.

13. Nathan Glazer, *The Social Basis of American Communism* (New York: Harcourt, Brace, and World, 1961), p. 3. Maurice Isserman estimates that in the years before World War II, there were 50,000 to 75,000 CPUSA members in the United States (Isserman, *Which Side Were You On? The American Communist Party During the Second World War* [Middletown, Conn.: Wesleyan University Press, 1982], p. 18).

14. Stanley Coben, *A. Mitchell Palmer: Politician* (New York: Da Capo Press, 1972), pp. 203-7.

15. "Russian Reds Are Busy Here," *New York Times*, June 8, 1919; Robert K. Murray, *Red Scare: A Study in National Hysteria, 1919–1920* (Minneapolis: University of Minnesota Press, 1955), p. 213; "The Red Assassins," *Washington Post*, January 4, 1920.

16. Roberta Strauss Feuerlicht, *America's Reign of Terror: World War I, the Red Scare, and the Palmer Raids* (New York: Random House, 1971), p. 108.

17. Theodore Draper, *The Roots of American Communism* (Chicago: Ivan R. Dee, 1957), p. 207.

18. Klehr, Haynes, and Firsov, *Secret World*, p. 21.

19. Ibid., p. 24.

20. In fact, the Soviet subsidies to American Communists continued into the 1980s, by which time the CPUSA scarcely existed. Moscow evidently did not realize this, perhaps assuming that most of the party members had gone underground—and inadvertently illustrating the truism that, in clandestine operations, it is ever difficult to check one's facts.

21. Ignazio Silone, *The God That Failed: Six Studies in Communism*, edited by Richard Crossman (London: Hamish Hamilton, 1950), p. 16.

22. Klehr, Haynes, and Firsov, *Secret World*, pp. 5, 7, 24–25. Robert A. Katzmann, who read a draft of the manuscript of this book, notes: "Gitlow was also a central figure in *Gitlow v. New York* (1925), in which Justice Edward T. Sanford, speaking for the Court, held that because 'a single revolutionary spark may kindle a fire that, smoldering for a time, may burst into a sweeping and destructive conflagration, [the state] may, in the exercise of its judgment, suppress the threatened danger in its incipiency' (268 U.S. at 669)."

23. Sidney Hook, *Out of Step: An Unquiet Life in the Twentieth Century* (New York: Harper and Row, 1987), p. 241.

24. National Security Agency, fourth Venona release, July 17, 1996, vol. 3, nos. 174–76 (December 29, 1943).

25. Hook, *Out of Step*, p. 281.

26. Ibid.

27. Ibid., p. 285.

28. David Riesman, *Abundance for What?* (Garden City, N.Y.: Doubleday, 1964; reprint, New Brunswick, N.J.: Transaction, 1993), p. 80.

29. Lionel Trilling, *The Middle of the Journey* (London: Secker and Warburg, 1975), p. viii.

30. Ibid., pp. x–xi. See also Daniel Patrick Moynihan, "Address to

the Entering Class at Harvard College, 1972," in *Coping: Essays on the Practice of Government* (New York: Random House, 1973), p. 405.

31. Trilling, *Middle of the Journey*, pp. xviii–xix.

32. Ibid., p. xix.

33. Ibid.

34. Daniel Patrick Moynihan, review of *Final Reports*, by Richard Rovere, *New Yorker*, September 17, 1984, pp. 134–40.

Chapter 4: The Experience of World War II

1. Art Ronnie, *Counterfeit Hero: Fritz Duquesne, Adventurer and Spy* (Annapolis, Md.: Naval Institute Press, 1995), pp. 208–9.

2. Ibid., p. 214.

3. Quoted in ibid., p. 2.

4. Publius [Alexander Hamilton], Federalist No. 9, in *The Federalist Papers*, edited by Clinton Rossiter (New York: New American Library, 1961), p. 72.

5. *The Harvard Encyclopedia of American Ethnic Groups*, s.v. "Germans," by Kathleen Neils Conzen.

6. Ibid.

7. Robert Edwin Herzstein, *Roosevelt and Hitler: Prelude to War* (New York: Paragon House, 1989), p. 189.

8. Ibid., p. 190.

9. Don Whitehead, *The FBI Story* (New York: Random House, 1956), p. 212.

10. By February 16, 1942, these numbers had expanded to a total of 2,192 Japanese, 1,393 Germans, and 264 Italians (Commission on Wartime Relocation and Internment of Civilians, *Personal Justice Denied* [Washington, D.C.: Government Printing Office, 1992], p. 55).

11. Ibid., p. 73.

12. Ibid., p. 81.

13. Franklin D. Roosevelt, "Authorizing the Secretary of War to Prescribe Military Areas," Executive Order 9066, *Federal Register* 7 (February 19, 1942): 38.

14. Commission on Wartime Relocation, *Personal Justice Denied*, p. 308.

15. Ibid., p. 287.

16. Stephen Fox, *The Unknown Internment: An Oral History of the Relocation of Italian Americans During World War II* (Boston: Twayne, 1990), p. 136.

17. Charles A. Horsky, having served as assistant prosecutor at the

Nuremberg war crimes trials, argued a case before the Supreme Court that challenged the wartime internment of Americans of Japanese ancestry. "I was trying to persuade the Court that there was no legitimate basis for the Army to arrest citizens," said Horsky in a 1989 interview with the *Washington Post*. "I couldn't get enough information to make it stick" (quoted in Irvin Molotsky, obituary of Charles A. Horsky, *New York Times*, August 24, 1997).

18. Civil Liberties Act of 1988, 102 Stat. 94. U.S. citizens of Aleutian descent were also relocated; of them the act said, "The United States failed to provide reasonable care for the Aleuts, and this resulted in widespread illness, disease, and death among the residents of the camps."

19. Quoted in Commission on Wartime Relocation, *Personal Justice Denied*, p. 82.

20. Richard Norton Smith, *The Colonel: The Life and Legend of Robert R. McCormick, 1880–1955* (Boston: Houghton Mifflin, 1997), p. 417.

Chapter 5: The Bomb

1. Maurice M. Shapiro, "Echoes of the Big Bang," *New York Times*, July 15, 1995.

2. Ibid.

3. J. Robert Oppenheimer's account is quoted in Richard Rhodes, *The Making of the Atomic Bomb* (New York: Simon and Schuster, 1986), p. 676.

4. Shapiro, "Echoes of the Big Bang."

5. "The Atomic Bomb," *Life*, February 27, 1950, p. 91.

6. Ibid., p. 100.

7. Weisband was convicted of contempt of court for failing to attend a grand jury hearing on Communist Party activity; in November 1950 he was sentenced to one year in prison (Robert Louis Benson and Michael Warner, eds., *Venona: Soviet Espionage and the American Response, 1939–1957* [Washington, D.C.: National Security Agency, Central Intelligence Agency, 1996], p. xxviii).

8. Max Weber, "Bureaucracy," in *Essays in Sociology*, translated and edited by H. H. Gerth and C. Wright Mills (New York: Oxford University Press, 1946), pp. 233–34.

9. Senate Committee on Foreign Relations, *The START Treaty: Hearings Before the Committee on Foreign Relations*, 102d Cong., 2d sess., S. Hrg. 102–607, pt. 1, p. 96.

10. George F. Kennan, *Memoirs: 1950–1963*, vol. 2 (Boston: Little, Brown, 1972), p. 191.

11. See, for example, Lillian Hellman, *Scoundrel Time*, with an introduction by Garry Wills (Boston: Little, Brown, 1976).

12. The three others were Edward R. Stettinius, Jr., secretary of state; H. Freeman Matthews, director of the Office of European Affairs; and Wilder Foote, assistant to the secretary of state (Edward R. Stettinius, Jr., *Roosevelt and the Russians: The Yalta Conference* [Garden City, N.Y.: Doubleday, 1949], p. 30).

13. Joseph Albright and Marcia Kunstel, *Bombshell: The Secret Story of Ted Hall and America's Unknown Atomic Spy Conspiracy* (New York: Times Books, 1997), p. 58.

14. Ibid., pp. 89–90.

15. Michael Dobbs, "Code Name 'Mlad,' Atomic Bomb Spy," *Washington Post*, February 25, 1996. See also Dobbs, "New Documents Name American as Soviet Spy," *Washington Post*, March 6, 1996.

16. Albright and Kunstel, *Bombshell*, p. 90.

Chapter 6: A Culture of Secrecy

1. Suslov joined the Politburo (then called the Presidium) in October 1952 but left in 1953 after Stalin's death. He rejoined in 1955 and remained a member until his death on January 25, 1982.

2. Daniel Patrick Moynihan, *A Dangerous Place* (Boston: Little, Brown, 1978), pp. ix–x.

3. Henry DeWolf Smyth, *A General Account of the Development of Methods of Using Atomic Energy for Military Purposes Under the Auspices of the United States Government, 1940–1945* (Washington: Government Printing Office, 1945). That same year Smyth published *Atomic Energy for Military Purposes: The Official Report on the Development of the Atomic Bomb Under the Auspices of the United States Government, 1940-1945* (Princeton: Princeton University Press, 1945); new editions of this work have been brought out by other publishers in 1976, 1978, and 1989.

4. Roscoe Pound, quoted in *Annual Report of the American Bar Association* 63 (1938): 340.

5. Erwin Griswold, "Government in Ignorance of the Law: A Plea for Better Publication of Executive Legislation," *Harvard Law Review* 48 (1934): 198. Griswold argued that, because administrative regulations "equivalent to law" had become so important in the ordering of everyday life, executive legislation should be published and thus made available to the public. A year after Griswold's essay appeared, Congress enacted the Federal Register Act of 1935, 49 Stat. 500.

6. Attorney General Tom Clark interpreted this exception to the APA's public-information provision in his 1947 *Manual on the Administrative Procedure Act:* "This would include the confidential operations

of any agency, such as the confidential operations of the Federal Bureau of Investigation and the Secret Service and, in general, those aspects of any agency's law enforcement procedures the disclosure of which would reduce the utility of such procedures. . . . It should be noted that the exception is made only to the extent that the function requires secrecy in the public interest. Such a determination must be made by the agency concerned. To the extent that the function does not require such secrecy, the publication requirements apply. Thus, the War Department obviously is not required to publish confidential matters of military organization and operation, but it would be required to publish the organization and procedure applicable to the ordinary civil functions of the Corps of Engineers."

7. *United States v. Curtiss-Wright Export Corporation,* 299 U.S. 304, 319 (1936).

8. Richard Frank, "Enforcing the Public's Right to Openness in the Foreign Affairs Decision-Making Process," in *Secrecy and Foreign Policy,* edited by Thomas Franck and Edward Weisband (New York: Oxford University Press, 1974), pp. 272–73.

9. Hatch Act, 53 Stat. 1148 (1953). Previously, under the Pendleton Act of 1883 and the Lloyd-LaFollette Act of 1912, civil service investigations of government employees had focused on issues of general character and ability. The 1912 act provided that employees could be removed only when doing so would promote the efficiency of the civil service. It also established specific procedures for notifying employees of any charges against them and allowing them to respond to such charges. The federal government's employment policies centered on the need to maintain a trustworthy and efficient civil service, one based on the core principle of "suitability" for federal employment, defined in the 1883 statute as "a requirement or requirements for government employment having reference to a person's character, reputation, trustworthiness, and fitness as related to the efficiency of the service" (22 Stat. 403 [1883]). Today, all government employees must still meet a standard of suitability that tracks the original 1883 definition; those requiring access to national security information must also be found "security-eligible" as defined in the Eisenhower Executive Order 10450.

10. Commission on Government Security, *Report of the Commission on Government Security* (Washington, D.C.: Government Printing Office, 1957), pp. 3–6; Eleanor Bontecou, *The Federal Loyalty-Security Program* (Westport, Conn.: Greenwood Press, 1953), p. 14.

11. Commission on Government Security, *Report,* p. 6.

12. Harold Green, "The Oppenheimer Case: A Study in the Abuse of Law," *Bulletin of Atomic Scientists* 33 (September 1977): 12, 61.

13. Among the critics were several Harvard law professors, including Zechariah Chafee, Jr., who had spoken out against Attorney General Palmer nearly three decades before, and Erwin Griswold, in

"The Loyalty Order: Procedure Termed Inadequate and Defects Pointed Out," *New York Times,* April 13, 1947. See also Bontecou, *Federal Loyalty-Security Program,* pp. 30–31.

14. Public Law 81–733, 64 Stat. 476 (1950).

15. Dwight D. Eisenhower, "Security Requirements for Government Employees," Executive Order 10450, *Federal Register* 18 (April 29, 1953): 2489.

16. Attempting to respond to the criticism, President Truman had amended his executive order in July 1951, lowering the standard of proof for disloyalty: "The standard for the refusal of employment or the removal from employment in an Executive department or agency on grounds relating to loyalty shall be that on all the evidence, *there is reasonable doubt* as to the loyalty of the person involved" (emphasis added; Harry S. Truman, Executive Order 10241, *Federal Register* 16 [April 28, 1951]: 3690). Then in 1952, the president convened a committee charged with merging "the loyalty, security, and suitability programs, thus eliminating the overlapping, duplication, and confusion which apparently now exist" (Truman, letter to the chairman of the Civil Service Commission, August 8, 1952, *Public Papers of the Presidents of the United States: Harry S. Truman* [Washington, D.C.: Government Printing Office, 1966], p. 513). But the often partisan attacks on his loyalty program persisted, and a single, unified program for reviewing applicants for government positions and existing employees was never established—even after the Wright Commission in 1957 criticized the Eisenhower structure as an "unnatural blend" and a "hybrid product, . . . neither fish nor fowl, resulting in inconclusive adjudications, bewildered security personnel, employee fear and unrest, and general public criticism" (Commission on Government Security, *Report,* p. 44).

17. Under Executive Order 10450, the *scope* of an investigation could vary, depending on an individual's position and how sensitive it was to national security.

18. Anthony Leviero, "New Security Plan Issued: Thousands Face Re-Inquiry," *New York Times,* April 28, 1953.

19. Ibid.

20. Edward A. Shils, *The Torment of Secrecy,* with an introduction by Daniel P. Moynihan (Glencoe, Ill.: Free Press, 1956; reprint, Chicago: Ivan R. Dee, 1996), pp. 213–14. Shils goes on to offer a strong critique of the system: "This seems a narrow and doctrinaire conception of the motives of treasonable conduct. It is this narrow doctrinairism which makes the present system so inefficient, even though it may well be fairly effective. Although it might catch a few potential spies, it hurts many innocent persons. The resources marshalled against the potential spy are usually almost equally dangerous to the innocent."

21. Public Law 304, 84th Congress.

22. *Congressional Record,* January 18, 1955, pp. 463–64.

23. Ibid.

24. Commission on Government Security, *Report,* pp. xiii–xiv.

25. Ibid., p. xvii.

26. Ibid., p. xxiii.

27. James Reston, "Security Versus Freedom: An Analysis of the Controversy Stirred by Recommendation to Curb Information," *New York Times,* June 25, 1957.

28. Commission on Government Security, *Report,* p. 688.

29. Max Frankel, "Top Secret," *New York Times Magazine,* June 16, 1996.

30. House Committee on Government Operations, *Availability of Information from Federal Departments and Agencies,* 86th Cong., 2d sess. (July 2, 1960), H. Rept. 86–2084, p. 36.

31. Commission on Government Security, *Report,* p. xvii.

32. In an even-tempered, respectful dissent to the proposal for establishing a central security office, former attorney general McGranery wrote of "the inherent evil of the pyramiding of administrative devices, the superimposing of agency upon agency and the empire-building proclivities which frequently go hand in hand with the creation of overseers," noting that "no problem is solved by shifting primary executive responsibility from agencies and officials having that primary responsibility to superimposed administrative creations," even those described as advisory (and for whom "the power to suggest too easily becomes the power to demand"). After all, there was no guarantee that a new agency would work any better than the old ones had. What was needed instead, McGranery continued, was a correction of existing procedures that failed to achieve national security "with minimum delay and maximum protection of the civil rights of the loyal employee," a desire to make the corrected procedures work, and a willingness to fix responsibility for mistakes of judgment and to seek to avoid their recurrence. "This can best be done," he added, "by holding accountable those officials and agencies having the primary responsibility" (ibid.).

33. Harold C. Relyea, *The Evolution of Government Information Security Classification Policy: A Brief Overview (1775–1973),* Congressional Research Service, September 11, 1973, p. 50; Robert O. Blanchard, "Present at the Creation: The Media and the Moss Committee," *Journalism Quarterly* 49 (Summer 1972): 272.

34. House Special Government Information Subcommittee, H. Rept. 85–1884 (1958), p. 152.

35. House Committee on Government Operations, *Executive Classification of Information: Security Classification Problems Involving Exemption (b)(1) of the Freedom of Information Act* (1973), H. Rept. 93–221, p. 21.

36. 5 *U.S. Code* 552 (1966).

37. Even so, significant concerns remain about both the effectiveness and the efficiency of the procedures used under the FOIA. For example, at a roundtable program on May 16, 1996, the Commission on Protecting and Reducing Government Secrecy heard testimony from journalist Terry Anderson concerning his efforts to use the FOIA to reconstruct the history of his seven years' captivity in Lebanon. What he encountered from his own government—outright denials of requested information and expressions of regret for the long delays, documents that had been completely blacked out, and piles of foreign newspaper clippings on Middle Eastern terrorism that had somehow come to be classified once they entered agency files—led him to tell the commission, "It's not the law that has to be changed but the culture of non-cooperation among the bureaucrats."

38. Commission on Government Security, *Report*, p. xx.

39. Defense Science Board, *Final Report of the Defense Science Board Task Force on Secrecy* (July 1, 1970). Ironically, given its tone and recommendations, the task force report was marked "For Official Use Only," apparently in an effort to control its distribution.

40. The task force noted that "never in the past has it been possible to keep secret the truly important discoveries, such as the discovery that an atomic bomb can be made to work" (ibid., pp. 3–4).

41. Ibid.

42. Glenn T. Seaborg, "Secrecy Runs Amok," *Science*, June 3, 1994, p. 1410.

43. Ibid.

44. Nick Cullather, letter to author, July 2, 1997.

Chapter 7: The Routinization of Secrecy

1. National Security Act of 1947, 61 Stat. 495.

2. Merle Miller, *Plain Speaking: An Oral Biography of Harry S. Truman* (New York: Berkeley, 1973), p. 392n.

3. Walter Pincus, "CIA Veteran Tapped to Run Operations," *Washington Post*, July 22, 1997.

4. James Q. Wilson, *Bureaucracy: What Government Agencies Do and Why They Do It* (New York: Basic Books, 1989), pp. 188–89.

5. Nicholas Cullather, *Operation PBSUCCESS: The United States and Guatemala, 1952–1954* (Washington, D.C.: Central Intelligence Agency, Center for the Study of Intelligence, 1994), p. 7.

6. Ibid., p. 84.

7. X [George F. Kennan], "The Sources of Soviet Conduct," *For-*

eign Affairs, July 1947, reprinted in Hamilton Fish Armstrong, ed., *Fifty Years of Foreign Affairs* (New York: Praeger, 1972), p. 197.

8. Ibid., p. 200.

9. Ibid., p. 203.

10. Robert M. Laskey, editor's introduction to NSC-68, *Naval War College Review* 27 (May–June 1975): 52.

11. Ibid., p. 51.

12. Peter Grose, *Gentleman Spy: The Life of Allen Dulles* (Boston: Houghton Mifflin, 1994), p. 347.

13. Paul H. Nitze, "Reflections on the Origins of NSC-68" (remarks delivered at a seminar, "Assessing the Soviet Threat: The Early Cold War Years," sponsored by the Central Intelligence Agency, Washington, D.C., October 24, 1997).

14. Ibid.

15. Laskey, "NSC-68," p. 62.

16. Ibid., p. 68.

17. In *Strategies of Containment* (New York: Oxford University Press, 1982), John Lewis Gaddis distinguishes among five "distinct geopolitical codes" between 1947 and 1980: Kennan's original containment strategy (1947–49); NSC-68 and the Korean War (1950–53); the Eisenhower-Dulles "New Look" (1953–61); the Kennedy-Johnson "flexible response" strategy (1961–69); and détente (1969–79). In describing the first of these, Gaddis notes Kennan's belief that "the breakup of international communism was an irreversible trend" because it "was subject to many of the same self-destructive tendencies of classic imperialism" (p. 47). Kennan's containment strategy was designed to exploit these weaknesses and hasten the decline of Soviet influence beyond its borders by applying U.S. economic and technological advantages in key areas of the world. NSC-68 represented the second distinct phase of containment strategy, one that emphasized much more strongly than Kennan had the buildup of U.S. military strength to counter that of the Soviet Union. Moreover, although the drafters of NSC-68 still recognized important Soviet weaknesses (including vulnerability to nationalism within its own borders and in "satellite" states), Nitze and his colleagues were more pessimistic about Soviet capabilities and what it would take to counter these. In addition, NSC-68 raised concerns about future trends in relative military strength, though it also emphasized the extent of U.S. economic superiority. Eisenhower's New Look strategy was premised on asymmetrical response—on reacting to an adversary's challenges in ways calculated to apply one's strengths against the other side's weaknesses, even if this meant shifting the nature and location of the confrontation. Kennedy's "flexible response" shifted back to a symmetrical response—to deter-

ring all wars, be they general or limited, nuclear or conventional, large or small. This philosophy also stressed a decreasing reliance on nuclear weapons in favor of conventional military deterrence and covert action. Gaddis describes the fifth stage of containment, détente, as seeking "to change the Soviet Union's concept of international relations, to integrate it as a stable element into the existing world order," by applying a combination of pressure and inducements that would, if successful, persuade the Russians that stability was in their interests (p. 289).

18. Richard M. Nixon, *The Real War* (New York: Warner Books, 1980), p. 2.

19. Roy Cohn, *McCarthy* (New York: New American Library, 1968), p. 64.

20. Quoted in Grose, *Gentleman Spy*, p. 346.

21. The members of the Task Force on Intelligence Activities were General Mark W. Clark, chairman; Richard L. Conolly; Henry Kearns; Edward V. Rickenbacker; Donald S. Russell; and Ernest F. Hollings, then lieutenant governor of and later a senator from South Carolina.

22. James H. Doolittle, "Report on the Covert Activities of the Central Intelligence Agency, September 30, 1954," located at the National Archives and Records Administration, College Park, Maryland.

23. Ibid., p. 7.

24. Task Force on Intelligence Activities, "A Report to the Congress by the Commission on Organization of the Executive Branch of the Government," June 1955, p. 14.

25. Frank O. Wisner to Colonel Matthew Baird, CIA director of training, memorandum, July 19, 1955, p. 3.

26. If real, as against nominal, growth rates are used, the "crossover" does not occur until 2021, but the Soviets would have, by any such calculation, long since established a potential military superiority.

27. Allen W. Dulles, "Dimensions of the International Peril Facing Us," address to the U.S. Chamber of Commerce, Washington, D.C., April 28, 1958, published in *Vital Speeches of the Day* 24, no. 15 (May 15, 1958): 454.

28. Walter W. Rostow, conversation with author, 1962.

29. John Prados, *The Soviet Estimate: U.S. Intelligence Analysis and Soviet Strategic Forces* (Princeton: Princeton University Press, 1982), p. 74.

30. The Gaither Report of 1957, formally known as U.S. Congress, Joint Committee on Defense Production, *Deterrence and Survival in the Nuclear Age*, 94th Cong., 2d sess., 1976, Committee Print, p. 25.

31. Prados, *The Soviet Estimate*, p. 80; Joseph Alsop, "Our Government's Untruths," *New York Herald-Tribune*, August 1, 1958.

32. Gaither Report, p. iii.

33. In 1997, for example, the Clinton administration began developing an $11 billion fleet of Boeing 747s equipped with lasers that could destroy enemy missiles from a few hundred miles away. Because this laser anti-missile technology is unsuitable for long-range attacks, it does not violate the Anti-Ballistic Missile Treaty, and so it has enjoyed some bipartisan support. But the laser fleet has been attacked by congressional investigators as being so flawed that it might not work in wartime. See William J. Broad, "Plan for Airborne Laser Weapon Is Attacked," *New York Times*, September 30, 1997.

34. Bryan Hehir, *The Uses of Force in the Post–Cold War World* (Washington, D.C.: Woodrow Wilson Center for Scholars, 1996), p. 3.

35. Senate Committee on Foreign Relations, *Estimating the Size and Growth of the Soviet Economy: Hearing Before the Committee on Foreign Relations*, 101st Cong., 2d sess., July 16, 1990, p. 49.

36. Ibid., p. 33.

37. Central Intelligence Agency, National Foreign Assessment Center, *Handbook of Economic Statistics, 1990* (Washington, D.C.: Central Intelligence Agency, 1990), p. 38.

38. Dale W. Jorgenson, letter to author, March 18, 1991.

39. While concluding that this failure of analysis was not unique to the intelligence community, Rowen has also noted at least four major aspects of the Soviet economy in which the CIA's assessments "differed markedly from those of observers outside the community": the Soviet economy's overall size, its performance, its military burden (as a proportion of the Soviet GDP), and what he calls the "costs of empire." See, for example, Henry S. Rowen and Charles Wolf, Jr., letter to the editor, "The CIA's Credibility," *National Interest* 42 (Winter 1995–96): 111–12, which was written in response to an article defending the CIA's analysis.

40. George Kennan, "Assessing the Soviet Threat: The Early Cold War Years," Center for the Study of Intelligence, Washington, D.C., October 24, 1997.

41. Stansfield Turner, "Intelligence for a New World Order," *Foreign Affairs*, Fall 1991, p. 162.

42. Anders Åslund, "The CIA Versus Soviet Reality," *Washington Post*, May 19, 1988.

43. *The Military Balance, 1996–1997* (London: Oxford University Press, 1996), pp. 306–11.

44. Former president Gerald R. Ford, address to the National Press Club at a luncheon for the Ford Foundation Journalism Awards for Presidential and National Defense Reporting, June 2, 1997.

45. Laskey, "NSC-68," p. 63.

46. George P. Shultz, *Turmoil and Triumph: My Years as Secretary of State* (New York: Charles Scribner's Sons, 1993), p. 703.

47. Senate Committee on Foreign Relations, *The START Treaty: Hearings Before the Committee on Foreign Relations*, 102d Cong., 2d sess., 1992, pp. 67–68. The questions were posed by the author.

48. See Daniel Patrick Moynihan, *Pandaemonium* (Oxford: Oxford University Press, 1994), p. 51.

Chapter 8: A Culture of Openness

1. Information Security Oversight Office, *1996 Report to the President* (Washington, D.C.: Information Security Oversight Office, 1996), p. ii.

2. Max Frankel, "Top Secret," *New York Times Magazine*, June 16, 1996.

3. Harold Edgar and Benno C. Schmidt, Jr., "The Espionage Statutes and Publication of Defense Information," *Columbia Law Review* 73, no. 5 (May 1973): 934, 936. See also Chapter 2.

4. John D. Morrison, "The Protection of Intelligence Data," as quoted in ibid., p. 1055 n. 346. The uncertainties surrounding the legislative intent of the 1917 act (as well as of its most significant amendment, in 1950) were to have significant consequences more than half a century later. Edgar and Schmidt note that "no prosecution premised on publication has ever been brought under the espionage laws" and that the abandoned prosecution of Daniel Ellsberg and his colleague Anthony Russo for unlawful retention of the Pentagon Papers "was the first effort to apply the espionage statutes to conduct preparatory to publication." In October 1984, Samuel Loring Morison, a civilian analyst with the Office of Naval Intelligence, was arrested for supplying a classified photograph—a picture of a Soviet nuclear-powered carrier under construction—to *Jane's Defence Weekly*, which subsequently published it. In October 1985, Morison became the first person convicted under the 1917 Espionage Act for an unauthorized disclosure of classified defense information to the press. His conviction was upheld in 1988, and the Supreme Court declined to hear the case.

The Morison prosecution remains unique; no other individual has been prosecuted on such grounds since. While the core provisions of the espionage laws have been used with some frequency to prosecute government and defense-contractor employees for actual or attempted communication of national defense information to a foreign agent as well as conspiracies toward that end (thus reaching the conduct of now-notorious spies like Aldrich Ames), according to data gathered by the Department of Justice, there were sixty-seven indictments under the espionage laws between 1975 and August 1996. Figures compiled by the Department of Defense Security Institute show eighty-six new espionage cases *reported* between 1975 and 1995. Ames was indicted under 18 *U.S. Code* 794(c) of the Espionage Act for conspiracy "to directly or indirectly communicate, deliver or transmit . . . documents and information related to the national defense . . . to a foreign government or a representative or officer thereof . . . with the intent or reason to believe such information could be used to the injury of the United States or to the advantage of a foreign government." His wife, Rosario Ames, was also indicted for conspiracy under a separate provision of the act, 18 *U.S. Code* 793(g): for "a willful combination or agreement" with her husband "to communicate, deliver or transmit . . . documents relating to the national defense . . . to persons not authorized to receive them." Both were also indicted for tax fraud. Both subsequently pled guilty. Aldrich Ames was sentenced to life imprisonment without parole; Rosario Ames, to a five-year term.

5. *New York Times Company v. United States,* June 30, 1971, in vol. 403 of *United States Reports,* compiled by Henry Putzel, Jr. (Washington, D.C.: Government Printing Office, 1972), p. 719.

6. Erwin N. Griswold, "Secrets Not Worth Keeping," *Washington Post,* February 15, 1989.

7. Leonard Garment, *Crazy Rhythm: My Journey from Brooklyn, Jazz, and Wall Street to Nixon's White House, Watergate, and Beyond* (New York: Times Books, 1997), pp. 296–97.

8. William Safire, *Before the Fall: An Inside View of the Pre-Watergate White House* (Garden City, N.Y.: Doubleday, 1975), pp. 358, 552.

9. Barry M. Goldwater, letter to William J. Casey, April 8, 1984, quoted in Daniel Patrick Moynihan, *Came the Revolution: Argument in the Reagan Era* (San Diego: Harcourt Brace Jovanovich, 1988), pp. 178–79.

10. Theodore Draper, *A Very Thin Line: The Iran-Contra Affairs* (New York: Hill and Wang, 1991), p. 22.

11. Theodore Draper, "Getting Irangate Straight," *New York Review of Books,* October 8, 1987, p. 47.

12. Lawrence E. Walsh, *Firewall: The Iran-Contra Conspiracy and Cover-Up* (New York: W. W. Norton, 1997), p. 531.

13. Ibid., p. 518.

14. Harold Hongju Koh, *The National Security Constitution: Sharing Power After the Iran-Contra Affair* (New Haven: Yale University Press, 1990), pp. 2–3.

15. Ibid., p. 2.

16. James Q. Wilson, *Bureaucracy: What Government Agencies Do and Why They Do It* (New York: Basic Books, 1989), p. 189.

17. Donald L. Robinson, "The Routinization of Crisis Government," *Yale Review* 63 (Winter 1974): 161.

18. Robert D. Novak, "China's Savior," *Washington Post,* February 24, 1997.

19. Anthony Downs, *Inside Bureaucracy* (Boston: Little, Brown, 1967), p. 19.

20. John F. Harris, "On CIA's 50th, Clinton Praises 'Quiet Patriotism,'" *Washington Post,* September 17, 1997.

21. Office of the Press Secretary, White House press release, "Remarks by the President at the Fiftieth Anniversary of the Central Intelligence Agency," September 16, 1997, www.whitehouse.gov.

22. James Q. Wilson, *The Investigators: Managing FBI and Narcotics Agents* (New York: Basic Books, 1978), p. 202.

23. Paul McMasters, quoted in Eleanor Randolph, "Is U.S. Keeping Too Many Secrets?" *Los Angeles Times,* May 17, 1997.

24. Dennis Cauchon, "Militiaman Convicted Under Anti-Terrorism Law," *USA Today,* August 26, 1997.

25. National polling data (from Gallup Organization; Louis Harris and Associates, ABC News/*Washington Post;* Time/CNN/Yankelovich; CBS News/*New York Times;* and Gallup/CNN/*USA Today* surveys) provided by the Assassination Records Review Board and on file with the commission. Congress in 1992 established the Assassination Records Review Board to review all records related to the Kennedy assassination and make them available to the public (subject to narrow exemptions) as soon as possible. It is likely that the efforts of the board will greatly clarify the historical record concerning the assassination and the activities of Oswald and others; it is far less likely, however, that they will have much impact on opinion.

26. Editorial, "The Amnesty Option," *New York Times,* July 6, 1997.

27. Evan Thomas, *The Very Best Men, Four Who Dared: The Early Years of the CIA* (New York: Simon and Schuster, 1995), p. 239, citing Thomas C. Reeves, *A Question of Character: A Life of John F. Kennedy* (New York: Free Press, 1991), pp. 217–18. See also Michael Beschloss, *The Crisis Years: Kennedy and Khrushchev, 1960–1963* (New York: HarperCollins, 1991), p. 103.

28. Lloyd A. Free, "Attitudes of the Cuban People Toward the Castro Regime," Institute for International Social Research, Princeton University, 1960, p. 26.

29. Hadley Cantril, *The Human Dimension: Experiences in Policy Research* (New Brunswick, N.J.: Rutgers University Press, 1967), p. 5.

30. "Russian Federation National Security Blueprint," December 17, 1997, printed in Moscow *Rossijskaya Gazeta,* December 26, 1997, translated by Foreign Broadcast Information Service, pp. 3–4.

31. Ibid., p. 8. The "National Security Blueprint" continues: "The factors intensifying the threat of the growth of nationalism and na-

tional and regional separatism include mass migration and the uncontrolled reproduction of human resources in a number of regions of the country. The main reasons for this are the consequences of the USSR's breakup into national-territorial formations, the failures of nationalities policy and economic policy, . . . and the spread and escalation of conflict situations based on national and ethnic grounds. Other factors are the deliberate and purposeful interference by foreign states and international organizations in the internal life of Russia's peoples, and the weakening of the role of Russian as the state language of the Russian Federation. The adoption by Russian Federation components of normative legal acts and decisions that are at variance with the Russian Federation Constitution and federal legislation is becoming an increasingly dangerous factor eroding the single legal area of the country. The continuing violation of Russia's single spiritual area, economic disintegration, and social differentiation provoke the escalation of tension in relations between the regions and the center, thereby constituting a patent threat to the federal structure of the Russian Federation."

32. Ibid., p. 10.

33. Ibid., p. 18. Russia rejected the "no-first-use" nuclear doctrine on November 2, 1993, when the "Basic Provisions of the Military Doctrine of the Russian Federation" was approved by President Yeltsin.

34. George F. Kennan, letter to author, March 25, 1997. The spell of secrecy is hard to break. Open sources are often discounted still. In May 1998, India detonated a number of nuclear devices, including a hydrogen bomb. The newly formed Hindu nationalist government had all but announced that it would do this. The Bharatiya Janata Party (BJP) 1998 Election Manifesto read, "The BJP rejects the notion of nuclear apartheid and will actively oppose attempts to impose a hegemonistic nuclear regime. We will not be dictated to by anybody in matters of security and in the exercise of nuclear option." When the option *was* exercised, the Department of State asked why the Central Intelligence Agency hadn't told them in advance. *Newsweek* reported, "The intelligence failure 'ranks right up there with missing the collapse of the Soviet Union,' says a senior State Department official" (Evan Thomas, John Barry, and Melinda Liu, "Ground Zero," *Newsweek*, May 25, 1998, p. 29).

Index

Boskin, Michael J., 197
Bradley, Omar Nelson, 70, 71
Brooks, Linton F., 200
Buckley, William F., Jr., 43
Bundy, William P., 186
Bureaucracy, 155, 181, 201; in federal government, 129, 165; and the Freedom of Information Act, 173; and intelligence, 80; Max Weber on, 142–43, 153; and secrecy, 60, 80, 152, 180
Burgess, Guy, 145
Burleson, Albert S., 106
Butler, George Lee, 78, 79

Cantril, Hadley, 222, 223
Carter, Jimmy, 8, 209
Casey, William J., 3, 210
Castro, Fidel, 57
Center for the Study of Intelligence, 76, 177
Central Intelligence Agency (CIA), 7, 9, 37–38, 43, 51, 76, 180, 187–90, 214; creation of, 76, 98, 180; and estimates of Soviet economy, 7, 13–14, 196–98; and Iran-Contra affair, 3, 210–12; and Kennedy assassination, 220–21; and NSC-68, 184; operations of, 213; and secrecy, 181, 185–86; and Venona, 15, 61. *See also* Center for the Study of Intelligence
Chadwick, James, 136
Chambers, Whittaker, 49, 53–54, 61, 68, 119, 121, 145
Chicago Tribune, 133–34, 204
Childs, Morris, 169–70
China, 188, 198
Church committee, 36–37, 46, 76, 207
Church, Frank, 36, 76
Civil Liberties Act of *1988*, 131
Civil Service Commission, 91, 110, 159, 161, 169, 172
Civil War (U.S.), 22, 82, 83
Clark, James Beauchamp (Champ), 92
Clark, Mark W., 187–89
Clarke, Carter W., 62, 70

classification procedures, 171–73. *See also* declassification procedures
Clinton, William Jefferson, 203, 215
COINTELPROS, 35, 37
Cold War, 9, 17, 90, 141, 178–79, 184, 190, 219–20, 226; and atomic bomb, 179; beginning of, 39–40, 141, 154; and Church committee, 36–37; and conspiracy theories, 21, 33, 36; Edward Shils on, 12–13, 15; and fascism, 44–45; in findings of Commission on Protecting and Reducing Government Secrecy, 16–17; history of, 16–20, 31, 55–58 *passim;* and Pentagon Papers, 31–34; and secrecy, 1–2, 34, 214, 217, 227; and Soviet military outlays, 74; and Joseph Stalin, 57, 58
Commager, Henry Steele, 104
Commission on Government Security (Wright commission), 60, 164, 167–68, 172, 175, 204; report of, 166
Commission on Protecting and Reducing Government Secrecy, 9–11, 16, 62–63, 143; on loyalty programs, 165–66, 168; conclusions and recommendations of, 14, 217–18
Committee on Administrative Procedure, 157
Committee on Classified Information (Coolidge committee), 170
Committee to Investigate the National Defense Program (Truman committee), 73, 95
Communism, 40, 86; domestic communism, 15–17 *passim,* 24, 62, 146. *See also* Communist Party of the United States
Communist International (Comintern), 23, 52–53, 113, 116–17, 122
Communist Labor Party, 113, 128
Communist Party of the United States (CPUSA), 25, 35, 52–53, 114, 117, 119, 124, 128, 154, 159,

Federal Bureau of Investigation (FBI) (*continued*) 48–49; criticisms of, 34–37, 46–47; files of, 2, 19, 41–45, 51; in findings of Commission on Protecting and Reducing Government Secrecy, 9–10; and J. Edgar Hoover, 24, 48, 62, 215–16, 221; and Venona, 16–17, 54, 142

Fermi, Enrico, 136

First Amendment, 93–94

Fletcher, Howard B., 70

Flynn, Edward J., 124

Flynn, Elizabeth Gurley, 87

Ford, Gerald R., 170, 198, 202

Foreign Relations Authorization Act for Fiscal Years *1994* and *1995*, 60. *See also* Committee on Protecting and Reducing Government Secrecy

France, 82, 84, 104, 198

Frankel, Max, 168, 203

Free, Lloyd A., 222

Freedom of Information Act (FOIA): and Administrative Procedure Act, 157; and FBI, 35, 41–42, 44, 47, 49; and federal bureaucracy, 174; and Moss subcommittee, 172–73

Freeh, Louis J., 70, 75

Fuchs, Klaus, 54, 144

Fulbright, J. William, 28

Gaddis, John Lewis, 55–57

Gaither, H. Rowen, Jr., 8, 190

Gaither report, 190–98

Gallinger, Jacob Harold, 93

Gardner, Meredith Knox, 61, 142, 151

Garment, Leonard, 206

German Communist Party, 25

German Americans, 18, 86, 104–6, 131

German-American Bund, 128, 159

Germany, 29; in conspiracy theories, 23, 25; during World War I, 85, 88, 90–91, 101–104; during World War II, 132–33, 150

Gilbert, W. S., 85

Gitlow, Benjamin, 117

Glazer, Nathan, 12, 86, 114

Gold, Harry, 144

Goldman, Emma, 111

Goldwater, Barry, 3, 28–29, 207, 210, 211

"Good Girl," 69. *See also* Bentley, Elizabeth

Gorbachev, Mikhail, 200

Gorelick, Jamie S., 75

Greenglass, David, 54, 144–45

Gregory, Thomas W., 90, 97, 106

Griswald, Edwin N., 205

Groves, Leslie R., 160

Guatemala, 181–82

Hague peace conferences, 125–26

Hall, Theodore Alvin, 54, 62, 147, 149, 151–52

Hamilton, Alexander, 101

Harding, Warren G., 109, 115

Hatch Act, 159

Haynes, John E., 68

H-bomb. *See* Nuclear weapons

Hehir, Bryan, 195

Hillenkoetter, Roscoe H., 71

Hiss, Alger, 64, 68–69, 74, 119, 121, 144, 146–47, 186; case against, 50, 52; trial of, 49

Hiss, Priscilla, 68, 121

Hitler, Adolf, 25, 123, 129, 134

Holmes, Oliver Wendell, 108

Hook, Sidney, 118–20

Hoover, Herbert, 187

Hoover, J. Edgar, 34, 43, 50, 54, 115, 126, 189; and Church committee, 46, 47; and FBI, 215–16, 221; and Francis Biddle, 129–30; and George E. Allen, 62–68; and secrecy, 22–24, 37, 40; and Truman, 70

Housekeeping Statute of *1789*, 173

House of Representatives, U.S., 9, 90–92, 207; and Defense Appropriations Committee, 198–99; and Foreign Operations and Government Information Subcommittee, 174; and House Un-American Activities Committee, 25, 70;

and Select Committee on Assassi-
nations, 40; and Select Commit-
tee on Intelligence, 41, 211; and
Special Government Information
Subcommitee of Government
Operations (Moss subcommit-
tee), 171–72
Humphrey, Hubert H., 164

India, 3, 88, 103
Industrial Workers of the World
(IWW), 87–88
Information Security Oversight Of-
fice (ISOO), 74, 202
Inouye, Daniel K., 132
Inter-Continental Ballistic Missile
(ICBM), 194
Iran-Contra affair, 3, 206–13

Jackson, Andrew, 82
Japan, 97, 198
Japanese Americans, internment of,
131–33
Jefferson, Thomas, 84–85
John Birch Society, 28, 29
Johnson, Hiram W., 95
Johnson, Lyndon B., 173, 195, 220;
administration of, 28–29, 33,
134, 176
Jorgenson, Dale W., 197

Kampelman, Max, 6
Kaufman, Irving R., 145
Kennan, George F., 57, 145,
182–84, 197, 198, 227. See also
containment doctrine
Kennedy, John F., 46, 48, 85, 168,
194; administration of, 28, 33, 176;
assassination of, 40, 41, 45, 219
KGB, 51, 61, 118
Khrushchev, Nikita, 79
King, Martin Luther, Jr., 220
Kissinger, Henry, 6, 32
Kristol, Irving, 190
Kuhn, Fritz J., 128, 129
Kunstel, Marcia, 150

Ladd, D. Milton "Mickey," 147
Lang, Hermann, 125–26

Lansing, Robert, 88, 112
Lea, Clarence, 130
League of Nations, 99
Lee, Robert E., 95
Lehman, Ronald F., 200
Lenin, 23, 56, 84, 112, 118, 155, 182
Leuchtenburg, William E., 104
"Liberal," 144. See also Rosenberg,
Julius and Ethel; Venona
Liberal Party, 124
Life magazine, 140–42
Lincoln, Abraham, 82
Link, Arthur, 107
Lippman, Walter, 186
Lipset, Seymour Martin, 74
Lodge, Henry Cabot, 95, 101, 204
Los Alamos, Atomic Research Lab-
oratory, 142, 147, 151, 155, 156,
160
Loyalty, 18, 111; and disloyalty, 18,
52, 105, 172; ensuring, 127; as
grounds for dismissal, 91; oath
of, 90; programs for, 15, 159, 161,
163, 165, 169; in report of Com-
mission on Government Security
(Wright commission), 166; and
secrecy, 98, 163

Maclean, Donald, 145
Madison, James, 84
Manhattan Project, 61, 136, 156
Marks, Herbert, 64, 68
Marshall, George C., 27, 57
Masses, The, 87, 113. See also New
Masses, The
Matsunaga, Spark M., 133
McCarthy, Joseph R., 16–17, 19, 27,
51, 70, 144, 163, 186, 189, 219
McCloy, John J., 64, 68
McFarlane, Robert C., 210
McKinley, William, 87
McNamara, Robert, 7, 28–29, 203
"Mlad," 150. See also Hall,
Theodore Alvin; Venona
Moorhead, William, 174. See also
Freedom of Information Act
Morison, Samuel L., 98
Moss, John, 172–74
Moss subcommittee, 172–74

National Archives and Records Administration, 10, 74, 202
National Declassification Center, 217–18
National Intelligence Council, 197
National Intelligence Daily, 180
National Reconnaissance Organization, 223
National Security Act of *1947*, 98, 179
National Security Agency (NSA), 7, 9, 60. *See also* Arlington Hall; Venona
National Security Council, 3, 179, 191, 193, 211
Naval Research Station, 135
Nazi-Soviet nonaggression pact, 123
Nazis, 120, 128
New Masses, The, 119
Nicaragua, 208–12
Nitze, Paul H., 57, 184
Nixon, Richard M., 35, 185–86, 203; administration of, 185–86, 203, 204; and Pentagon Papers, 32–33, 204–5; and Watergate, 33, 206
Norden, Carl L., 125–26
North Atlantic Treaty, 179
North Korea, 55
NSC-68, 183–85, 199
Nuclear weapons, 28, 42, 51, 183–84, 195, 225–26; and the atom bomb, 135–42, 150, 179, 195; and the H-bomb, 137–40, 174; Soviet espionage in, 143–44; in wartime, 78, 144, 190
Nutter, G. Warren, 193

Office of Naval Intelligence, 98
Office of Strategic Information, 171
Office of Strategic Services, 77
Operation PBSUCCESS (Cullather), 177, 181
Oppenheimer, J. Robert, 136, 160, 163
Overman, Lee Slater, 89, 95

Palmer, A. Mitchell, 23, 115
Palmer Raids, 115–16, 152

Panuch, J. Anthony, 68, 69
Papen, Franz von, 101–2
Pearl Harbor, 142
Pentagon Papers, 29, 31–33, 40, 47, 203–6
Pepper, Claude D., 73
Philby, Kim, 16, 54, 114
Pike, Otis, 36
Pike committee, 36, 37, 207
Podesta, John D., 203
Pound, Roscoe, 157
Powers, Richard Gid, 74, 146, 219
President's Science Advisory Committee, 190, 192
Press: censorship of, 91, 96, 106, 133, 167; freedom of, 37, 93–94
Proxmire, William, 194

Reagan, Ronald, 210; administration of, 8, 209
Reed, John, 87–88, 113–14; and Communist Labor Party, 114; and John Reed Society, 149
Regulation: secrecy as, 13, 59, 79, 164; in wartime, 154
Reston, James, 167–68
Ritter Ring, 125–26
Roosevelt, Franklin D., 25, 38, 167; administration of, 85, 120, 130, 150, 157; war plans of, 133
Roosevelt, Theodore, 105
Rosenberg, Julius and Ethel, 49, 51, 54, 144–45
Rossi, Bruno, 147
Rostow, Walt, 193
Rowen, Henry S., 197
Rovere, Richard, 123
Ruina, Jack P., 175
Rumsfeld, Donald, 173
Russell, Richard B., 180
Russia, 22–23, 84, 107, 111–13 *passim*, 188, 198–99, 224–26. *See also* Soviet Union
Ruthenberg, Charles Emil, 114

Sakharov, Andrei, 138
Sarbanes, Paul S., 212
Sax, Saville, 147, 149
Schmidt, Benno C., 92, 204

Seaborg, Glenn T., 176-77
Secrecy, 1, 12, 27, 41, 45-47, 185, 203, 212, 222, 227; and Administrative Procedure Act, 158; and bureaucracy, 111, 153; and CIA, 186; and classification decisions, 11, 74-75, 172; after Cold War, 80, 202; during Cold War, 15-20, 58, 74, 154, 214; and conspiracy, 50, 98; cost of, 218; culture of, 154, 206, 221, 223, 226; and declassification decisions, 170-77, 217-18; and findings of Commission on Protecting and Reducing Government Secrecy, 10, 14; and Freedom of Information Act, 42; in government, 11, 47, 49, 73, 168, 202; as government regulation, 13, 59, 79, 164; and the legislature, 213, 216; and national security, 3, 8; and nuclear weapons, 136, 141, 195; power of, 21-22; and the presidency, 133, 211; as ritual, 29, 43; routinization of, 180, 198; and science, 174-75; in Soviet Union, 112; during Watergate era, 29-33, 35
Security Resources Panel, 190
Sedition Act of *1918*, 97. *See also* Alien and Sedition Acts of 1798
Seitz, Frederick, 175, 227
Senate, U.S., 9, 81, 90-95; Judiciary Committee, 157; Committee on Foreign Relations, 195-97, 200, 202; Select Committee on Intelligence, 3, 210; Joint Resolution *21*, 164
Seward, William H., 85, 87
Shapiro, Maurice M., 135
Sheehan, Neil, 29-32
Shevchenko, Arkady M., 155-56
Shields, John Knight, 93-94
Shils, Edward, 12-15, 18, 21, 163, 218
Shultz, George P., 199-200
Silone, Ignazio, 117
Slany, William Z., 83
Smith, Jeffrey, 78
Smyth, Henry DeWolf, 156

Smyth report, 156, 174
Social Security Administration, 181
Solzhenitsyn, Alexander, 5-6
Soviet Union, 117, 155, 178, 181-82, 213, 226-27; archives of, 52-53, 80; and CIA, 181-82, 190; and Cold War, 44, 46, 49, 78, 183-85; and Comintern, 113-14; economy of, 4-8, 13-14, 79, 190-93, 195-201; and espionage, 51-56, 90, 119-20, 140, 143, 163, 165; U.S. relations with, 39, 43; and Venona, 60, 150-52
Spender, Stephen, 190
Sputnik, 9
Stalin, Joseph, 25, 39, 55-58, 137, 167
Stennis, John C., 164-65
Stimson, Henry L., 131
Stone, Earl E., 71
Stone, Harlan, 24
Story, Joseph, 93-94
Strategic Air Command, 194
Strategic Arms Reduction Treaty I (START I), 6, 199-200
Strategic Arms Reduction Treaty II (START II), 226
Strategic Command, U.S., 78
Studies in Intelligence, 77
Supreme Court, U.S., 158, 206

Teller, Edward, 139
Thomas, Charles S., 92-93
Thomas, Evan, 221
Torment of Secrecy, The (Shils), 12
Trilling, Lionel, 120-23
Trotsky, Leon, 118, 214
Truman, Harry S., 17, 45, 54, 57, 62-63, 70-71, 73, 137, 159, 161, 180; administration of, 15, 38, 49, 160, 162; Executive orders of, 159-61
Turner, Stansfield, 79

Ulam, Stanislaw, 139
United States v. Curtiss-Wright Export Corporation, 158
United Nations, 4, 137, 155, 167